JERUSALEM

right: An impression of Jerusalem in a
Hebrew Marriage Contract from Venice,
1750. The Hebrew caption is from Psalm
125, 'As the mountains are round about
Jerusalem'.

frontispiece: The southeast corner of the
city wall, with large Herodian masonry in
its lower courses. Mount Ophel is in the
foreground. The small domed structure,
top right, is the Dome of the Chain, in
design and decoration an exact model of
the large Dome of the Rock, to its left.

endpapers: Jerusalem 1967, by the Israeli
artist Shalom of Safad.

JERUSALEM

sacred city of mankind:
a history of forty centuries

Teddy Kollek and Moshe Pearlman

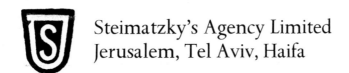

Steimatzky's Agency Limited
Jerusalem, Tel Aviv, Haifa

Designed by Felix Gluck for George Weidenfeld and Nicolson Ltd
Phototypeset by BAS Printers Limited, Wallop, Hampshire
Printed by Officine Grafiche Arnoldo Mondadori, Verona, Italy

Contents

1	The Mists of Antiquity	2000–1000 BC	11
2	The City of David	1000–961	27
3	Solomon's Jerusalem	961–922	43
4	The Divided Kingdom	922–722	55
5	Isaiah and Hezekiah	715–687	61
6	The Fall . . .	587	67
7	. . . and the Rise	537	73
8	Hellenism	332–167	79
9	The Maccabees (Hasmoneans)	167–63	85
10	Herod the Great	37–4	95
11	Jerusalem and Jesus		111
12	The Great Revolt	AD 66–70	125
13	Bar Kochba, Hadrian and Aelia Capitolina	132–5	137
14	Christian Jerusalem	324–638	145
15	Moslem Jerusalem	638–1099	155
16	The Crusader Kingdom	1099–1187	175
17	Under the Mamelukes	1250–1517	189
18	Ottoman Jerusalem	1517–1917	199
19	Jerusalem of the Mandate	1917–48	235
20	Capital of Israel	1948	249
21	Jerusalem Reunited	June 1967	259
	Main Events in the History of Jerusalem		277
	Acknowledgements		282
	Index		283

The hills round
Jerusalem; in the
distance is the city,
spread along the topmost
ridge.

Jerusalem, with a recorded history of some four thousand years, has been more familiar to more people for a longer period than any other place on earth. It is a city of enchantment, perched high amid the Judean hills, some forty miles inland from the Mediterranean coast. It stands in the centre of Israel, roughly midway between the country's southern tip, Eilat, gateway to the Red Sea, and Metullah, in the north, on the Lebanese border.

This is the city of David, who in the tenth century BC unified the country and proclaimed Jerusalem the capital. This is the city of Solomon's Temple. This is the city where the giant prophets Isaiah and Jeremiah uttered thoughts which influenced the moral and religious attitudes of half the human race. This was the scene of Jesus' last ministry, and here that he was crucified. Moslems, too, consider Jerusalem holy, believing it to be the site from which Mohammed ascended to heaven.

The history of Jerusalem from earliest times is the history of man, a history of war and peace, of greatness and misery, of splendour and squalor, of lofty wisdom and of blood flowing in the gutters. But the golden thread, the consistent theme running through that history, is the unshakeable association of the Jewish people with the city.

The story of this association is repeatedly interrupted by a succession of conquerors – Egyptians, Assyrians, Babylonians, Persians, Seleucids, Romans, Moslem Arabs, Seljuks, Crusaders, Saracens, Mamelukes, and Ottomans. Yet throughout the three thousand years since David made it the seat of Israel's authority, the spiritual attachment of the Jews to Jerusalem has remained unbroken. It is a unique attachment.

Throughout the centuries of their dispersion, in whatever far corner of the earth they found themselves, the Jews prayed for the return to Zion, the biblical synonym for Jerusalem. Their synagogues, wherever in the world they were built, were oriented towards Jerusalem (and the practice is followed to this day). When a Jew built a house, part of a wall would be left unfinished to symbolise the temporary nature of the dwelling – until the owner could return to Jerusalem. History has no parallel to this mystic bond. Without it, there would be no State of Israel today.

Jewish pilgrims crossing the forecourt to approach the Western Wall shortly after the war in June 1967.

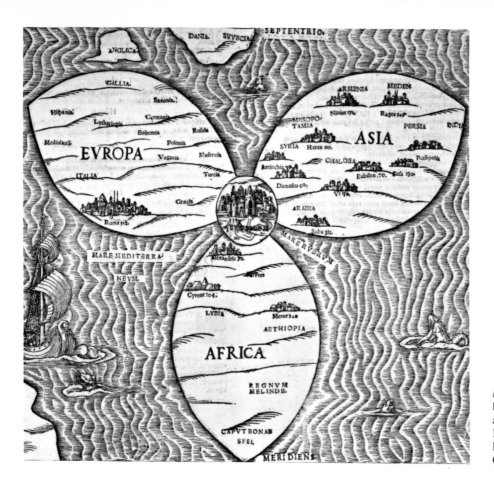

left: Jerusalem has long been represented in maps as the 'Centre of the Worl Here it is shown in a late sixteenth-century German map.

Archaeologists and historians have long wondered why Jerusalem should have been established where it was, and why it should have become great. It enjoys none of the physical features which favoured the advancement and prosperity of other important cities in the world. It stands at the head of no great river. It overlooks no great harbour. It commands no great highway and no cross-roads. It is not close to abundant sources of water, often the major reason for the establishment of a settlement, though one main natural spring offered a modest supply. It possesses no mineral riches. It was off the main trade routes. It held no strategic key to the conquest of vast areas prized by the ancient warring empires. Indeed, it was blessed with neither special economic nor topographic virtues which might explain why it should ever have become more than a small, anonymous mountain village with a fate any different from that of most contemporary villages which have long since vanished.

It had, and still retains, certain qualities not given to all settlements. It is a city of beauty, its hilly landscape wild and rugged. It is suffused with colour, the soft hues of autumn and spring, the sharp pigments of a cloud-less summer. It enjoys a most equable climate. Even on the hottest day, the heat is dry. The nights are always cool. The air is fresh. There is a luminous quality to the light. Strangers from other climes feel as though a film were suddenly removed from their eyes. Often throughout the year, with the

right: Street scene in the Old City after the June 1967 war, where Arab kefiya meets the fur-trimmed 'streimel' of the orthodox Jew. Top right, the Hebrew direction sign to the Western 'Wailing' Wall.

12

going down of the sun, a halo of radiance briefly crowns the hilltops before darkness closes in. Perhaps this awed the ancients and moved them to religious wonder.

These features are a boon to inhabitants and visitors. Allied to the height of the location, which gave it a degree of natural defence, and the presence of some water, they explain perhaps why Jerusalem should have been a feasible and attractive site of early settlement – but not why it should have become important.

The importance of Jerusalem sprang from the cultural geniuses of old, the Jewish philosopher-kings and biblical prophets, who made Jerusalem their centre. From Jerusalem they gave forth their wisdom to the world – and changed it. As Isaiah proclaimed: 'For out of Zion shall go forth the law, and the word of the Lord from Jerusalem.' Monotheism, the concept of good and evil, brotherly love, and the rule of law, these were the challenging precepts of the ancient Hebrews. Jerusalem was the platform from which they were launched.

*First mention of
Jerusalem in
written records*

The origins of the city are lost in the mists of antiquity, but from the style and make of pottery discovered on and around the site, and by additional scientific reasoning, archaeologists have concluded that the first settlement was established at the beginning of the third millennium BC. Its first appearance in the written records occurred a thousand years later, at the beginning of the second millennium BC, as a city of the Canaanites.

At that time, the land of Canaan was not a unified country but an agglomeration of semi-nomadic tribal confederacies and a few cities, each ruled by a 'king' who was usually a vassal of one of the two great empires vying for hegemony of the Middle East. One was the Egyptian, in the south, the other was the Assyrian in the north. Canaan lay in between, and was thus a frequent battleground. Whichever empire was dominant at a particular period controlled Canaan. The vassals paid tribute to it, and were expected to be politically loyal to their overlords. They rarely were – particularly when they sensed that power was shifting, that the scales of strength were swinging to the other side, and that in the next conflict, the rival empire might win. This was always a cause of anxiety to the imperial monarchs.

One of the devices which Egypt used to keep her vassals in line was what has come to be known as the Execration Texts. Two sets have been discovered, and the Egyptian hieroglyphs deciphered. The first, belonging to the nineteenth century BC, are inscriptions on bowls. The second, written in the eighteenth century BC, are inscribed on clay figurines representing bound captives. These texts consisted of lists of names of distant cities and nomadic clans and their chiefs who were subordinate to Egypt. They are thus of considerable scholarly importance, since the existence of many of these cities at so early a period of history would not otherwise have been known.

Through these texts, the Egyptians sought to exercise political witchcraft, an early form of psychological warfare, against their actual or potential enemies. Smashing the bowl or figurine was held to smash the power of the enemy whose name was inscribed on the pottery. No doubt the threat to

View of the walled city
from the southeast. The
twin domes at the top right
belong to the Church of the
Holy Sepulchre.

15

do so was considered to be sufficient. The mood of the times was hardly one of scepticism towards witchcraft. The knowledge by a provincial 'king' contemplating disaffection that it was in the power of the pharaoh to do him harm by violent execration might well have prompted him to think twice and possibly influence him to remain friendly to Egypt.

The name of Jerusalem appears in the nineteenth-century BC group of Execration Texts: '. . . the Ruler of Jerusalem, Yaqar-'Ammu, and all the retainers who are with him; the Ruler of Jerusalem, Setj-'Anu, and all the retainers who are with him; . . .' (In Egyptian hieroglyphs, Jerusalem appears as *Urushamem*. In the Akkadian tongue it was *Urusalim*). It has long been believed that Jerusalem means 'City of Peace', the Hebrew name, *Yerushalayim*, as it appears in the Bible, stemming from the two Hebrew words *Ir*, which means city, and *Shalom*, which means peace. Modern historians, however, consider that the derivation is probably *yara*, which means founded, and *Salem*, which was the name of the local god, so that the meaning would be 'Founded by the god Salem'.

Meaning of the name 'Jerusalem'

The city seems to have had strong religious associations even for its earliest settlers, and there are clues to this in the Bible. The Patriarch Abraham appears on the scene in the eighteenth century BC and he meets 'Melchi-zedek king of Salem', as recorded in Genesis XIV, 18. The Bible adds that Melchi-zedek was 'the priest of the most high God', which suggests a central place for the city in the religion of the time.

Zedek is the Hebrew word for righteousness. It appears to have been a standard component in the name of the priestly rulers of Jerusalem and supports the thesis of the city's religious importance even in the pre-Judaic times. In the period of Joshua, the name of the king is given in the Bible as 'Adoni-zedek' (Joshua X, 1). Here, incidentally, he is referred to as 'king of Jerusalem'; no longer is Salem used.

Decline of Egyptian power

The eighteenth century BC saw the decline of Egyptian power, due primarily to internal political dissension and weakness. The provinces were quick to take advantage of enfeebled imperial control. In Canaan, moreover, the semi-nomadic chieftains had begun to settle down, establish townlets and emerge as petty kings. Jerusalem in the previous century had been one of the few cities in the land – as is evident from the first group of Execration Texts. In that list, there is identifiable mention of only Jerusalem and Ashkelon as towns in Canaan; the rest are names of nomadic clans. In the eighteenth-century texts, however, the list of cities is longer.

With Egyptian weakness, the kings of these towns felt increasingly independent, and pharaonic control, loose at best, virtually ceased. Jerusalem, too, at this time, took advantage of the lax central authority.

But not for long. Soon, the city was to become subservient once again – to a new master who came from the north. Disintegration in Egypt had been felt not only by the petty vassals in Canaan but, more important, by a powerful northern people called the Hyksos, whose origins are somewhat obscure. Their empire however is believed to have extended as far north as the river Euphrates. They were evidently well organised, and archaeological evidence shows that they had fashioned new military techniques by the use of revolutionary new weapons – the horse-drawn chariot and the

17

composite bow. The chariot, used for the first time as an efficient tactical weapon, gave them a new mobility, and the new bow gave them heavier 'fire-power' and greater range. No one at the time had anything to match these weapons, and the Hyksos were thus able to thunder down south through Canaan and Egypt, and subjugate them. The Hyksos' mastery of the region was to last some hundred and fifty years.

In the middle of the sixteenth century BC, a revived Egypt began a series of campaigns against the northern empire and defeated the Hyksos. We know that towards the end of the fifteenth and beginning of the fourteenth centuries, pharaoh Amenhotep III, who ruled Egypt at the zenith of her civilisation, was recognised by his only possible northern rivals, the kings of Mesopotamia and Babylonia, as sovereign of Syria, and drew the obedience of his Asian vassals. These included the vassals of Canaan. With the Hyksos' departure, Egypt had re-established control over the country.

It is in the period of Amenhotep III and his son Amenhotep IV, otherwise known as Ikhnaton, who reigned from 1379 to 1362 BC, that Jerusalem appears in the written records as more than just the name of a city. From them we learn something of its political life. The records are the Tel el-Amarna letters, clay tablets inscribed in the cuneiform script consisting of the correspondence between the two pharaohs and the vassal princes of the Egyptian empire. (Amarna is the site where the royal archives were found. It was excavated in 1891–2.)

Reference to Jerusalem in the Tel el-Amarna letters

Eight of the letters are from the local ruler of Jerusalem, and are typical, with duplicity, intrigue, and cunning apparent beneath the fulsome veneer of sycophancy. Each vassal was suspicious of his neighbour, often with justice, and would write to the pharaoh affirming his own loyalty, charging the other vassals with treachery and vehemently denying any such practice on his own part. The ruler of Jerusalem at the time and signatory to the letters is Abdu-Heba, and he opens his first letter with the usual terms of self-prostration and adulation of the pharaoh, continues with a defence against the accusations of a neighbouring chief that he has been rebellious, and ends with a plea for help if his lands are to be saved:

'To the king, my lord: Thus Abdu-Heba, they servant. At the two feet of my lord, the king, seven times and seven times I fall . . . They blame me before the king, my lord, saying: "Abdu-Heba has rebelled . . ." Behold . . . the arm of the mighty king brought me into the house of my father! Why should I commit transgression against the king, my lord? . . . Let the king take care of his land . . . The lands of the king have all rebelled; Ilimilku [the ruler of Gezer, west of Jerusalem] is causing the loss of all the king's land . . . let the king, my lord, send out troops of archers . . . if there are archers here in this year, the lands of the king, my lord, will remain intact; but if there are no archers here, the lands of the king, my lord, will be lost.'

In his other letters, Abdu-Heba continues to repudiate the slanders against him, warns of continued threats to Jerusalem and repeats his pleas for military aid. Several of them, however, contain references to incidents which offer enlightening clues to the political, military and economic cir-

Greek Orthodox priest in the Old City. Gatepost of the Zion Gate is visible through a shell-hole in the arched chamber.

cumstances of Jerusalem and to the powers of its local ruler. One speaks of the revolt of the Egyptian garrison. Another complains that Egyptian mercenaries have plundered the ruler's own house and almost murdered him. There is a reference to the tribute paid by Jerusalem: 'I have sent gifts to the king, my lord, ... captives, five thousand silver shekels and eight porters for the caravans of the king.' That Abdu-Heba could send a caravan to Egypt suggests a certain importance to his own status and that of Jerusalem. That it was sometimes hazardous, reflecting an absence of order in the country, is indicated by the cry in one of his letters that a caravan was 'captured in the plain of Ajalon. Let the king, my lord, know that I cannot send a caravan to the king, my lord. For thy information.'

These are the last documentary records which mention Jerusalem until we reach the biblical account of the Joshua conquest in the middle of the thirteenth century BC. Jerusalem was not taken by the Israelites at that time. It was held by the Jebusites, a people whose origins have been the subject of considerable scholarly speculation but still remain unclear.

It is true that the first chapter of the Book of Judges says that 'the children of Judah had fought against Jerusalem, and had taken it, and smitten it with the edge of the sword'; but biblical scholars explain away this apparent contradiction by suggesting an inaccuracy in the brief summary of previous events contained in the first sentences of this chapter. They are agreed that for the two hundred and fifty years between Joshua and David, Jerusalem remained in Jebusite hands.

Just about the time when Joshua was engaged in the conquest of the hill country of Canaan, another people were entrenching themselves in the coastal region. These were the Philistines, a 'sea people' who are believed to have come from Crete and Asia Minor. They enjoyed a comparatively high standard of material culture, and were the first in the region to use iron weapons, which gave them the advantage over their adversaries. Palestine, derived from Philistina, was one of the names by which the country was known thereafter.

Establishing themselves along the coast, they soon began to push inland in an obvious campaign to take the entire country. In so doing they came up against the tribes of Israel, and, indeed, the Book of Judges is full of accounts of conflict and battle between the two nations. The period of Israelite settlement following the Joshua conquest would have been slow and difficult even if conditions had been ideal. What was required was a complete change in the Israelite pattern of living, adaptation to an independent and settled life of agriculture after generations of slavery, years of wandering in the wilderness and fighting on the move. But conditions were far from ideal. And what made matters worse were the inter-tribal quarrels and dissensions. It was inevitable that the Philistines should have registered significant successes in attacks on the territories of individual tribes; and there were periods when the Philistines had the upper hand in the country.

These were not circumstances which favoured an Israelite venture against the Jebusites of Jerusalem, and Jerusalem remained a hostile enclave within the Israelite settlement.

Eventually, however, the sharpening common danger from the Philistines led to closer cooperation between the Israelite tribes, and culminated in the general acceptance of a king, Saul, to reign over them. Monarchy was against the Israelite tradition, but it seemed the only means to secure the central authority necessary to meet the Philistine threat.

The early part of Saul's reign, in the latter half of the eleventh century BC, was marked by a series of spectacular successes against the Philistines and some of the other hostile neighbours. But, from the biblical account, it seems that Saul was more soldier than statesman, a gifted leader on the battlefield but with little skill in fashioning a cohesive nation. With the immediate danger over, inter-tribal quarrels began to re-emerge, a feature which the Philistines, when they had recovered, were quick to exploit. Saul finally went down to defeat in the disastrous battle on Mount Gilboa.

Nova urbis Hierosolymitanæ descriptio, qua forma & situ nostro seculo se conspiciendam præbet.

Saul's dynasty was continued briefly, and weakly, through one of his surviving sons, Ishbosheth, but he drew the loyalty only of the northern tribes.
The southern Israelites, the powerful men of Judah, rallied to David, who
now moved his headquarters to Hebron. During the next few years, they
fought each other as much as they fought their hostile neighbours, the
southerners becoming stronger, the House of Saul becoming weaker. The
people, too, were wearying of the senseless civil strife, which could benefit
only their common enemies. After the violent death of Ishbosheth, 'Then
came all the tribes of Israel to David unto Hebron, and spake, saying,
Behold, we are thy bone and thy flesh . . . and king David made a league
with them in Hebron before the Lord: and they anointed David king over
Israel' (II Samuel v, 1–3). This occurred in the last decade of the eleventh
century BC, near the year 1000.

It was David who completed the unification of the settled tribes of Israel
started by Saul. It was he who finally shattered the power of the Philistines.
It was he who, by a judicious combination of diplomatic alliances and the
waging of a series of successful campaigns against threatening neighbours,
firmly secured his frontiers. He was king of a united Israel that was now,
as it was not in Saul's day, in command of the entire country.

But not quite. There was still a hostile site that had not been reduced –
Jerusalem, and David resolved to take it.

The actual sequence of events, whether he went up against the Jebusites
at the beginning of his reign, or even before his accession to the united
sovereignty, or only after he had subdued the Philistines, is not clear from
the biblical record, and has thus been the subject of much scholarly speculation. Even more baffling has been the method of the city's capture. If the
account had been limited to verse 7 II Samuel v: '. . . David took the
stronghold of Zion [Jerusalem]: the same is the city of David', that would
have been that: a simple statement of the capture, and anyone's guess as to
how it had been effected. But the preceding and succeeding sentences add
some information – not enough to explain, just enough to puzzle. And
biblical scholars have been arguing ever since.

avid wielding the sword
Goliath after the duel.
rom a fifteenth-century
lustrated Hebrew manu-
ript, from Florence, now
the Israel Museum,
rusalem.

Verse 6 says: 'And the king and his men went to Jerusalem unto the Jebusites . . . which spake unto David, saying, Except thou take away the blind and the lame, thou shalt not come in hither: thinking, David cannot come in hither.' Verse 8 reads: 'And David said on that day, Whosoever getteth up to the gutter, and smiteth the Jebusites, and the lame and the blind . . . he shall be chief and captain . . .' I Chronicles xi, 6, adds: '. . . So Joab the son of Zeruiah went first up, and was chief'.

One problem was 'the gutter'. To what could this have referred? Most scholars held that this was the specially constructed water tunnel which gave the inhabitants access to the outside Gihon spring without being detected, in time of war, by the besiegers. David's stratagem would thus have been to get his men inside the city walls through the tunnel. But there were difficulties with this explanation. The tunnel was too narrow for manoeuvre, had a vertical incline, and could be negotiated by attackers only in single file which would have left them easy prey to the defenders when they emerged at the other end. Other scholars have sought to overcome this difficulty by suggesting that 'touches' is a more accurate translation of the original biblical Hebrew than 'getteth up', and arguing that the attackers 'touched' or held the upper entrance to the tunnel and thus cut off the city's water supply. One scholar has made the more revolutionary and feasible suggestion that 'gutter', too, is the wrong translation of the Hebrew, and that the meaning is 'trident', a kind of pitchfork in use at the time. The sentence would thus read: 'Whosoever, with his trident, smiteth the Jebusites . . .'

However, more puzzling to scholars was the reference to 'the blind and the lame'. What did that mean? Until very recently, there was grudging acceptance of the meaning given in the first century AD by the historian Josephus that this was a gesture of derision by the Jebusites. When David and his men appeared, the inhabitants of the city closed their gates and led out their maimed persons upon the ramparts 'out of contempt', as if to say that 'the very lame themselves would hinder' David's entrance; and relying, too, on the strength of their walls.

The acceptance of this meaning, as we say, was grudging, because it seemed to later scholars to be unreasonable to expect the Jebusites to be so sure of themselves and so contemptuous of the strength of David. He was, by then, in a strong position, commanding more support than Saul had ever had, and his prestige as a military commander must have been high even outside the community of Israel. The Jebusites must also have been aware of David's capture of or alliance with cities not far from Jerusalem. Their position, indeed, may well have been considered hopeless once David decided to march upon them, and it was therefore improbable that the Jebusites would have responded with the contemptuous presentation of their lame and their blind as defenders.

It was the brilliant reasoning of the Israeli archaeologist Professor Yigael Yadin which resulted in a satisfying solution to the biblical conundrum. He recalled the texts of early Hittite clay cuneiform tablets found early in this century at Boghaz-Koy, a Turkish village in the centre of Anatolia, which was the site of the Hittite capital in the second millennium BC. They referred

The bleak southern end of the valley of Hinnom.

28

to the solemn ceremonies in which Hittite soldiers swore allegiance to king
and country. The officiating priest would use symbolic devices to instil fear
into any who might contemplate betrayal, such as heating wax in front of
the parading troops and crying out: 'Whoever breaks these oaths . . . let
him melt like wax.' One of the Boghaz-Koy documents gives this description
of one of the rites:

> 'They parade in front of them a blind woman and a deaf man and you
> speak as follows: "See! here is a blind woman and a deaf man. Whoever
> does evil to the king and queen, let the oaths seize him! Let them make
> him blind! Let them make him deaf! . . . Let them annihilate him, the
> man himself together with his wife, his children, and his kin!" '

In his book *The Art of Warfare in Biblical Lands*, Yadin says: 'In the context
of this ceremony, it seems to me that we can now understand what the
Jebusites were trying to do as David and his men massed to attack their
city. Recognising the hopelessness of their plight, incapable of withstanding
an assault, they tried to deter David from making the attempt. This they

did by stationing a number of lame and blind people on the wall or near
the gate and staging something similar to the Hittite ceremony, using the
same ritual symbolism to strike fear into the hearts of David's men, crying:
"Except thou take away the blind and the lame, thou shalt not come in
hither" .... The Jebusites felt that David would not dare attempt an
assault against the power of the oath and the magic. And apparently their
threatening curse – and *not* their derision – had its effect on David's men,
so that he was compelled to offer a substantial reward to the man who
would perform an act of heroism. And what was this heroic act? Not
breaching the wall and capturing the city, but doing just one thing: being
the *first* to rise and go forward, the first to strike the Jebusites, the blind and
the halt, and demonstrate thereby to the whole army that they need not
fear to defy the power of the oaths and witchcraft of the Jebusites: "So
Joab the son of Zeruiah went first up, and was chief." '

By taking Jerusalem, David wiped out the last alien enclave in the hill-
country of the Hebrews and reduced the one hostile fortress that stood
between the two portions of the Israelite kingdom. Moreover, Jerusalem,

while not commanding the trunk road which ran through them, was not far from it, and finally, the city lay near the head of one of the passes which led up from Philistine territory. The capture of Jerusalem was thus as necessary to Israel's independence of the Philistines as it was to the unification of the northern and southern Israelite tribes.

These and other reasons were also behind the spectacular move which David now took, and which was to have so long and great an impact on history – making Jerusalem the capital of Israel. He could not remain in Hebron. It was too far south, and too closely associated with the southern

tribes alone, and for a similar reason he could not choose a northern site. His capital had to lie between the two. Jerusalem fulfilled this requirement. It had not been conquered previously, so it was not part of the settled territory of any of the tribes, and this very neutrality gave it an additional advantage.

It was from this capital that David ruled an increasingly vigorous kingdom, perhaps the most powerful State lying between the temporarily weakened rival empires, the Egyptians in the south and, now, the Babylonians in the north. Subduing the Philistines gave him complete control of the Mediterranean coastal plain. Capture of Damascus brought his dominions up to the Euphrates. Conquest of the eastern and southern territories gave him an outlet to the Red Sea, through the Gulf of Aqaba. His son and successor, Solomon, was to reap the full benefits of these military and political achievements.

And it was to this capital that David brought the Ark of the Law, to give it a permanent resting place. This symbol of his people's God, the mobile shrine and sanctuary, had accompanied the Israelites throughout their wanderings, had been carried by them into battle. Never had it had a permanent home, a special site with which it was associated. It had been captured a generation before by the Philistines, and after its rescue, had lain in Kirjath-jearim (near today's Abu Ghosh), some ten miles to the west of Jerusalem. David now 'brought in the ark of the Lord, and set it in his place, in the midst of the tabernacle that David had pitched for it.' (II Samuel, VI.) Thus was the most scared national and religious symbol of Israel brought to Jerusalem. Jerusalem was now not only the political and military capital of the country. It became, and was to remain for all time, the religious centre of the nation.

Permanent home for the Ark of the Law

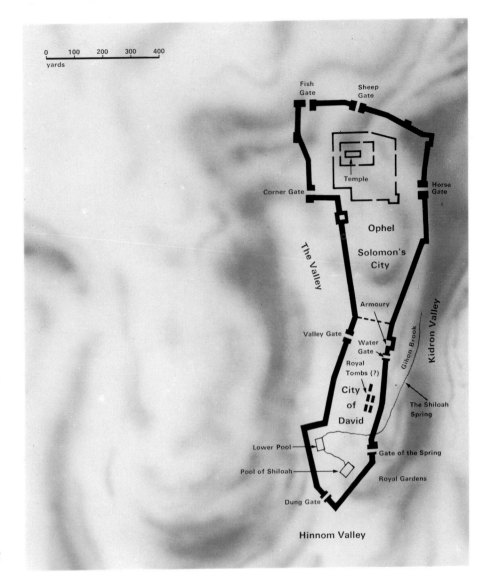

Position of David's city

The Bible describes some of the structures in the city erected by David. He built himself a residence of stone and cedar, with the aid of Phoenician workmen, for he had concluded an alliance with Hiram of Tyre – today's Lebanon. He also built barracks for his garrison and accommodations for the members of his family, the priests and the royal officials, as well as a royal tomb for himself and his dynasty.

There has long been speculation as to the nature of these buildings and their exact location – the location, indeed, not just of David's buildings but of his entire city. The best modern opinion, however, puts the City of David to the south of today's Old City, due south of the Temple compound which Solomon was to build. Recent archaeological excavations show that its northern wall was some 650 feet south of today's southern wall. Its southern boundary was the pool of Shiloah (Siloam).

The City of David was long and narrow, its defences based, as they had

been in the previous centuries, on the steep natural inclines to the east, south and west, and on a fortified rampart on the vulnerable north side where the city was linked to the plateau. The valley of Kidron lay below on the east, the valley of Hinnom on the south, and the central valley on the west. (The southeast part of the Kidron is also sometimes referred to as the Shiloah valley.) The main source of water came from the Gihon spring at the foot of the eastern wall – and was the principal reason for the siting of the city at that precise location. (The 'spring' of En-Rogel further south, just below the junction of the Kidron and Hinnom valleys, was one of several wells in the area which served as subsidiary sources.)

The names of the valleys bounding the city are sometimes confusing to the layman because the later, enlarged Jerusalem was also protected on the east, south and west by natural inclines, but they clearly could not be the same as those guarding David's city. The one constant, to this day, is Kidron, on the east. The names and whereabouts of the other two may best be understood in relation to the topography of the area.

The Valleys of Jerusalem

Think of two parallel ridges, east and west, lying north to south. They are divided by a central valley, which was later, in the first century, called the Tyropoeon valley. On the extreme east lies the Kidron. On the extreme west, i.e. on the west of the western ridge, but also curving round south, lies the valley of Hinnom. David's city covered the southern portion of the eastern ridge, and was thus bounded by the Kidron and central valleys with Hinnom touching its southern tip.

Later, when the western ridge was included in the entire city, Hinnom became the western and southern boundary (as it is today), and the central valley was inside the walls. Gradually, this central valley became filled in with debris and its level rose, so that now it seems an ordinary street in the Old City with no division between eastern and western ridges.

left: Lighting a candle in the antechamber of the traditional Tomb of David on Mount Zion.

right: The traditional Tomb of David (immediately beneath the mosque) on Mount Zion.

We know that David did considerable work on the city's defences, but there is no detailed indication in the biblical record of what this was. We are told that 'David dwelt in the fort . . . and . . . built round from Millo and inward'. Scholars agree that Millo was not the name of a place but the Hebrew word for filling. Some hold that it meant simply the piling of earth to provide a base for the new fortifications. Most, however, consider that it refers to the area just north of David's city, between that city and the later Temple compound, close to another high feature on the eastern ridge known as Mount Ophel.

In David's time, the Ark of the Law was still covered by a nomad's tent. He wished to build a permanent shrine, but it was not given to him to do so. The task of building the Temple fell to David's son, Solomon.

'It is easy to exaggerate,' says George Adam Smith, 'David's share in the making of Jerusalem. Her full influence and sacredness were a Divine achievement, which required the ages for its consummation. The

Prophets and the Deuteronomic legislation were perhaps the greatest factors in the development of the City; much of her glory, which the later literature throws back upon David, is only the reflection of their work. Nevertheless, it was his choice of her which started everything; which brought history to her walls and planted within them that which made her holy. The Man, whose individual will and policy seem essential to the career of every great city, Jerusalem found in David. He made her the capital of a kingdom; he brought to her the shrine of Israel's God; he gave her a new population. . . . But besides thus standing behind the City and providing the first impetus to her career, the figure of David stands out among the early features of her life more conspicuous than any of them. . . . Of all the actors on that stage . . . there is none who moves more clearly, whether under the stress of the great passions or through the details of conduct and conversation. . . . The drama of Jerusalem is never more vivid than while David is its hero.'

SEPTENTRIO

Stephano Bolton Civi Londinensi. T.E.
Hinc æstimeverum, vir ingenue, quantos Somp
tus Solomon fecerit hanc Structuram, cujus vel
Umbra hanc vult delineationem. Quæ in me
Munificentia tanti constitit.

ATRIA
Templi
Solomon

Equi Solis

MERIDIES

David was a hard man to follow. But Solomon proved equal to the challenge. Few great leaders in history have been succeeded by men of equal calibre. Yet Solomon carved out a name for himself comparable to that of his father. Their characters were vastly different, and so the fields in which their individual greatness expressed itself differed the one from the other. Both were statesmen, but David was also the great warrior. Solomon had to fight no great battles, and could concern himself with the economic development of a peaceful country, a peace made possible by the successful wars fought by his father. David emerges from the biblical record as a very human individual, with human foibles and weaknesses. We see him in temptation and in penitence, in grief and in ecstatic joy as he dances in front of the Ark. He is the self-made man, rough, rugged, volatile. Solomon is the suave heir, aloof, sophisticated, viewed always through his majesty and grandeur. He is 'Solomon in all his glory', and, as one historian observed, 'we see the glory, but are dazzled as to the man behind it.'

David brought all the tribes together, bequeathing to his son a united nation. Solomon consolidated it – though in the process sowed the seeds for its disruption. Solomon continued his father's alliance with Hiram of Tyre, and also 'made affinity with Pharaoh king of Egypt, and took Pharaoh's daughter, and brought her into the city of David'. With his frontiers secure, he applied himself to advancing the material prosperity of the country. He mined copper in the southern tip of the Negev. From the nearby port at the head of the Gulf of Aqaba, outlet to the Red Sea, 'he made a navy of ships' and, together with his Phoenician ally Hiram, developed a considerable maritime trade. Gold and silver and ivory were brought by sea from Ophir, and formed part of the overland commerce with Israel's northern neighbouring states. Imports from these states were traded for goods from Egypt, linen from that country, horses from Cilicia. Solomon seems to have been the tycoon of the area, or, in the more sober phraseology but exaggerated terms of the biblical description, 'So king Solomon exceeded all the kings of the earth for riches and wisdom.'

At the centre of this trade stood Jerusalem, recipient of its revenues. In

K

E

H

I   I   I

Stadt Ierusalem

the process, the vastly enriched city underwent a great expansion, its physical features matching its economic, political and religious status as the most important site in Israel. To the wealth brought by distant trade was added the labour of the whole nation, both being applied to embellishing Jerusalem with buildings which raised her above every other town in the country.

How was the national labour secured and harnessed for the aggrandisement of Jerusalem? Solomon divided the kingdom into twelve provinces, and each province was responsible for the upkeep of the royal court for one month a year. They also had to provide workmen for the buildings in the city, notably, as we shall see, for the Temple and the royal palace. They also had to contribute taxes for the construction of 'chariot cities' and forts to protect the trade routes and the approaches to Jerusalem. The biblical report, in I Kings IV, of the towns and districts called upon to make these contributions does not include Jerusalem itself, Bethlehem and Hebron – the seats of Solomon's family – as if they had been relieved of the national duty. This may have been a contributory cause of the defection of the northern tribes following the death of Solomon.

'In the fourth year of Solomon's reign over Israel . . . he began to build the house of the Lord' (I Kings VI, 1), and its construction was his most spectacular act. Nothing in the Bible is described in such great detail as the preparations for and the actual building of this Temple.

The site chosen was the highest spot on the hill-city, the 'threshing floor

: The Temple forecourt, envisaged by a sixteenth-tury German engraver.

ht: A sixteenth-century presentation of Abraham's would-be sacrifice of Isaac Mount Moriah, ditional site, later, of the mple Mount.

of Araunah the Jebusite' (II Samuel XXIV), which King David had insisted on buying and for which he had paid 'fifty shekels of silver'. He thus acquired ownership of the land on which he himself erected an altar and upon which his son Solomon would later erect the permanent shrine. It was located to the north of the city compound as it existed in David's day, where it stood within its own huge court. Tradition associates this site with Mount Moriah, scene of Abraham's would-be sacrifice of Isaac, and to this day the Temple Mount is also referred to as Mount Moriah.

Biblical description of Solomon's Temple

The whole of chapter VI and most of chapter VII in the First Book of Kings are given over to a detailed description of the architecture and interior decorations of the Temple. It was a thick-walled, rectangular building of squared stones and cedar beams, lying from east to west, about one hundred and ten feet long, forty-eight feet broad (the measurements include the wall-thickness), and more than fifty feet high. A huge porch extended on its eastern side and 'side chambers' were built against the other three sides. A partition wall inside the Temple marked off the main hall from 'the oracle . . . to set there the ark of the covenant of the Lord'. This 'oracle', later called the Holy of Holies, was a cube of thirty feet, panelled, as was the main hall, with richly carved cedar, and floored with 'planks of fir'– probably cypress wood. Lighting of the hall was through high lattice windows above the side chambers. The 'oracle' was dark, lit by a single lamp. Overhanging the Ark were 'two cherubims of olive wood, each ten cubits [15 feet] high', and the Bible details numerous other decorations.

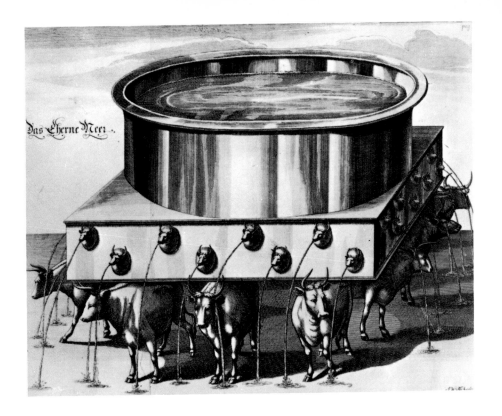

Das Eherne Meer.

above: The 'molten sea', supported by twelve
oxen, that stood in the Temple of
Solomon as described in 1 Kings 7:23–26.

below: Court of the Priests in Solomon's
Temple, as imagined by a sixteenth-century
German theologian.

*: Ivory figure of a
ierub', discovered in
maria. It is said to be
hilar to the figures of
erubs' placed in the
oly of Holies in Solomon's
mple.

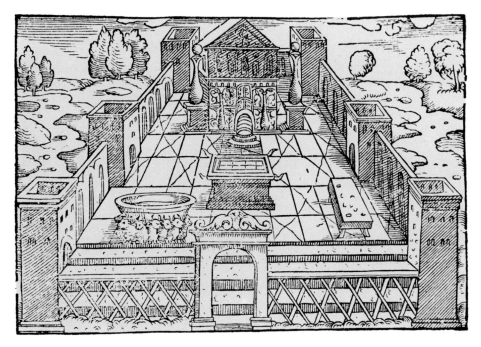

left: A medieval engraving after the description by Josephus, of the garments worn by the high priest (left) and ordinary priests (right).

With its completion came the great day of dedication. And in the biblical description of the dedication ceremony may perhaps be found the answer to those who have suggested an incongruity between this sumptuous House of the Lord and the traditional simplicity with which the Hebrews had launched and nurtured the new, radical idea of monotheism. This was the only contemporary religion which fashioned no material shape or image of God. The heart of the Temple was the 'oracle', the gloomy cubicle containing the Ark, which from the days of Sinai was believed to have been 'inhabited' by the Supreme Being. He was represented by no image. The Ark was reverently laid in the darkness of the inner chamber. 'And it came to pass, when the priests were come out of the holy place, that the cloud filled the house of the Lord.' Towards this sombre and image-less shrine, the people of Israel, crowding the sunlit court outside, worshipped His presence, while Solomon pronounced the nature of the One God (I Kings VIII.)

Through his words and those of the later prophets, the Temple and Mount Zion, the city of Jerusalem in which it stood, were to be invested with a unique sacredness, fount of the Jewish religion and central inspiration of the Jewish nation, long after the Temple had been destroyed, and throughout all the centuries of the Jewish exile.

Below the Temple (but also on high ground, believed to be Mount Ophel), and separated from it by a wall, rose another formidable building, the 'House of the King'; and below that, Solomon constructed a large complex of royal buildings. They are described in I Kings VII. From these

The dedication ceremony

right: Temple area from the southeast. Left, the city wall joins the wall of the Temple compound. Middle left, Mount Ophel and the recently excavated ancient wall of Ophel.

50

biblical details and from the contours of the site, we can recapture the appearance of this handsome cluster of structures, and a truly imposing spectacle they must have presented. On the highest point of the hill-city loomed the Temple, surrounded by its huge court. Below it, in a series of terraces and standing in their own courts, rose the royal palace and the 'house for Pharaoh's daughter'; the 'porch of pillars'; the 'porch for the throne'; and the large 'house of the forest of Lebanon', so named, presumably, because its cedar beams rested upon forty-five pillars also of cedar wood brought from the Lebanon. The latter buildings served as the business quarters of the palace, offices where state affairs were conducted, assembly rooms, and the hall where Solomon sat in judgement. In addition to the walled courts in each of the terraces, the entire complex was encircled by a strong wall of stone, so that it must have appeared as a separate citadel in Jerusalem.

There are only fragmentary references to Solomon's work on the fortifications of the city, nothing beyond the fact that he built 'the wall of Jerusalem round about' – we cannot trace its line – and that he also 'built Millo, and repaired the breaches of the city of David'. Millo, as we have already indicated, may have been the area between the Temple compound and David's city. There is no clue as to what and where the breaches were that he repaired.

The walls of
Solomon's city

Many and considerable were the achievements of Solomon, statesman, diplomat, builder, trader, industrialist, administrator, philosopher, poet, man of peace, and man of God. Undoubtedly, his greatest act was the building of the Temple and the consolidation of Jerusalem as the religious centre of his people.

However, in the process of his formidable work of national development, he displeased many sections of the population, notably – and the experience is not uncommon in our own day – by his taxation policy. By the strength of his personality he held the nation together, in a united Israel. On his death, the stresses proved too strong for his successor. He had reigned, like his father, some forty years. He died in the year 922 BC.

4 The Divided Kingdom

Shortly after the death of Solomon, political catastrophe struck the country, tearing it apart – literally. The northern tribes revolted against the Davidic dynasty, centred in Jerusalem, and now represented by Solomon's weak son, Rehoboam. They seceded, setting up their own state which they called Israel. Jerusalem was now the capital only of a truncated State to the south, formed mostly by the territory of the tribe of Judah. The united kingdom, founded by David and made prosperous by Solomon, was now divided into the Kingdom of Israel and the Kingdom of Judah.

The bitter tribal squabbles whose eruption had led to the split were sharpened after the secession, and for the next fifty years Israel and Judah were at war with each other. This civil war could give comfort – and opportunity – only to their enemies. Egypt's pharaoh Shishak moved up through the Negev, attacked Judah and, though he did not take Jerusalem, mounted sufficient pressure to draw ransom from her.

Political and economic decline of Jerusalem

The political decline of Jerusalem was matched by a decline in its economic fortunes. The buildings of David and Solomon remained, but the transactions conducted therein were no longer the affairs of a large and prosperous country. Jerusalem no longer controlled the outlet to the Red Sea in the south, and Israel lay as a barrier between it and its former Phoenician trading companion in the north. Revenues from maritime commerce and overland caravans no longer flowed into Jerusalem's coffers. The steady stream of people from all over the land to visit the Temple now ceased. Most of the men of Israel did not enter Judah.

But some did. These were 'the priests and the Levites' (the priestly tribe); for Jerusalem retained the one great symbol which sanctified the city as the spiritual centre of the nation – Solomon's Temple. And this may well have been the principal element which sustained Jerusalem through its misfortunes, eventually led to the Israel-Judah rapprochement, and ultimately brought about the restoration of the city's status, power and influence over the Hebrew nation. Certainly the arrival of the priests from Israel strengthened the religious importance of Jerusalem in the sombre years immediately following the division of the kingdom.

Rock carved tombs in the Kidron valley. The tomb on the right is called the Tomb of the prophet Zechariah'.

Rehoboam was followed by his son Abijah who was succeeded by his son Asa, and it was Asa, during his long reign from 913 to 873, who seems to have exercised a stronger hand than his father and grandfather in safeguarding both the religious purity of Jerusalem and the borders of Judah, even extending them somewhat at the expense of Israel. This, together with the rise in Israel of the energetic house of Omri in the final years of Asa's reign, paved the way for peace between the two kingdoms.

Omri ascended the Israel throne in the year 876, and he set out to make Israel great. He it was who established a new capital which he hoped would rival Jerusalem. This was Samaria, on the western face of Mount Ephraim, commanding the principal pass in the area to the Mediterranean coast. He was also concerned in developing the wealth of his country, and this could be done only within peaceful borders. If he could be sure of his southern frontier, he would be less likely to fear attack from his Syrian neighbours in the north. He was thus in the mood to consider some kind of non-aggression pact with the kingdom of Judah.

Neither he nor Asa lived long enough to consummate it. But their sons did – Asa's son Jehoshaphat, who came to the throne of Judah in 873, and Omri's son Ahab, who became king of Israel in 869. Despite their wide differences in character and religious outlook, they both had an understanding of politics, and 'Jehoshaphat . . . joined affinity with Ahab'. At last the war between Israel and Judah came to an end.

Jehoshaphat, in the twenty-four years of his leadership of Judah, proved to be the most inspiring influence in Jerusalem since the days of Solomon, regulating religious life, advancing justice throughout the land, and heightening the position of the city in the eyes of all Israel. On the military and economic fronts, with his northern border secured through his alliance with Israel, he was able to subdue his southern neighbour, Edom, and thereby re-take the Negev and the access port to the Red Sea. He had little success in reviving Solomon's maritime activities, but there were renewed revenues from the overland caravan trade, and Jerusalem benefited accordingly.

Improved conditions under Jehoshaphat

The Bible makes no mention of any special structural work undertaken by Jehoshaphat in Jerusalem, and so we may assume that the city skyline was no different from what it was in Solomon's time. What went on beneath the skyline, however, was marked by a vibrant spirit, mood, prosperity and sense of order that had not been known for two generations.

Jerusalem under his three successors reached a low ebb, but it flourished under his great-grandson Joash (837–800), who carried out the first extensive repairs to the Temple.

The Davidic line was continued with the accession of Joash's son Amaziah in the year 800. He prospered at first, and, anxious to open the road to the south, fought a successful battle against the Edomites (who had revolted after Jehoshaphat's death). Fresh from his victory, he boastfully challenged the king of Israel, and there followed the last military engagement between the two Hebrew kingdoms. Amaziah was defeated at the battle of Beth Shemesh, and, we are told, the king of Israel pressed on to Jerusalem. He attacked the city from the north, the side where the fortifications were not

bounded by ravines, 'and brake down the wall of Jerusalem from the gate of Ephraim to the corner gate, four hundred cubits'.

The greatest fortification programme in Jerusalem since the time of Solomon was undertaken by the son of Amaziah. This was Uzziah, who ruled from 783 to 742, and under him Jerusalem entered a long and prosperous period. One of his first acts was to restore the alignment with the kingdom of Israel which his father had broken. With their common frontier no longer an area of concern, both kingdoms could tackle their hostile neighbours without fear of assault on their rear. Israel pressed north, defeated the Syrians and 'recovered Damascus'. Uzziah moved south. His father had won a battle against Edom but had apparently not subdued her. Uzziah did, recapturing the Negev and regaining an outlet to the Red Sea. 'He built Elath, and restored it to Judah.' As a result, the two kingdoms between them soon commanded the territory from the southern tip of the Negev right up to the borders of Phoenicia and Damascus in the north, and both flourished. The effect on Jerusalem was to revive much of the prosperity she had enjoyed under Solomon.

II Chronicles XXVI recounts the deeds of Uzziah in varied fields. So impressive were his military campaigns against foes on every side that 'his name spread abroad even to the entering in of Egypt.' He also built cities, raised fortresses in the desert, dug wells, developed farming 'for he loved husbandry', and, above all, strengthened the city of Jerusalem.

He may well have been concerned about the comparative ease with which Jerusalem's defences had been breached in his father's time. He set about ensuring the safety of the capital. 'He built towers in Jerusalem at the corner gate' – probably at the extreme northeast – 'and at the valley gate' – believed to be on the southwest of the city – 'and at the turning of the wall, and fortified them.'

What did the city look like at the time, and what was its pattern of life? Fortunately, there are additional biblical accounts of the period which offer illuminating indications; for it is during Uzziah's reign that there are

written records of the words of the great contemporary prophets, Isaiah, Amos, and Hosea, whose utterances have come down to us through the ages. The pictures of national life presented by Isaiah and Amos have a pastoral background; but against this background we also view an extraordinary enterprise in building and trade. This, of course, with its attendant concern for material values, wealth and luxury, is bitterly censured by the prophets. But in so doing, they tell us of society at the time. Trade with the nations of the Middle East brought many foreign products and inventions into Judah and Israel, and contact with foreign ways and customs. Isaiah mentions the ships of Tarshish and the 'treasures upon the bunches of camels', showing the flourishing maritime and overland commerce; and he cries out that Judah and Jerusalem are 'replenished from the east . . . and they please themselves in the children of strangers'. Amos describes an excessive zeal in buying and selling. Hosea attacks northern Israel as a very 'Canaan', a deceitful merchant who gives short weight and 'loveth to oppress'. All three condemn the people's materialism, the striving for luxury, the covetousness, and the threat to religious – or ethical – values.

It is evident from all this that there was an influx of foreign elements into Jerusalem, alien traders who were no doubt accommodated outside the city walls. Within the walls, the inhabitants were probably more crowded than ever, with more buildings going up in more compact quarters. Towering above them stood the Temple; but the call to righteousness was sounded more eloquently and passionately on the tongues of the prophets.

Uzziah's son Jotham, who reigned from 742 to 735, also 'built cities in the mountains of Judah, and in the forests he built castles and towers'. But the only reference in the Bible to his additions to the Jerusalem structures is: 'He built the high gate of the house of the Lord, and on the wall of Ophel he built much.' The 'high gate' was the northern gate of the inner court of the Temple. The 'wall of Ophel' lay to the south of the Temple and the palace compound. The probability is that Jotham now strengthened this in the style of his father's fortification work.

Fortifications added by Jotham

58

These fortifications were to be tested in the reign of Jotham's son Ahaz (735 to 715). In the year 744, a strong new ruler, Tiglath-Pileser III, had reached the throne of Assyria, with powerful imperial ambitions and the military strength to achieve many of them. One was to subjugate the two Hebrew kingdoms. The northern one, Israel, was nearest to him, and it soon became a vassal state. This heightened the pressure on Judah, whose king sought to propitiate Tiglath-Pileser both by paying tribute and adopting idolatrous ways.

For a time it seemed to work – but only because Tiglath-Pileser was preoccupied with conquests to the north of Assyria. Israel and Syria (not to be confused with Assyria, which was to its west, north and east) decided to take advantage of this preoccupation, and formed a league against Tiglath-Pileser which they wanted Judah to join. Ahaz, newly ascended to the throne, refused, as his father had done before him, whereupon they decided to move against him. 'And it came to pass . . . that Rezin the king of Syria, and Pekah . . . king of Israel, went up toward Jerusalem to war against it.'

This brought panic to Jerusalem, and the Bible records that the hearts of Ahaz and the people were gripped with fear. Then rose the prophet Isaiah to instil courage into the king, and he went 'forth now to meet Ahaz . . . at the end of the conduit of the upper pool in the highway of the fuller's field', to tell him 'fear not, neither be fainthearted' (Isaiah VII, 3, 4). Scholars suggest that Isaiah found Ahaz inspecting the water supply *outside* the city wall – because he had to 'go forth' to the conduit – to devise means of preventing its use by the approaching invaders. There are several theories as to where exactly was this 'upper pool' and what and where was 'the fuller's field', but all are speculative.

Apparently the fortifications of Ahaz' predecessors Uzziah and Jotham were too strong for Pekah and Rezin, for they 'could not prevail against it [Jerusalem]'.

Tiglath-Pileser took action against the league of rebellious vassals, and soon most of northern Israel was conquered and eventually occupied. Samaria alone, the capital and vaunted rival of Jerusalem, held out. Tiglath-Pileser's son and successor, Shalmaneser V, laid siege to it, yet the city withstood attack for more than two years. Shalmaneser died while the siege was in progress, and was followed by Sargon II. It was to this Assyrian ruler that Samaria fell. The year was 722 BC. Many thousands of the surviving Israelites were exiled to Upper Mesopotamia and Media.

The northern Hebrew kingdom was destroyed, its people banished. Judah alone was preserved, remnant of the nation in its own land, with Jerusalem now the sole national capital, home of the central sanctuary, the Temple, and sole trustee of the hopes of the people of Israel.

Jerusalem now enters a pregnant phase in her history, a period marked, on the one hand, by deadly menace from the victorious Assyrians who were now right on the borders of Judah, and, on the other, by a tremendous spiritual upsurge. The two figures who play a giant role in this Jerusalem phase are the prophet Isaiah and King Hezekiah (715 to 687).

We have seen something of the part played by Isaiah in Ahaz' day in stiffening the resolve of Judah's ruler. His role in the political and military spheres, as well of course as in the religious, was to be more formidable in the reign of Ahaz' son and successor, Hezekiah. The central scene where this role was played was Jerusalem, and the Book of Isaiah offers us glimpses of life in and around the city as intimate and colourful as some of those in the Book of Samuel in the time of David, some 250 years earlier.

Isaiah grew up and dwelt in Jerusalem, living with its sights and sounds and patterns for some fifty years. He was familiar with and conditioned by its history. This was his heritage. In return, he was to give to Jerusalem – and, through Jerusalem, to civilisation – a prize of measureless worth, powerful moral precepts in sublime language. His concern was immediate and local – developing Jerusalem's spiritual forces, rallying her military strength, arresting her threatened destruction. The impact was timeless and universal.

In his prophetic pronouncements, Isaiah draws upon the landscape of the region and the common scenes he encountered inside the city as he walked its streets and watched from his housetop. And so we read of the bleak surrounding hills and 'the desolate valleys' and 'the holes of the rocks' – much as they are today; of the fruitfulness nearer home – the wheatfields of 'the valley of Rephaim' (now a broad Jerusalem street bearing the same name) where 'the harvestman gathereth corn', the vineyards where they 'gleaned grapes' and the groves where they 'shook the olive tree'. Inside the city, which he also calls 'Mount Zion', we get a detailed description of the crowds in the Temple court and the milling multitudes in the narrow lanes, the horses and chariots, the 'tumult' and the 'movement' there, the lust for material riches, for silver and gold, which so outrages the prophet, and the indulgence in carse festivities with 'the harp, and the viol, the tabret, and the pipe, and wine . . . but they regard not the work of the Lord'.

Over all this hangs the grim threat of invasion. Isaiah, through his burning words, rouses the king and people to meet it not only by making the fortifications more secure, but above all by a strengthening of the spirit.

cenes from the life of Isaiah :
p, he has the vision of the
ord ; centre, an angel
urges him with a living
al from the altar, and
ottom, he is shown
ealing the king
f his sickness.

He emphasizes the moral and religious significance of Jerusalem, the spiritual fountain it was and must again become, 'the faithful city . . . full of judgement [and] righteousness'. It has been debased, but the Lord has not forsaken it. Later, when the battle is joined, his words take on a crucial urgency – and, at the critical moment, decide the issue.

Meanwhile, Hezekiah got to work on the physical strengthening of Jerusalem. The new Assyrian ruler, Sennacherib, was smashing his way even further southwards, and although Hezekiah could and did put off the confrontation by various alliances with kingdoms equally threatened by the Assyrians, he knew that eventually Jerusalem would be attacked.

Hezekiah's physical improvements to the city

It is evident from the Bible that he was much preoccupied with the water system, and from this ancient record – as well as from a remarkable archaeological discovery some ninety years ago – we know that he devised a plan to secure his own water supply and at the same time deny water to the enemy. However strong his fortifications, he would never withstand siege if his water ran out. By the same token, a besieger could not long maintain his pressure on the city if, in the arid surroundings in which his men would be encamped, the main local source of water were cut off.

Hezekiah accordingly 'made a pool, and a conduit, and brought water into the city' (II Kings xx, 20). He 'also stopped the upper watercourse of Gihon, and brought it straight down to the west side of the city of David' (II Chronicles xxxII, 30). Gihon, as we have seen, was at the foot of the eastern wall and was the main source of the city's water. What Hezekiah did, therefore, was to seal the Gihon cave in which the spring issued, thus denying it to an invader. At the same time, he cut a 600 yard tunnel (preserved to this day) which led the water under the southeastern part of the city and out to a reservoir or pool inside the city at a point where the ground is lower. This is known as the pool of Siloam (or Shiloah).

In 1880, the biblical record was confirmed by the discovery in the rock wall of the lower entrance to the tunnel, south of the Temple area, of a Hebrew inscription on how the underground passage was excavated. The language is perfect classical Hebrew prose, its contents and script pointing to the reign of Hezekiah. The words were inscribed on a prepared surface of the wall, like the surface of a tablet, but the top part of the inscription was missing. Six lines alone remained, enough to tell the story of how the tunnel was dug by two teams of miners starting at opposite ends, working towards each other and meeting in the middle. It is known as 'The Siloam [or Shiloah] Inscription'. In its standard English translation, it reads as follows:

'[. . . when] (the tunnel) was driven through. And this was the way in which it was cut through: – – while [. . .] (were) still [. . .] axe (s), each man toward his fellow, and while there were still three cubits to be cut through, [there was heard] the voice of a man calling to his fellow, for there was an overlap in the rock on the right [and on the left]. And when the tunnel was driven through, the quarrymen hewed (the rock), each man toward his fellow, axe against axe; and the water flowed from the spring toward the reservoir for 1,200 cubits, and the height of the rock above the head(s) of the quarrymen was 100 cubits.'

The upper entrance, near the Gihon spring, of Hezekiah's Tunnel, eighth seventh century BC.

ancient pool of Siloam,
he southern tip of the
in the time of David.

Hezekiah also set about strengthening the fortifications of the city, re-organising the armed forces and the reserves, and re-equipping them to meet the inevitable Assyrian attack. He 'built up all the wall that was broken, and raised it up to the towers, and another wall without, and repaired Millo in the city of David, and made darts and shields in abundance. And he set captains of war over the people. . .'.

While all these works were being undertaken, he introduced radical religious reforms, repairing the Temple, purifying it, breaking up the idols that had made their appearance in the previous reign, and outlawing pagan worship and the barbaric forms this sometimes took. When he roused his people, it was with the 'Lord God of Israel' on his tongue, and 'the people rested themselves upon the words of Hezekiah'.

Jerusalem defies
Sennacherib

In the year 701, Sennacherib struck. The powerful Assyrian monarch had already accomplished a victorious march southwards and reduced all the territories to the west, north and northeast of Judah. He had also cut deeply into the Hebrew kingdom and had 'come up against the fenced cities of Judah, and took them'. Jerusalem alone remained. Sennacherib now proceeded against it.

The mighty conquests which had brought him so close to Jerusalem, coupled with the sacking of all the other principal cities of Judah, prompted Sennacherib to attempt to cow Hezekiah into surrender without having to fight. He sent his Chief Minister Rabshakeh together with an army which encamped near the ramparts of the city, and they tried with threatening words to demoralise the Jerusalemites into submission.

Hezekiah sought advice from Isaiah, and it was the prophet's rallying words which stiffened his people's resolve to resist and saved Jerusalem. The biblical record condenses them into a few sentences. His key exhortation was: 'Be not afraid of the words which thou hast heard.' The surrender appeal was spurned. The siege was withstood. The attackers eventually left and returned to the Assyrian capital.

Jerusalem was untaken. Its miraculous survival against so mighty a foe, the one fortress to remain standing when all others in the path of the conqueror had fallen, gave it a special mystique. Here alone the Assyrians had been held. The Temple was intact. At a crucial moment the words of Isaiah, the man of God, had saved the city. The feeling spread that Jerusalem was inviolable. In physical terms, this article of faith was to receive a tragic jolt 114 years later. In spiritual terms – Jerusalem in the heart of the Jew – it remains alive to this day.

Acknowledged was the greatness of Jerusalem, the greatness of Isaiah, and the supremacy of Jerusalem as the centre of the Hebrew nation. In its defiance of Sennacherib, Jerusalem knew one of its finest moments.

Hezekiah died in 687 and was followed by his son, Manasseh. With the departure from the Jerusalem scene of two such outstanding personalities as Hezekiah and Isaiah, who died about the same time, there was a reaction to the religious reforms they had introduced and to the spirit of political resistance they had firmly upheld. It is clear from the contemporary records that Manasseh soon became a vassal of the Assyrians even though their power was now on the decline, and it may have been with the desire to please his masters that he reverted to the idolatrous ways of his grandfather. Indeed, though his reign was long, he receives comparatively brief mention in the Bible, and this is largely a list of his evil deeds. The most barbaric of them was that 'he caused his children to pass through the fire in the valley of the son of Hinnom' – a reference to child sacrifices. (This is the origin of the currently used term Gehenna as a synonym for hell, or a place of burning or of torment; it derives from the Greek corruption of the original biblical Hebrew for 'valley of Hinnom' which is *Gai-Hinnom*.)

Josiah, 'the righteous king', was Manasseh's grandson. His reign (640–09) was marked by a powerful religious revival, reminiscent of the time of his great-grandfather. Hezekiah's contemporary had been the prophet Isaiah. The prophet in the period of Josiah was the great Jeremiah.

Effect of biblical discovery on Josiah's reign

Josiah's departure from the pagan ways of Manasseh and his efforts to restore the purity of the Jewish religion received a dramatic spur by the discovery of a sacred 'book of the law' in the Temple. It is generally accepted by scholars to have been some form of the biblical Book of Deuteronomy, and it was apparently discovered while the Temple was being repaired and renovated. The High Priest handed it to the king's scribe and the scribe brought it to Josiah and read it before him. The king was overwhelmed by the stern denunciations in the Book against the neglect of its laws, and was moved to take urgent measures to fulfil its commands. His first step was to assemble 'all the men of Judah and all the inhabitants of Jerusalem with him, and the priests, and the prophets, and all the people, both small and great' in the Temple compound, and 'he read in their ears all the words of the book of the covenant which was found in the house of the Lord.'

outheast angle of walls of
e Temple compound.
ecent clearance of debris
ncovered part of the
djoining ancient city wall.

What followed swiftly was the destruction of all the pagan altars and places of idolatrous worship in the territory 'from Geba to Beersheba' – the limits of Judah – and a rigid ban on pagan practices, particularly child sacrifice, 'that no man might make his son or his daughter to pass through the fire to Moloch.'

National worship was centralised in Jerusalem and recognition of the one sanctuary for the One God, the Temple, weakened with the split of the kingdom after Solomon, was now settled once and for all. Jerusalem was the shrine of the one great system of ethical and intellectual monotheism in the ancient world.

Three times every year, the manhood of the people made the pilgrimage to Jerusalem, a practice which continued throughout the centuries. The occasions were the three religious festivals – Passover, marking the exodus of the Children of Israel from Egypt and their liberation from bondage; Tabernacles, recalling the temporary booths which gave them shelter during their wanderings through the wilderness; and the Feast of Weeks, the celebration of the granting of the Torah to Moses on Mount Sinai. These gatherings did much to promote national unity and discipline. They also offered a convenient means of instructing the people in great causes. Jeremiah chose these occasions for the delivery of his prophecies, being able to address the country's masses in the Temple courts.

Beginning of religious pilgrimage to Jerusalem

The people of Judah worshipped in Jerusalem. Josiah was anxious that the Hebrews in the former kingdom of Israel should do the same. His great-grandfather, Hezekiah, had had a similar wish, and had appealed to those living in the original tribal provinces to celebrate the Passover in Jerusalem. Josiah could elicit a greater response, for he was living in the period of Assyrian decline, when control by this northern power over the former province of Israel had slipped. Josiah accordingly marched north and annexed these territories, and the Hebrews again became one. At the next festival celebrations in Jerusalem, with the people of both Israel and Judah taking part, 'there was no Passover like to that kept in Israel from the days of Samuel the prophet; neither did all the kings of Israel keep such a Passover as Josiah kept, and the priests, and the Levites, and all Judah and Israel that were present, and the inhabitants of Jerusalem.' Josiah may well have considered this the crown adorning his life's achievement.

The Assyrian decline, which Josiah had exploited, was to prove his own downfall, and shortly afterwards, the temporary downfall of Judah and Jerusalem. Contenders for the succession of the great Assyrian empire were Babylon in the northeast and Egypt in the southwest. Judah, lying between them, was crushed in the ensuing struggle, in which the Babylonians eventually came out on top.

By the year 602, Judah had become a vassal state within the Babylonian empire. The young king Jehoiachin (grandson of Josiah), his mother, notables, craftsmen and artisans were deported to Babylon. The king's uncle, Zedekiah, was left behind as puppet ruler in Jerusalem. For several years, Judah remained submissive, the mood of revolt kept at a low key. Elements urging resistance were restrained. But these later got the upper hand, and in about the year 588 they rebelled. The Babylonians moved

Pilgrimage to Jerusalem: men near the Western Wall wear tefillin, phylacteries, forehead and left arm during a service.

68

south to crush them, and encamped outside the gates of Jerusalem.

There was no surrender, the people resolving to defend the city. No immediate attempt was made to storm its ramparts. Instead, the Babylonians built a siege wall round it to starve the inhabitants, but they abandoned it in the middle in order to deal with a threat from Egypt. They soon returned to Jerusalem, however, and resumed their blockade.

For many months Jerusalem held out. There were times when Zedekiah thought of surrender. The prophet Jeremiah, too, thought resistance futile – but for a different reason: he foresaw the temporary fall of Jerusalem because of its iniquities. The people, however, listened to neither, and stubbornly insisted on holding out.

In mid-summer of the year 587, the walls of the starving city were breached, the battering rams piercing the northern defences. The king and some of his guards 'fled by night by the way of the gate between two walls, which is by the king's garden'. They were pursued, and Zedekiah was captured 'in the plains of Jericho'. His end was cruel. Brought before Nebuchadnezzar, he was made to witness the slaying of his sons, and then his eyes were put out. He was carried off in chains to Babylon and there he died.

A month after the fall of the city, Nebuchadnezzar sent one of his commanders to Jerusalem with instructions to level it. 'He burnt the house of the Lord, and the king's house, and all the houses of Jerusalem . . . and brake down the walls of Jerusalem round about.' The precious Temple ornaments 'and such things as were of gold . . . the captain of the guard took away.' Some of the prominent citizens (who had escaped the earlier deportations) were executed. The rest were deported to Babylon.

Thus fell Jerusalem, and thus was the Temple destroyed. In its carnage and ruin, bereft of its people, Jerusalem became the desolate city.

In the hearts of its exiles, however, Jerusalem continued to live. In the misery of their banishment, it haunted their thoughts, and all hopes were centred on its resurrection. It was 'by the waters of Babylon' that their cry was uttered which echoed through all the centuries of Jewish history:

'We hanged our harps upon the willows in the midst thereof
For there they that carried us away captive required of us a song;
And they that spoiled us required of us mirth,
Saying, Sing us one of the songs of Zion.

'How shall we sing the Lord's song in a strange land?
If I forget thee, O Jerusalem, let my right hand forget her cunning.
If I do not remember thee, let my tongue cleave to the roof of my mouth;
If I prefer not Jerusalem above my chief joy.' (Psalm 137).

A burial cave of the secon century BC, discovered b chance in 1956 during house-building in the residential district of Rehavia. It is called 'Jas Tomb' because this nam was found carved within

Less than fifty years later, the great Babylonian empire fell as suddenly as it had arisen, overwhelmed by Cyrus, founder of a new Persian empire. Cyrus was a rare leader – a brilliant military figure and a wise and enlightened ruler. Unlike the Assyrians – and most other ruling nations of the region at the time – who brutalised their subject peoples and sought to terrorise them into conformity with the reigning régime, Cyrus from the very beginning offered cultural autonomy to his heterogeneous subjects; respected – and gave protection to – their creeds and their customs; and, where possible, entrusted their administration to one of their own leaders. Indeed, Persian troops were given specific orders not to interfere with the religious rites of the vanquished.

Babylon, the capital, was taken at the end of the year 539 BC, and by 538 the entire empire came under Persian control, right up to the frontier of Egypt. Jerusalem and Judah were thus brought within Cyrus' rule.

In the first year of his reign, Cyrus, in accordance with the liberal aims which he applied to all his communities, issued a decree about the Jews which was to have a momentous impact on history. He proclaimed himself in favour of the restoration of the Jewish community and religion in their own land. All Jews in Babylonian exile who wished to return to Judah would be permitted to do so. They could rebuild their Temple in Jerusalem, and his royal treasury would contribute towards the building expenses. The holy Temple vessels taken away by Nebuchadnezzar would be restored. Jews who remained in Babylon would be encouraged to aid the returnees and contribute to the rebuilding of their Jerusalem sanctuary.

Placed in charge of this 'Return to Zion' movement was 'Sheshbazzar, the prince of Judah'. Scholars consider that Sheshbazzar was a son of Jehoiachin, the boy-king of Judah who had been carried into captivity in the deportations of 598, and he was thus the legitimate heir to the throne of Judah. Cyrus appointed him Governor, and he applied himself immediately to the task of building the new Temple on the site of the old. Exactly how much was done by him and how much under his successor is obscure, for the biblical report telescopes the accounts of Sheshbazzar and his nephew, Zerubbabel, who followed him as 'Governor of Judah', crediting most of the work to Zerubbabel.

It is evident that little progress was made in the first few years. Rebuilding a ruined city with a thin population would have been slow work under the best of conditions. Conditions were far from ideal. The newcomers were harassed by poverty and the struggle for existence, and aid from the Persian treasury was apparently inadequate. They were also harassed by local hostility and by the traditional enmity of the neighbouring territories. By the time Cyrus died, killed during one of his campaigns in 530, little more than the foundations had been laid of the Second Temple. And not much more had been accomplished by the year 522, when Cambyses, son and successor to Cyrus, took his life.

Yet seven years later, in March of the year 515, the Temple was completed. 'And the children of Israel, the priests, and the Levites, and the rest of the children of the captivity, kept the dedication of this house of God with joy.' This was during the reign of the third Persian monarch Darius I.

As large as the First, though less ornate, the Second Temple may yet have seemed more impressive to the people at the time. For it was now the sole great edifice in a city whose walls were still in ruins. Solomon's Temple had risen amid a formidable complex of royal buildings, the king's palace, the judgement hall, the barracks, the arsenal, all enclosed within a single large compound. None had been rebuilt. The Second Temple thus stood alone upon the high ground, set in its own courts and surrounded by its own wall. As George Adam Smith points out, it was a kind of 'religious Capitol . . . without civic or political rival'; and this could not be without its impact on the spiritual mood of the people.

For the next seventy years, the history of Jerusalem is obscure, though from the prophetic writings it is apparent that the community failed to live up to the high hopes of the first and second waves of returnees from Babylon.

Only with the coming of Nehemiah and Ezra do the tides turn – and the mists lift upon the chronicles of the period. The detailed record of activities in Jerusalem and the development of the city and the community under their leadership appears in the Bible, in the books bearing their names.

Leader of the third wave of returnees from Babylon and one of the giant figures in Jewish history was the remarkable Nehemiah, who arrived in Jerusalem in about the year 440 as Governor of Judah.

By the second half of the fifth century BC, the Jews of Babylon had become well established, boasting scholars, men of commerce and high officials of the Persian régime. Devout adherents of their religion, their eyes turned to Jerusalem, they were deeply concerned with its welfare, and gravely disquieted by continued reports of its suffering.

The Persian monarch at this time was Artaxerxes I (465–24), son of Xerxes and grandson of Darius I, and Nehemiah was an official at his court. 'In the twentieth year of Artaxerxes' – that is, in the year 445 – Nehemiah was visited by a delegation from Jerusalem, headed by 'Hanani, one of my brethren', who reported that the people there 'are in great affliction and

The building of the Te[m]
An illumination from a
fifteenth-century Catal[an]
manuscript.

*Completion of the
Second Temple*

reproach: the wall of Jerusalem also is broken down, and the gates thereof are burned with fire.'

Nehemiah, after reporting this to the king and expressing his anxiety to go to Jerusalem to rebuild it, was sent there as Governor.

On arriving in Jerusalem, Nehemiah lost no time in tackling the city's problems, the most urgent of which was the safety of the community. After only 'three days . . . I arose in the night, I and some few men with me', and made a secret survey of the city walls to see what needed to be done. He details (Nehemiah II, 13–15) his inspection tour, leaving through 'the gate of the valley', going to the 'dung port', 'the gate of the fountain', the 'king's pool', then up 'by the brook, and viewed the wall, and turned back'. He then assembled the Jewish leaders, called to mind 'the distress that we are in, how Jerusalem lieth waste', shook them out of their apathy, told them 'the king's words that he had spoken unto me' – the implications of which could not have been lost on them – and roused them with 'come, and let us build up the wall of Jerusalem.' Their response was: 'Let us rise up and build.'

Labour for the work of reconstruction was provided by contingents from the city and village communities in Judah, each being assigned a specific part of the wall. Such heart and spirit did the Jews put into their work that the wall was erected 'in fifty and two days'. (The first-century historian Josephus writes that the final wall, complete with battlements and gates, took about two and a half years.)

While the wall was going up, the kingdoms bordering on Judah tried to hinder the work, subjecting the Jews to frequent harassment. Nehemiah's answer to their raids was to organise his people into two formations. All were armed, but one maintained the defences while the other continued with the work. As soon as the raiders appeared, a trumpet was sounded at the point of danger and all rushed to stave off attack. Nehemiah was with them all the time, tireless, resourceful, encouraging them, overseeing their labours, checking the defences, moving from post to post with the trumpeter at his side so that he could personally give the alarm at the last feasible moment before attack so as not to waste any working time. As Nehemiah writes:

'. . . half of my servants wrought in the work, and the other half of them held both the spears, the shields, and the bows, and the habergeons [coats of mail]. . . . They which builded on the wall, and they that bare burdens, with those that laded, every one with one of his hands wrought in the work, and with the other hand held a weapon. For the builders, every one had his sword girded by his side, and so builded. And he that sounded the trumpet was by me.'

Nehemiah ends this episode with the following human touch: 'So neither I, nor my brethren, nor my servants, nor the men of the guard which followed me, none of us put off our clothes, saving that every one put them off for washing.'

Nehemiah's details of the wall's construction – and the speed of the accomplishment – show that his men followed the line of the old Jerusalem ramparts, those destroyed by Nebuchadnezzar. Destruction had been heaviest along the eastern and northern walls, the gates and wall here had to be built from the foundations. The work on other sections was largely reconstruction. All gates were fitted with new beams, doors, locks and bars.

The prophet Ezra read the Law.

The site enclosed by Nehemiah's walls again included from south to north, the pool of Siloam, the City of David, Ophel, and the Temple Mount. There were eight gates: the Dung Gate in the extreme south; the Fountain Gate a little higher up, in the southeast corner; the Water Gate in the east, just above the Gihon Spring; the Horse Gate in the northeast, just above Ophel and southeast of the Temple; the Sheep Gate in the north; the Fish Gate in the northwest corner; the Corner Gate in the northwest, opposite the Horse Gate; and the Valley Gate in the west.

Area enclosed by Nehemiah's walls

The Book of Nehemiah is more than a description of Jerusalem's walls. An exciting narrative of a momentous period in Jewish history and a sociological document on the fashioning of a people, it is the personal story of a most remarkable leader who vastly enriched the long drama of Jerusalem. He explains his policies and describes his conduct with a wealth of circumstance and detail, setting them in a descriptive context of life in the city. We thus get a lively picture of Jerusalem at the time from passing mention, as he tells his narrative, of such items as the atmosphere in the Temple court during a festival; the night vigil of the guards; the gates at dawn with fish-dealers waiting to get in (and being turned away on the Sabbath); the hospitality of the Governor's table (though he himself lived frugally 'because the bondage was heavy' upon his people) – at which 'one ox and six choice sheep; also fowls' were provided for upwards of 150 persons; and a typical scene of asses ambling into the city laden with the produce of the countryside – 'sheaves . . . wine, grapes, and figs, and all manner of burdens'.

There is a description of a late summer, early autumn, month in Jerusalem, the month of Iyar (September or October), after the completion of the walls, when the Jews were to celebrate (and do to this day) the Festival of Succot (tabernacles or booths). This festival recalls the improvised booths which the Children of Israel used in their wanderings through the wilderness after the Exodus from Egypt.

Nehemiah writes that this festival had not been kept, though it was 'written in the law which the Lord had commanded by Moses, that the Children of Israel should dwell in booths in the feast of the seventh month.' The people were then accordingly told to 'Go forth unto the mount, and fetch olive branches, and pine branches, and myrtle branches, and palm branches, and branches of thick trees, to make booths, as it is written. So the people went forth, and brought them, and made themselves booths, every one upon the roof of his house, and in their courts, and in the courts of the house of God, and in the street of the water gate. . .' (A similar sight may be seen each year during the Succot Festival in today's Jerusalem, with families gathered for meal times in their balcony booths, and, during the preparatory days, bearing 'pine branches' and 'palm branches' and myrtle leaves through the streets to their homes.)

The festival of Succot

Nehemiah had come to a Jerusalem that was largely in ruins and to a community that was disillusioned and lax, at the mercy of corrupt officials, and on the verge of disintegration. Nehemiah revived the community, gave it dignity and uncorrupt rule, cohesion and political status.

But there was one area of communal life which had become equally lax and which Nehemiah felt himself unqualified to reform – religion and religious practice. The man who was – and who did – was the man whose name ever after was to be linked to that of Nehemiah, and who shares with Nehemiah the credit for the total reorganisation of the Jewish community, setting it on the course it was to follow in the succeeding centuries. That man was Ezra the Scribe.

Ezra had secured permission from the Persian monarch to lead a great company of priests and Levites to Jerusalem in order to instruct the Jewish community in the Torah, to reform worship and customs which had been abused, and to introduce honesty and order into their religious life.

With the political stability and sound administration provided by Nehemiah, Ezra set about establishing a firm spiritual basis for the Jewish community, one that would hold not only for the Jews of Jerusalem and Judah, but for Jewish communities wherever they lived. That basis was the law, the Torah, in the form in which it had evolved in Babylonia since the exile and governed the community there. What Ezra did, in fact, was to establish Judaism, Judaism as practised ever after, in its basic form, by orthodox Jews throughout the world.

Ezra and the company he brought with him from Babylonia were not priests in the parochial sense, nor was he an ordinary scribe. Rather were they teachers, expounders, guardians and interpreters of the written law, and it was Ezra who set the tradition whereby those who guided the community in the law, who declared its meaning, developed its details and applied them to particular cases, were the men of learning, the sages. To this day, among Jews, it is the rabbi as scholar who commands respect, not necessarily the rabbi as priest or minister.

Through Ezra, the Torah became the accepted constitution of the Jewish community. Henceforth, wherever the Jews lived, whether in Jerusalem or in the Diaspora (the Jewish communities outside Israel), whether in a subject Judah or in a free and independent state, they would possess and preserve their own special identity. For more than five hundred years Jerusalem had been the physical capital of Jewry. Through the towering impact of Ezra it also became the spiritual capital of Jews in their dispersion, and was to secure their future as a people when the great exile occurred some five hundred years later.

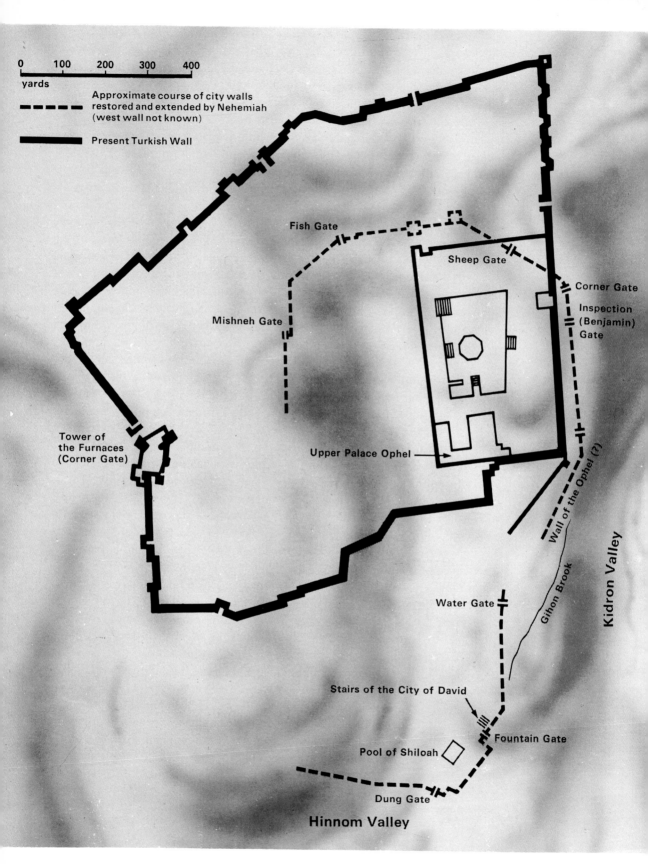

0   100   200   300   400

yards

- - - - - Approximate course of city walls
restored and extended by Nehemiah
(west wall not known)

━━━━━ Present Turkish Wall

Fish Gate

Sheep Gate

Corner Gate

Inspection
(Benjamin)
Gate

Mishneh Gate

Tower of
the Furnaces
(Corner Gate)

Upper Palace Ophel

Wall of the Ophel (?)

Kidron Valley

Water Gate

Gihon Brook

Stairs of the City of David

Fountain Gate

Pool of Shiloah

Dung Gate

Hinnom Valley

There are almost no written records enabling us to reconstruct the history of Jerusalem for the next hundred years, up to the fall of the Persian empire before the youthful wonder king of Macedonia, Alexander the Great, in the year 332 BC. What is known however is that Jerusalem was now the capital of a considerably truncated Judah, the Jewish region within the larger Persian satrapy (colonial province) called Abar-Naharah (Aramaic for 'beyond the river'). It appears to have experienced rather less turbulence than the previous years, and from the prophet Joel we get a picture at the beginning of the fourth century of a pastoral and God-fearing people. Beyond the city walls, Jewish farmers tend their olive groves, vineyards and cornfields. Above the Temple Mount rises the smoke of sacrifice. And at the great annual festivals come the murmur of the throngs at prayer in the Temple courts and the shout of their responses.

From the history of the area we know that at this time the influence of the Greeks, great seafarers and traders, was making itself felt in the Middle East, and Judah could not have been immune. This Hellenistic influence was given wings by the phenomenal military successes of Alexander, who had conquered western Asia, including India, before he died in 323 BC at the age of thirty-two.

Alexander left Jerusalem untouched, but with his death came the disintegration of his newly-won empire, his generals quarrelling among themselves. Two of them vied with each other for the control of, among other areas, the land of Judah. The two were Ptolemy, who had seized Egypt and set up his capital in newly established Alexandria, and Seleucus, who after some years had become master in the north, with capitals in Antioch in Syria and Seleucia in Babylonia. After a series of battles fought between former comrades-in-arms, Ptolemy won, and for the next century Jerusalem came under the authority of his dynasty.

Ptolemy took back with him to Egypt a large number of Jewish prisoners, and from this nucleus there grew the important Jewish community of Alexandria, soon to become the greatest centre of Diaspora Jewry. Beyond this, however, Ptolemaic rule in Jerusalem and Judah was on the whole

Map showing the area of Nehemiah's city.

benevolent, and the Jews enjoyed almost complete autonomy, though they paid an annual tribute. This period, the third century BC, was one of comparative stability – though the Seleucids tried several times to take the country and were driven back by the Ptolemies – and Jerusalem developed and prospered. Contemporary Greek writings dwell on the thriving agriculture of Judah and the strength of Jerusalem, its community well organised and administered. The Temple and its worship continue to dominate Jewish national life.

Incidentally, it was under Ptolemy II's patronage that the translation of the Bible into the Greek language was inaugurated in Alexandria. The result was the Septuagint – so called because the translation was believed to have been done by seventy notable Jewish scholars brought specially to Alexandria from Jerusalem for the purpose. The project was initiated by the Jewish community of Alexandria so that their Greek-speaking children could remain familiar with their own sacred writings.

To these Jews of Alexandria, as indeed to the growing Jewish communities in other cities of Egypt and elsewhere in the world, Jerusalem remained the city of their devotion, and the Temple the target of their spiritual loyalty. Exile enhanced their fervour towards the Holy City – just as it had to the Babylonian deportees. When they prayed, they turned to Jerusalem. Each year they sent their half-shekel for the support of national worship as Temple tribute. Whenever they were able, they went on pilgrimage to Jerusalem on the annual 'pilgrim' festivals. This was to be the pattern continued by Diaspora Jewry after the Great Exile in AD 70.

right: Kindling the Channukah lights to commemorate the Maccabean liberation. An illumination from an Italian–Hebrew manuscript dated 1470.

left: The Jewish prayer 'Next Year in Jerusalem' and a representation of the city as central motif, on a plate presented by London Jewry to the Lord Mayor in 1730.

overleaf: An early nineteenth-century *succah* (booth) from South Germany, with a landscape of Jerusalem painted on the rear wall, now in the Israel Museum, Jerusalem

הנסים ועל הפרקן ועל
הגבורות ועל התשועות
ועל המלחמות שעשית
לאבותינו בימים ההם ובז
ובזמן הזה בימי מתתיה
כהן גדול חשמונאי ובניו
וחשמונאי ובניו כשעמדה מלכות יון הרשעה על עמך
ישראל להשכיחם מתורתך ולהעבירם מחקי רצונך ואתה ברחמיך
הרבים עמדת להם בעת צרתם רבת את ריבם דנת את דינם נקמת
את נקמתם מסרת גבורים ביד חלשים ורבים ביד מעטים וטמאים
ביד טהורים ורשעים ביד צדיקים וזדים ביד עוסקי תורתך ולך
עשית שם גדול וקדוש בעולמך ולעמך ישראל עשית תשועה גדולה
ופרקן כהיום הזה ואחר כך באו בניך לדביר ביתך ופנו את
היכלך וטהרו את מקדשך והדליקו נרות בחצרות קדשך וקבעו
שמנת ימי חנכה אלו להודות ולהלל לשמך הגדול   ועל כלם

לפורים

הנסים ועל הפרקן ועל
הגבורות ועל התשועה
ועל המלחמות שעשית
לאבותינו בימים ההם ובז
ובזמן הזה בימי מרדכי
ואסתר בשושן הבירה בשן
כשעמד עליהם המן הרשע בקש להשמיד להרג ולאבד את כל
היהודים מנער ועד זקן טף ונשים ביום אחד בשלשה עשר לחדש
שנים עשר הוא חדש אדר ושללם לבוז ואתה ברחמיך הרבים הפרת

fes les roi haditacions en
une ate pres de ierlin que
lon apeloit modin. for la
roit z de grant aier. ensi
com uos portes oir en lestoi
re. la quel su entaillee. por
lor grant boute. z por lor

le rei uaine. z helozas le spie
en cui tens la ate de ierlin
z le temple su reedesiez.
lxr. ans. apres ce que Ja
buchodonolor. lor destruite
z gastee. si com oin truepe
en la sin dou liure des rois.

In the year 198 BC, the Seleucids under Antiochus III succeeded, where his predecessors had failed, in meeting and routing the Ptolemaic Egyptian army, driving them from Asian soil, and annexing the land between, Palestine. Jerusalem, having lived for more than a century under the 'Greeks of Egypt', the Ptolemies, now came under the 'Greeks of Syria', the Seleucids.

The first years were benevolent, the Jews of Judah being granted a large measure of autonomy and complete freedom of worship. With the accession of Antiochus IV, Epiphanes, in the year 175, however, this policy was drastically changed. With cultural unity as his aim, and idolising Greek ways, he sought to impose a standard pattern of life upon his heterogeneous vassals and to advance the worship of Greek gods.

Desecration of the Temple

In Jerusalem, some Jews responded favourably to Hellenism. This caused sharp internal conflicts in which the emperor often intervened. In 169, he seized the opportunity of 'restoring order' during one such clash to enter the Temple, plunder it, and carry off its holy and precious vessels and treasures. This touched off city-wide riots, and Antiochus sent in a stronger force who slaughtered many of the inhabitants and partially destroyed the walls and a number of buildings. He followed up this action by erecting a Hellenistic fortress, called the Akra, on the western hill, opposite the Temple Mount, garrisoned by Seleucid troops.

Then came the final phase of his attempts to Hellenise the Jews. The Temple, 'that was to be called thenceforth after the name of Olympian Zeus', was defiled. Within its sacred precincts, Greek troops practised heathen rites, introduced the image of Zeus, sacrificed swine upon the altar, destroyed the Scrolls of the Law. The observance of customs special to the Jewish religion, such as the Sabbath, traditional feasts, circumcision, was punishable by death. So was failure to observe idolatrous Hellenistic practices. Jews were executed for refusing to eat pig's flesh, or bow down to Greek images, or partake of the monthly sacrifice in honour of the king.

This brutality was met at first by passive resistance on the part of the orthodox Jews, known as the Hassidim, Hebrew for 'pious'. They continued

enes of the Maccabees' olt. From a richly minated thirteenth- tury French nuscript.

observance of the Jewish law in secret. When caught, they were slain. Ordered to 'conform with Greek manners', they preferred death to submission. Persecution mounted and resistance now became active. This in turn was met by more brutal repression which, in its turn, brought more intensive and widespread rebellion. Soon all Judah was in armed revolt.

In the year 167, the Jews struck back at their oppressors in a national war of resistance which was to constitute one of the heroic chapters in Jewish history. The liberation and 'cleansing' of Jerusalem and freedom of worship – which now meant freedom from Seleucid rule – was the aim of the campaign. The strategy of the Jewish rebels was thus to isolate the Jerusalem garrison of occupying troops by seizing key positions commanding all the approaches to the city. It was, inevitably, a guerrilla campaign on the part of the poorly armed Jews against the regular forces of Antiochus' régime.

The start of the revolt

The action which sparked the revolt occurred in the village of Modin (17 miles northwest of Jerusalem, and just east of today's international airport of Lod).

There, a Jewish priest named Mattathias, of the House of Hasmon, had settled after leaving Jerusalem to escape the religious restrictions. He was a courageous and patriarchal figure, and his five sturdy sons, Johanan, Simon, Judah, Eleazar and Jonathan, were fashioned in his mould.

Into Modin one day rode the officers of Antiochus. They assembled the populace, announced that there would be public worship of the pagan god by the sacrifice of swine's flesh, and called upon Mattathias to 'come forward first, and carry out the order of the king . . . then you and your sons will be counted among the friends of the king. You and your sons will be honoured with silver and gold and many gifts.' Mattathias solemnly refused: 'We will not listen to the decree of the king by going astray from our worship, either to the right or to the left.'

Another Jew then came forward to comply with the heathen order, whereupon Mattathias 'brought courage to decision, and running up he slew him upon the altar. The king's man who was enforcing the sacrifice he also killed at the same opportune time, and pulled down the altar. . . . Then Mattathias shouted out in a loud voice in the town, saying, "Let everyone who is zealous for the Law, and would maintain the covenant, follow me." He and his sons fled to the mountains, and left whatever they possessed in the town' (I Maccabees II, 15–28).

Soon joined by the Hassidim and other Jews who had resolved to resist the tyrant, Mattathias and his sons formed guerrilla bands and, operating from the hills, they began to harry the Seleucid troops, destroy pagan altars, and give heart to the small Jewish communities in the countryside. Many of these quickly followed the standard of revolt, swelling the guerrilla ranks.

Some months later, Mattathias died, and leadership passed to his son Judah, nicknamed the Maccabee – Hebrew for 'hammer'. He, his brothers and their followers are therefore known as the 'Maccabees'; but the dynasty they founded is called 'Hasmonean', after Hasmon, who, according to Josephus, was the great-grandfather of Mattathias.

Judah the Maccabee

Judah was clearly a born military leader, courageous, resourceful, inspiring, and it was he who transformed his guerrilla bands into a national

liberation army with independence as his objective. The Book of Maccabees
mentions four major battles, and these show the Seleucid aim of crashing
through to Jerusalem and Judah's strategy of blocking their entry. Jewish
reconnaissance patrols first bring news that General Apollonius is muster-
ing 'a large force from Samaria, to wage war against Israel'. Judah goes
out to meet him while he is still getting organised 'and struck him down
and killed him. Many were killed, and the rest fled.'

Then came General Seron 'with a strong expedition' and tried to break
through from the northwest. He was met and routed by the Maccabees at
the pass of Beth-Horon, just southeast of Modin, and some twelve miles
northwest of Jerusalem. A third expedition was routed at Emmaus, some
fifteen miles west of Jerusalem, and a fourth at Beth Zur, the same distance
south of the city.

The approaches to Jerusalem were now free, and there was little immediate fear of another expeditionary force. The Maccabees thereupon 'gathered
together and went up to Mount Zion'. They beheld a sorry sight on the
Temple Mount, the sanctuary desolated, the altar profaned, the gates
burned, the priests' chambers torn down, weeds growing in the courts 'as
in a forest or as on one of the mountains'. Seleucid troops were still behind
their fortified walls in the Akra citadel, so 'Judah appointed certain men
to fight against the garrison . . . until he could cleanse the sanctuary.'

All traces of the cult of Zeus were removed, a new altar was installed, and
new sacred vessels were brought in. The Temple was then re-dedicated.
The date was 'the twenty-fifth day of the ninth [Jewish] month', corre-
sponding to the month of December. It was three years to the day after it
had been desecrated.

'Judah and his brothers and the entire congregation of Israel decreed
that the days of the dedication of the altar should be kept with gladness

A late nineteenth-centu[r]
Channukah lamp, mad[e]
limestone, from the Yem[en]

and joy at their due season, year after year, for eight days from the twenty-fifth of the month of Kislev' (I Maccabees IV, 59). To this very day, Jews throughout the world celebrate the Feast of Channukah (Channukah is Hebrew for 'dedication') by the kindling of lights, lighting a candle on the first night and an additional one on each successive evening, and by reading from the Book of the Maccabees. Most modern celebrants are familiar with the Talmudic story of the 'miracle of the oil' as the reason for the eight day feast: that when the Hasmoneans came to re-dedicate the Temple, there was only enough pure (undefiled) oil in the cruse to burn for one day, yet, through the blessing of God, it lasted for eight days, when a fresh supply became available.

It is evident from the Maccabean story that Judah and his men re-occupied not the whole city of Jerusalem but only the Temple Mount. (From the state in which he found it, its courts overgrown with shrubs, it seems that the Greeks must have tired of abusing the sanctuary.) The town seems to have remained in the possession of the Greeks and the apostates, guarded by the garrison in the Akra citadel. The rest of the original population, loyalist Jews who had escaped massacre, had long joined the faithful villagers of Judah who had flocked to the Maccabean banner in the hills and wastes of the surrounding countryside.

The city itself thus continued to serve as a Seleucid base. The Temple Mount continued to serve as a Jewish outpost. For the next twenty-three years, the Greeks and the Jews were to face each other from the walls of their fortresses, the Akra and the Temple Mount, only a few score yards apart. They could harass each other, but neither could breach the other's fortifications. Numerous and fierce were the engagements in the years that followed, with intervals of truce when pressure on the Maccabees was lightened by power struggles for the Seleucid throne after the death of Antiochus Epiphanes in 163.

Judah the Maccabee was killed in battle at Elasa (some twelve miles northwest of Jerusalem) in the year 160. Maccabean leadership now passed to his brother Jonathan who carried on the struggle for liberation. This, plus sharpened internal conflict among the Seleucid hierarchy, together with their realisation that trying to suppress the Jewish religion was futile and a moderate policy might prove more fruitful, prompted the imperial rulers to yield. Jonathan entered Jerusalem in the year 152, not only as military leader but also as High Priest, and virtual Governor of Judea. To this post he was appointed by King Demetrius, who had seized the Seleucid throne in 162, and was now being challenged by a rival. Each sought the help of the rebel Judean leader, and Jonathan enjoyed far-reaching concessions.

The city of Jerusalem was now in the possession of the Maccabees. Jonathan began to rebuild and refortify it, and also to extend independent Jewish rule over an increasingly wide area of Judah. Among the cities that fell to him were Jaffa, Ashkelon and Ashdod. Jerusalem once again had its outlet to the Mediterranean. The Akra citadel, however, remained a Greek stronghold, some scholars suggesting that its disbandment was one concession the king was not prepared to make.

Jonathan was treacherously killed by a Seleucid general in 143, and was succeeded by his last surviving brother, Simon. (Johanan had been killed earlier, and so had Eleazar, dying a spectacular death on the battlefield.) In the year 141, the Akra citadel capitulated. 'The yoke of the heathen' was lifted, and a formal Jewish assembly in Jerusalem confirmed Simon in the titles of 'High Priest and General and Ruler of the Jews'. These titles were to be hereditary, and under his successors they developed into the rank of kingship. Issue of a Jewish coinage under Simon marked the completeness of his sovereignty. (The coins did not bear his head.)

The Hasmonean dynasty With Simon there begins the Hasmonean dynasty, which lasted until the Roman conquest in 63 BC – and a further brief spell from 40 to 37 BC. The early Hasmoneans added a golden chapter to the history of Jerusalem and to the history of the Jews, but later it was gravely tarnished by bitter factional conflict. Their dynasty at first provided strong and comparatively stable administration, and, taking advantage of Seleucid decline and the consequent imperial rivalries in the Middle East, they succeeded eventually in encompassing within independent Jewish rule almost the entire area which had constituted the undivided kingdom of Israel under David and Solomon. As a consequence, Jerusalem, the religious and political capital, also prospered physically, growing in population and acquiring more buildings. Life in the city became busier than ever, with more and more pilgrims from the country and from the Diaspora visiting the Temple, and merchants using trade routes now within control of the Jewish State arriving to arrange their affairs.

John Hyrcanus Simon was murdered in 135 and was succeeded by his son John Hyrcanus, who, with Seleucid decline, was free to develop his independent state. Under him, territories regained included part of Transjordan in the east, Samaria in the north, and the land of Edom (Idumea) in the south. (The Idumeans, who were converted to the Jewish religion, were later to produce the celebrated king, Herod the Great.)

Internally, there was trouble between two rival Jewish factions, the

Sadducees and the Pharisees, which was to become more bitter as time went on, and was to have its impact on the fate of Jerusalem on the eve of its fall in 63 BC, and of its destruction in AD 70. Volumes have been written on the detailed differences between these two groups, religious, political and economic. Two generalisations will suffice us here. The Sadducees were firm adherents of the written commandments of the Torah, saw the Temple as the centre of religious life, were supporters of the priestly class, and approved of the combined political and religious leadership of the High Priest. The Pharisees wanted the separation of religion and politics, gave importance to the oral Law as well as to the written, respected non-priestly expounders of the Torah more than they did the rigid Temple priests (as did the generations which followed Ezra the Scribe) – and with all this were more concerned with religious values than with political independence.

Judah Aristobulus   The conflict became more pronounced when Hyrcanus died in 104 and was succeeded by his son Judah Aristobulus, who promptly proclaimed himself king – the first Hasmonean to use this title. He reigned only one year (though in that year he managed to regain the rest of Galilee) and was followed by his brother, Alexander Jannai. Under him, the rift between his people widened, erupting eventually into civil war, and he dealt with his opponents, the Pharisees, most cruelly. A number had joined the Seleucid king, Demetrius III, to fight against Jannai, and when some were captured, Jannai had them publicly executed in the centre of Jerusalem and massacred their families. For such treatment, and for his general harsh and intemperate behaviour, the reign of King Alexander Jannai, who was also known as Jonathan the High Priest, is a blot on the Hasmonean record, even though he widely extended the frontiers of the state. By the time he died, in 76 BC, Jewish sovereignty covered – in the terminology of today – the whole of the Mediterranean coastal plain (with the exception of Ashkelon) from Mount Carmel in the north to the southern end of the Gaza Strip in the south; the entire country west of the Jordan and of the Dead Sea, from the northern Negev in the south to Galilee in the north (thus including the 'West Bank'); and a considerable belt of territory east of the Jordan, from western Syria in the north to just beyond the southern end of the Dead Sea.

Though he had two eligible sons, Alexander Jannai designated his wife, Salome Alexandra, as his successor, and she reigned from 76 to 67 BC.

Of the two sons she had borne Jannai, she appointed the elder, Hyrcanus, High Priest. He was, says Josephus, 'but little qualified for the management of state affairs . . . and of a more tractable disposition than Aristobulus, who was of an active and enterprising temper'.

The power of the Pharisees rose during her nine year reign, to the point where some Sadducees were put to death on the charge of having abetted Jannai in his massacre of Pharisee captives. In the year 67, during the final days of Salome's life – she was nearly eighty – Aristobulus, with Sadducee backing, proclaimed himself king. War ensued between the two brothers, and the younger emerged the victor, starting a four-year reign as Aristobulus II which was to end with the loss of Jewish independence.

There was a brief reconciliation between the two rivals. But then Antipater *Antipater's advice to Hyrcanus* (father of the future Herod the Great), the leading Idumean and counsellor at the Jewish court, advised Hyrcanus to seek the aid of Aretas, king of the Nabateans (whose capital was Petra in Transjordan), in winning back his kingdom. Hyrcanus did so, fleeing to Petra, and joined Aretas in the invasion of the Jewish State in 64 BC.

The force was too strong for Aristobulus, and he was pressed back inside Jerusalem, finally fortifying himself within the walls of the Temple Mount. It was in imminent danger of falling when the power of Rome intervened.

Rome's conquering hero, Pompey, was leading a successful campaign in Armenia at the time, and had despatched a force southwards to take Damascus. When that city fell, he sent his commander Marcus Scaurus to take over. Scaurus, when he reached Damascus, heard of the trouble further south, in the land of Judah, and promptly went to investigate, losing no time in seizing this golden – in the literal sense – opportunity where two rivals would be bidding for his aid. Aristobulus won – '400 talents' was the price – and Scaurus immediately threatened Aretas 'with Pompey and the Romans' unless he raised the siege on Jerusalem. Aretas quickly retired, and back to Damascus went Scaurus, heavily laden with bribes.

But the respite enjoyed by Aristobulus – and Jerusalem – was brief indeed. Pompey came on into Syria, conferred in Damascus, and resolved to continue marching southwards. He entered Judah, took Jericho, and advanced on Jerusalem. Josephus writes that Aristobulus, shaken by the impossible odds, went out to present his submission; but his supporters were bent on resistance, and when Pompey's officer came to receive the surrender, they refused to allow him even to enter the city. Pompey accordingly put Aristobulus in custody and appeared in force before Jerusalem.

Pompey's advance on Jerusalem

Strife then broke out in the city between the supporters of Aristobulus, who called for war and the rescue of the king, and the partisans of Hyrcanus, who thought the chances hopeless and submission the most prudent course. The former, outnumbered, retired into their Temple stronghold, destroyed the bridge linking the Temple to the Upper City, 'and prepared to fight to the death'. The supporters of Hyrcanus, on the other hand, concentrated in the Upper City, opened their gates to Pompey.

What Pompey saw, in reconnoitring the possible lines of attack, were the strong outer walls of the Temple compound with steep natural slopes on all except the north side, and access from the western, or city, side now denied by the destruction of the bridge. He accordingly resolved to attack from the north, though even here there was a broad and deep ditch, dug by the defenders, and protected by huge towers. (The well-travelled first-century BC Greek geographer and historian, Strabo, says the ditch was 60 feet deep and 250 feet broad.)

Pompey set his troops to filling this ditch, a formidable task, says Josephus in his book, *The Antiquities of the Jews*, because of its size and also because the Jews harassed them from the towers above. When the ditch was filled, Pompey rolled across it the siege engines and battering rams which he had brought up from Tyre, and began attacking the wall, his stone-throwers trying to prevent interference from the besieged. Neverthe-

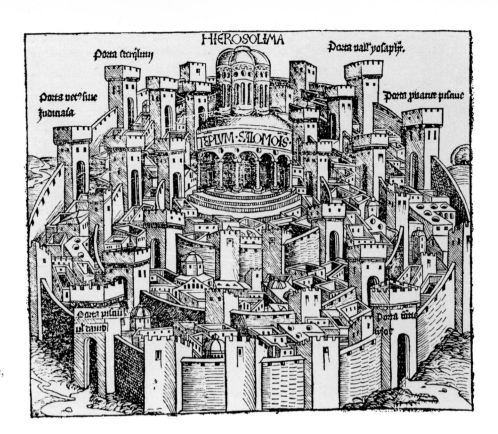

HIEROSOLIMA

Porta ccclinij   Porta vall' yosaphť.

Porta vet'sive judiaala

TEPLVM·SALOMOIS·

Porta pilani ul' dauid

Porta pianie pisane

Porta tñt' stor

less, for weeks he could make no headway. Only when the siege was in its third month did the Romans succeed in effecting a breach and swarming through. 'The Temple was taken on a fast day. . . On entering the place the enemy made a general massacre; but even this cruelty did not deter those at the altar from proceeding in their devotions, as they deemed it preferable to fall into the hands of an inveterate foe than to abandon the rights of their religion.'

Pompey put Jerusalem under tribute to Rome; placed the administration of the conquered territories in the hands of his commander Scaurus; reinstated Hyrcanus as High Priest – which made him the puppet ruler in Jerusalem; executed the surviving leaders of the Jewish resistance; and then left in triumph for Rome, carrying captive Aristobulus and his sons Alexander and Mattathias Antigonus. The year was 63 BC.

93

Roman conquest and Roman might did not bring quiet to Judea. For the next twenty-three years the country seethed with rebellion and battle, until the last of the Hasmoneans briefly regained the throne, Jerusalem, and Jewish independence.

Young Alexander had escaped en route to Rome, and in time assembled a considerable force of Jewish resistance groups who overran a good deal of Judea and advanced as far as Jerusalem. But they were compelled to retreat before overwhelming Roman strength. One of the Roman generals who opposed them was Mark Antony. And one of the forces under Antony was led by Antipater, 'manipulator' of Hyrcanus and now the real power in Jerusalem. It was he indeed who greatly aided the Romans in suppressing revolts by Hasmonean-led rebels, and in so doing greatly advanced his own position, and that of his son Herod.

Not long thereafter, Aristobulus and his other son, Antigonus, escaped from Rome, and soon they too were rallying Jewish forces in Judea to regain independence. But they, too, after a series of stiff battles, were defeated.

Rome continued to rule, and Antipater to wield local power, managing by his subtlety to enjoy imperial backing no matter who was the Roman master. Though Pompey had been his patron, when the struggle between Julius Caesar and Pompey ended in Caesar's victory in the year 48, and particularly after Pompey's assassination some months later, Antipater changed sides and courted Caesar. He was rewarded with the appointment of Commissioner of Judea, with Hyrcanus, now *his* puppet, confirmed as High Priest. He appointed his eldest son, Phasael, Governor of Jerusalem and district, and his next son, Herod, Governor of Galilee. With his death (he was poisoned) in 43, his two sons shared his powers – though Herod's share was the larger – as well as what meagre political power Hyrcanus had commanded.

By now, the only independent Hasmonean still alive was Mattathias Antigonus. His father Aristobulus and brother Alexander had both been killed. He, the rebel outlaw, had not given up hopes of independence, and he now turned to the Parthians for help. They were the one significant

The three huge towers, Phasael (right), Mariamne (centre) and Hippicus, built by Herod the Great to protect his palace. Scale model reconstruction by Professor Michael Avi-Yonah in the garden of the Holyland Hotel, Jerusalem.

power in the Middle East who still held out against Rome. In the year 40, a Parthian force together with Antigonus' followers marched on Judea and advanced to Jerusalem, capturing it after fierce fighting in the Temple stronghold and in the city. Herod managed to escape. Phasael was caught, and committed suicide while in custody. As for Hyrcanus, Antigonus, his nephew, ordered that his ears be cut off, so as to incapacitate him permanently as High Priest, because the holder of this office had to be a person 'without blemish'. Antigonus became king, and Jerusalem and Judea were again independent under a Hasmonean.

Freedom was shortlived. Herod, whose road to kingship had been so carefully paved by his father, and by Roman favour, and who, by his own ambition and cunning, had come so close to gaining it, was not prepared to concede the prize. But there was little he could do, alone, in Judea itself. He could not rally the people of the land he sought to rule and exhort them to march with him against Mattathias Antigonus. The people of the land were Jews, and Antigonus was their king, a Hasmonean. Herod, on the other hand, was despised. He, like his father, was an outsider. They had wormed their way into high positions in Jerusalem, usurped authority, and maintained it by servile fawning upon the occupying Roman power, hated by the Jews. There was only one course for Herod if he wished to depose Antigonus and put himself on the throne – secure Roman help; and Roman help would also be required to keep him on the throne over an unwilling population.

Herod made his way to Rome, where he was warmly received by friends, like Mark Antony, whom he and his father had helped in the battles to crush the Jewish rebellions. Antony, seeing in Herod a pliable representative, one who would make Judea safe for the Romans, accordingly proposed to the Roman Senate, says Josephus, that 'it would be a prudent measure to appoint Herod king of Judea; and in this proposition the Senate unanimously concurred. They deviated from their usual practice in thus conferring sovereignty upon a person not of royal descent.'

Herod returned to the Middle East and started his long and fierce campaign against Antigonus, aided by two Roman legions, units of mercenaries, Syrian auxiliaries and formations from his kinsmen, the Idumeans. Not until the third year of his being named king by the Romans did he reach Jerusalem and bring his army up to its walls. The next four months were months of bitter siege and battle, but the walls remained intact. Herod was then reinforced by the Roman general Sosius, whom Antony had appointed Governor of Syria and had instructed to assist Herod.

In the fifth month of the siege, the combined forces of Herod and Sosius broke into Jerusalem, taking the first wall, then, some days later, the second wall, the outer quarters of the Temple and the lower town. The Jews retired to the middle of the Temple compound and the Upper City and continued the fight from there. But theirs could only be a delaying operation. The besieging armies poured in and carried out a grim carnage. (Herod is said to have tried to restrain the excesses of the Romans, but without success.) Mattathias Antigonus was carried away by Sosius and put to death.

Herod, king of the Jews by Roman title, was now king of Judea also in

General view today of the interior of the Citadel, also known as the 'Tower of David', containing Hasmonean, Roman, Byzantine, Crusader, Mameluke and Ottoman ruins.

fact. The year was 37 BC. He was to reign until 4 BC and to leave his mark on Jerusalem.

Herod's character

Herod has been spared not a single unflattering adjective by the various historians and writers, ancient and modern, who have dealt with his character and activities. Cruel, cunning, savage, explosive, are a few, and his deeds assuredly justify such epithets. Upon his accession, he executed the leading adherents of Antigonus, which wiped out more than half the members of the Sanhedrin, supreme religious and civil council of the Jews. During the course of his reign, he executed or arranged to have murdered his wife Mariamne – who was a Hasmonean; her grandfather (old Hyrcanus); his popular brother-in-law; his mother-in-law; his two sons by Mariamne; and his eldest son. Apart from this palace slaughter, he was utterly faithful to his Roman overlords and rigidly suppressed any sign of rebelliousness among his subjects. In Jerusalem, he always had Roman legionaries on hand.

With it all, however, Herod was undoubtedly a most efficient administrator and brilliant organiser. Above all, he possessed a remarkable talent and passion for building. It was he who built the amazing fortifications on the top of Masada which were recently excavated; he who built the city of Caesarea on the Mediterranean coast – of such opulence that the Romans later used it as their capital; he who built other cities as well as fortresses and palaces all over the country. This genius he also brought to Jerusalem – relics of his handiwork may be seen to this day in the Old City – and completely changed its skyline.

Herod's huge building projects in Jerusalem may have been prompted by the wish to curry favour with his sullen subjects; to preserve himself from their anger and strengthen internal security – as we shall see from the siting and design of two of his structures; and to glorify his name by the physical association of his works with the great city.

Scholars agree that he must first have repaired and strengthened the old walls which had suffered at his own hands during the siege, but we have no account of this. We do, however, have an account of his new structures – and the physical remains of some. The first was a magnificent royal palace which he built in the northwest corner of the Upper City (that is, on the southwest hill), close to today's Jaffa Gate. At the northern end of the palace he erected three huge towers which 'he consecrated to the memory of his brother, his friend and his wife' and which were accordingly known as the Phasael Tower, Hippicus Tower and Mariamne Tower. Each was built on a high, solid base of huge stones, with a revetment. The towers were provided with battlements and turrets. All that can be seen today is the base of the Phasael Tower, just inside the Jaffa Gate. Its stones are set closely to each other without mortar. The dimensions of the masonry approximate to those given by Josephus: each stone a cube of just over four feet. Visitors to Jerusalem see this Herodian ruin but may not know it as such, because some centuries after Herod's death someone called it the Tower of David, and the name stuck.

Herod built a fourth tower, about a thousand yards to the northwest, which he named Psephinus. It was isolated from the other three, but later, in the time of King Agrippa (AD 41–4), they were connected by the new city wall he built, known as the Third Wall.

Herod's royal Court or Palace was also, in fact, a citadel. Its north and west sides were bounded by the old wall, the First City Wall, and to complete the enclosure, matching walls were erected on the east and south sides. Two huge halls (each with couches for a hundred guests) and numerous chambers were set amid large open courts with colonnades and shrubberies. It received its water from a high level aqueduct.

Palace and towers dominated the entire Upper City. From them one could observe the local happenings; and in the event of trouble, the king would be well protected.

Herod had built well; so well, in fact, that his palace became the residence of his immediate successor and of the Roman procurators; a stronghold of the Jewish resisters in the great battle for Jerusalem in AD 70 where they were to hold out for one month after the rest of the city had fallen; the site of the Roman legion camp thereafter; the castle of the Byzantines; the fortress of the Moslems; the 'Tower of David' of the Crusaders; and the Turkish citadel right up to our own times.

It is possible that Herod's building of his great palace on this location, which moved the centre of the city's authority from the east to the southwest hill, gave rise to the eventual tradition that this southwest hill had been the site of the ancient stronghold of David. Modern scholars are all agreed that the City of David lay in the southeast, south of what later became the Temple Mount.

The second structure built, or rather enlarged, by Herod with internal security well in mind was the Antonia fortress. It replaced the Baris, the fort of the Hasmoneans, at the northwest corner of the Temple compound, and was named in honour of Mark Antony. He erected here a massive castle set upon a huge base with precipitous sides, carrying four huge towers at its corners. The southeastern one was higher than the others and served as a vigilant eye looking down upon the Temple. It was manned by a Roman infantry unit, and, particularly at Jewish festival times which drew crowds of worshippers, they would appear fully armed 'to watch for any sign of popular discontent'. A secret staircase and passageway led from the fortress to the grounds of the Temple.

The interior of Antonia, says Josephus, 'contained every kind of dwelling and other convenience, colonnades, baths and broad courts for encampments, so that in possessing all manner of utilities it seemed a city, but in sumptuousness a palace'. This powerful Antonia fortress was also to play a key part in the successive battles of Jerusalem, and to figure, according to prevailing tradition, in the trial of Jesus at the beginning of the following century.

Many were the buildings which Herod raised in Jerusalem. But the pride of them all, and the one which was to leave the Herodian mark on the city to this day, was his reconstruction of the Temple. He started building it in 20 BC, the eighteenth year of his reign, and the House itself, the sanctuary, was completed very rapidly – in eighteen months. The cloisters and outer enclosures took another eight years, and work on the rest of the structure continued long after his death. It was finished only a few years before AD 70, when the whole edifice went up in flames, never to be replaced.

Why should the impious Herod, his heart strange to Judaic interests, have applied his hand to the glorification of Jewry's central shrine? It was clearly a gesture of appeasement to the Jews, already hostile, and made more angry by his Hellenistic and Roman temples in the new cities he had established and the pagan games and spectacles he had introduced to Jerusalem. Here was something he would do for Judaism – and indulge his

right: Pompey commits the sacrilege of entering the Temple's Holy of Holies. From a French manuscript illuminated by Fouquet in 1470.

overleaf: A late sixteenth-century pictorial map of Jerusalem made in Cologne, with views of the city and illustrations of early biblical scenes and of outstanding events at the time of Jesus.

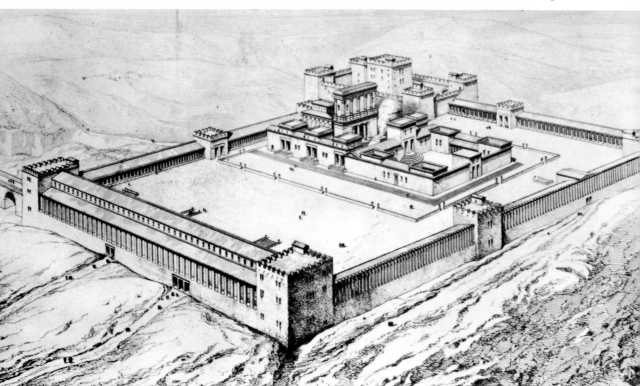

passion for buildings of magnificence. To appease them further, he trained a thousand priests as masons and carpenters to work on those parts of the sanctuary which profane hands were not allowed to touch.

The ground-plan and interior arrangements of the Temple proper, the house of worship itself, were exactly the same as before. These could not be altered. They were fixed by the Bible. But Herod doubled its height and vastly amplified the porch, so that the building seemed to soar. This impression was heightened by its being set atop a series of descending terraces with huge courts, colonnaded and walled. The Temple was built of large blocks of white stone, its façade plated with gold, so that at a distance 'it appeared like a mountain covered with snow'.

In order to provide an appropriate base for his immense architectural enterprise – the sanctuary towering above broad terraced courts, all located

above: A reconstruction of the Temple of Herod made by the Comte de Vogüé in the nineteenth century.

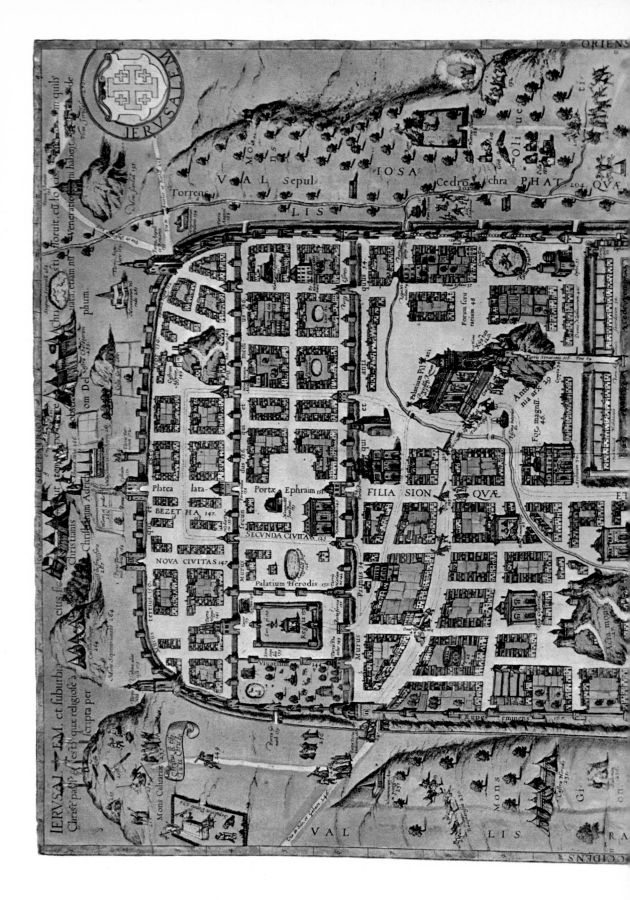

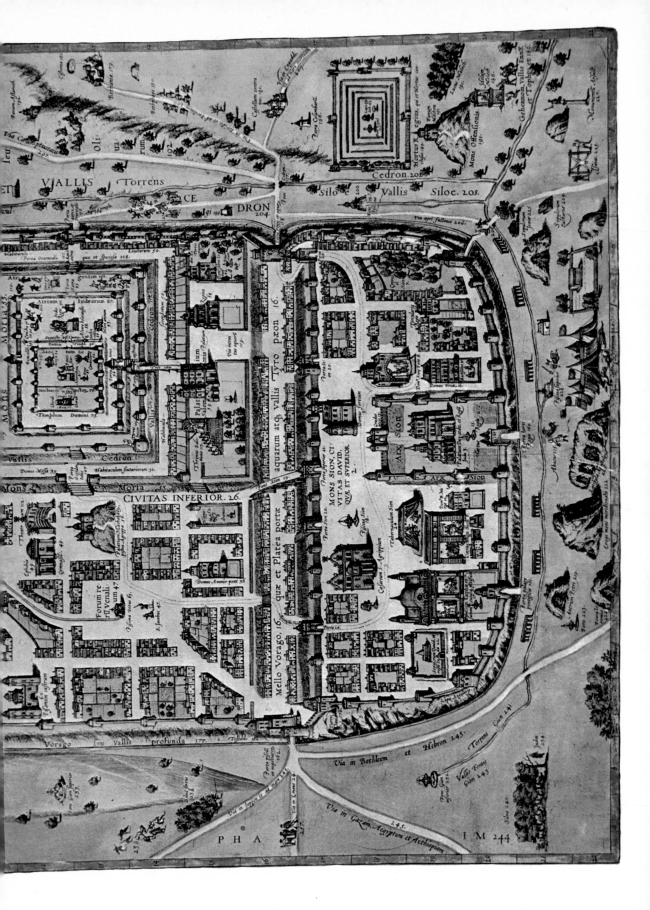

on a hill – Herod built a most formidable platform, a great rectangular esplanade some 400 by 300 yards, supported by substructures and great buttress walls rising from the ravines that bounded the Temple Mount. The 'Wailing Wall' or 'West Wall', revered by Jews throughout the world for the last 1900 years as their most sacred Holy Place, is one of these walls.

Standing high above the vast stone stage was the gold-façaded House of Worship, divided into the Holy Place – furnished with the Altar of Incense, the Table of Shewbread, and a seven-branched candelabrum – and the Holy of Holies, now bare, but which in Solomon's Temple held the Ark of the Law. One mortal alone was allowed to enter the Holy of Holies – the High Priest – and even he only one day in the year, the solemn Day of Atonement (Yom Kippur).

Beyond the façade extended the now enlarged Porch. Twelve broad steps led down to the Altar Court, the Court of the Priests and the Court of the Israelites, which may all have been one large court with the appropriate sections marked off. The altar was of great unhewn stones. Priests alone performed the sacrifices. The Court of the Israelites was for male Jews who were offering sacrifices and who were required to watch the ceremony.

A stone wall bounded the eastern side of the Court of the Israelites, and through an impressive bronze gate in its centre one descended fifteen steps to the Court of Women. (Since it was on a lower terrace, it may have held a gallery to enable women to view the services in the upper court.) Despite its name, the Court of Women could be entered by all 'ceremonially clean' Jews, men and women, and this indeed was also where the administrative affairs of the Temple were conducted. This court had large chambers in its corners and from this level there was access to the vaults beneath the Court of the Israelites holding the Temple treasures and Temple dues offered by Jews from the country and from the Diaspora.

The courts and buildings mentioned so far all constituted the Inner Temple, and were enclosed in a high, towered and gated wall, which in turn was surrounded by a narrow terrace and ritual fence. It was a fortress in itself, and indeed in AD 70, the Jews held out in this separate citadel for some time after the Roman Titus had penetrated the Outer Court.

This Outer Court, also known as the Court of the Gentiles, was fourteen steps lower down and constituted the floor terrace of the esplanade. It ran right round the Inner Temple, and was broader in the south and the east, so that the Sanctuary and Inner Temple were sited not in the centre of the esplanade but in the northwest. Into this court came the crowds entering mostly through the south gates. Among them were also Gentiles from many lands who were permitted inside this enclosure alone; inscriptions on stone in Latin and Greek warned them against passing through the ritual fence to the Inner Temple, on pain of death.

This Outer Court was deeply cloistered, two rows of columns skirting the north, west and east sides, and a splendid colonnade of four rows, comprising 162 Corinthian columns, forming what was known as the Stoa Basilica or Royal Cloister, on the south side. Each column was fashioned from a single, massive block of stone, locally quarried. (One, apparently broken in the handling, was left on the site of the mishap where it has remained to this day. From it one can gauge the extraordinary dimensions of the original building. The site is now Jerusalem's Russian Compound.)

Surrounding the Outer Court and enclosing the entire Temple platform was a massive wall with strong gates. The gate in the north overlooked the suburb of Bethesda, that in the east wall the Kidron valley. In the south, facing the Lower City and the site of David's City, there were at least the two 'Gates of Huldah', one double, one triple. Set low in the wall they gave entry to passages which led beneath the Royal Cloister and emerged on to the Outer Court. These were the entrances most widely used, and their remains may be seen today. The wall in the west, according to Josephus, had four gates which gave on to the Upper City. Two of them offered access to two bridges which linked the East Hill to the West Hill, that is the Temple Mount to the Upper City. The arch of one of these bridges and the foundations of another have been preserved to this day. They were named after the men who discovered them in the last century and are known respectively as Wilson's Arch and Robinson's Arch.

Such, then, was the marvel of Herod's rebuilt Temple. Herod may have been hated by his subjects, but they must certainly have been powerfully impressed by the reconstructed shrine. We learn from the Talmud that the rabbinical sages, who could say of the wonders of Jerusalem that it was 'the city blessed with nine measures of beauty', made this observation on the architecture of the despised monarch: 'He who has not set eyes upon the structure of Herod has not seen a structure of beauty in all his life.'

Herod's gory death in the year 4 BC was the signal for a Jewish uprising which was harshly suppressed by Roman legions personally led by the Roman Governor of Syria, Varus. Following the rebellion, Varus appointed one of Herod's sons, Archelaus, puppet ruler of Judea. He lasted ten years (4 BC to AD 6) before the Romans removed him and resolved to put Judea under open and direct Roman rule. It became an annexed possession. Henceforth, except for the years AD 41-4, Judea was governed by Roman officials, who were called procurators.

Death of Herod

The interruption of their administration in AD 41 came with the appointment of Agrippa as king of Judea. The mad Caligula had become emperor of Rome, and Agrippa, who had been raised at the Roman court, was a boyhood friend. Agrippa was the grandson of Herod and Mariamne – son of the father whom his grandfather had murdered – and so, through Mariamne, a Hasmonean. As such he was beloved of the Jews; and as friend of the emperor, he was accepted by the Romans. His dealings with both were such that his brief reign was one of unmixed popularity. It must be added, though, that the enthusiasm of his Jewish subjects stemmed also from his sedulous worship, his strict adherence to the Torah, his benevolence and his magnanimity. He was deeply concerned in furthering the interests not of Rome but of the Jews. There is reason to suppose that this soon became recognised by Rome. When he died, suddenly, in AD 44, there was a reversion to rule by procurator.

Agrippa's major physical contribution to Jerusalem was his construction of a new city wall, known as the Third Wall, in the north. His intention was to give protection to the new northern suburb of Bethesda, which had

A typical doorway in Old Jerusalem.

Robinson's Arch: all that remains today of one of the bridges that, in Herod's time, linked the Temple Mount with the Upper City.

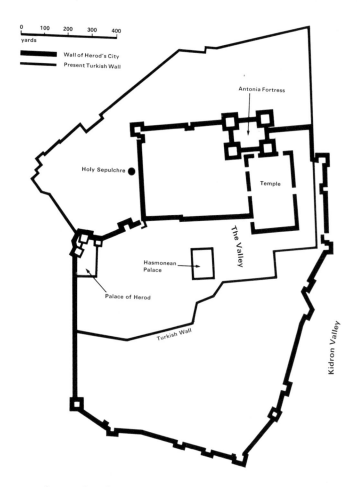

left: Map showing positi of main buildings in Herod's Jerusalem.

0 100 200 300 400
yards

▬▬ Wall of Herod's City
▬▬ Present Turkish Wall

Antonia Fortress

Holy Sepulchre ●

Temple

The Valley

Hasmonean Palace

Palace of Herod

Turkish Wall

Kidron Valley

sprung up and was developing outside the walls, and strengthen that side of the city which was so vulnerable to outside attack – the northern side. Agrippa's wall ran from Herod's Hippicus Tower northwest to the Psephinus; from there it turned northeast to a point called the Corner Tower – and along this stretch stood what Josephus terms the 'Women's Towers'; and from there southwards to the Kidron, towards the northeast corner of the Temple platform. It enclosed the whole of Bethesda, and had a ditch on its outer side. (The foundations of the 'Women's Towers' and the 'Corner Tower' were discovered some years ago. From her latest excavations, British archaeologist Kathleen Kenyon reaches the conclusion that the course of Agrippa's wall was roughly that followed by today's northern wall. This is disputed by other archaeologists, who still hold that Agrippa's wall lay much further north, and the only ancient wall matched by the line of today's wall is that of Hadrian, in the second century AD.)

Agrippa was not allowed to complete this wall, although most of it was up before the Romans ordered him to stop work. He and his subjects were in too close harmony for his act of fortification not to be suspected as a prelude to insurrection.

right: Another view of the model of Herod's palace. Today's Citadel stands on the site of this palace.

II Jerusalem and Jesus

One of the Roman procurators who served before the accession of King Agrippa was Pontius Pilate. His name would have died with him were it not for an execution warrant he signed during his term of office, AD 26–36. In order to reduce the status and importance of Jerusalem, hoping thereby to lessen its influence as the fount of Jewish rebellion against Roman rule, the procurators shifted the seat of their administration to the Herodian-built city of Caesarea on the Mediterranean. But they would visit Jerusalem on the principal Jewish festivals, the Pilgrim Festivals, when the Temple drew vast numbers of worshippers from the country and the Diaspora and the consequent dangers of insurrection were greatest.

It was on the Passover Festival, the traditional 'freedom festival' of the Jews, when they recall their exodus from Egypt and liberation from slavery, that Pontius Pilate came to Jerusalem. It was while he was there that he ordered the crucifixion of a Galilean Jewish preacher, Jesus of Nazareth, little dreaming of the effect upon mankind his action was to have.

The year was AD 33. Jesus and his disciples, observant Jews, had come to Jerusalem to celebrate the festival. He had been making the pilgrimage since boyhood. 'When he was twelve years old,' we read in Luke (chapter 2) 'his parents [who] went to Jerusalem every year at the feast of the Passover' took him along. On their way home, after staying through the days of the feast, they missed the youngster, but thought he was with their kinsfolk. They had gone a day's journey when they found that he was not with their group, and they returned to Jerusalem to look for him. They searched for three days, and then 'they found him in the Temple, sitting in the midst of the doctors, both hearing them and asking them questions. And all that heard him were astonished at his understanding and answers.'

That was Jesus at the age of twelve. He went on to learn and study and argue and preach, becoming versed in the Torah and familiar with the teachings and sayings of contemporary and earlier rabbis. All that he learned and saw made him one with the people, moved by poverty, angered by repressive Roman authority, contemptuous of priestly Temple administration which he considered was more attentive to ceremonial than religious

ancient grotto beneath
e chapel of the Sixth
ation of the Cross.

content. He wandered round the country giving utterance to his views, expressing the ethical values of the Old Testament and the Hebrew prophets in simple language and parables of telling directness. A man of charismatic power and magnetic leadership, his exhortations on the biblical concepts of human brotherhood, kindness, charity, and the equality of rich and poor before God were balm to the meek and hungry. The authorities hated him.

The Last Supper

By the time he came to Jerusalem on what was to be his last Passover, he was already well known – and marked as a dangerous rebel. He was aware of the threat to his life if he forsook the comparative safety of Galilee and made this pilgrimage, when Jerusalem would be thronged with visitors and the Romans would be on the alert for revolt. He knew that many rebellious preachers before him had ended up on the cross, the traditional manner of execution by the Romans and hated by the Jews, who saw it as a cruel expression of a cruel tyranny. But Jesus came nevertheless.

What made his pilgrimage even more dangerous was the repeated claim that he was the Messiah. This angered most Jews, including the Jewish leadership with their experience of 'false Messiahs', and who also considered the idea of the 'Son of God' most blasphemous. But the Romans feared that he might be greeted as an angel of liberation come to free his people from foreign oppression, and they would certainly take action against him.

Walking south from Galilee with his disciples, he reached Jericho and made the ascent to Jerusalem, going through Bethany and Bethphage, crossing the shoulder of the Mount of Olives and suddenly coming upon the Temple crowning the Mount, the courts, the esplanade, and the city itself. Like the thousands of other pilgrims, he came a short time before the festival, spending his days in and around the city and the nights with his friends in Bethany or bivouacking, 'as his custom was' on the tree-covered slopes of his favourite place, the Mount of Olives.

The eve of the Passover Festival approached. It was marked then, as it is to this day by Jews all over the world, by a ritual meal called the 'Seder' when the story of the exodus from Egypt is recited and certain foods are taken which symbolise the dramatic events of that liberation. The bread eaten (matzah) is unleavened – to symbolise the haste of the Israelite departure so that there was no time for the dough to rise; the tasting of bitter herbs is a reminder of the harsh life and labour suffered by the Israelite slaves; a shank bone represents the slaughtered paschal lamb whose blood was sprinkled on the doorposts of Israelite dwellings just before the exodus so that the angel of death would 'pass over' them when he went to slay the Egyptian first-born. Four glasses of ritual wine are drunk during the recital.

Such was the Passover meal celebrated by the Jew, Jesus, and his disciples, the meal that was to be known very much later, with the rise of Christianity, as The Last Supper, and out of which was to grow the ritual of the Mass.

The meal was held in the 'Upper Room' of a certain house, and there was to be much controversy in later centuries as to its exact location. The Gospels offer no clue, simply telling us that when his disciples asked him 'Where wilt thou that we go and prepare that thou mayest eat the Passover?', he told them to go into the city, follow a man with a pitcher of water, enter the house which he entered, and say to the owner, 'The Master saith,

he Coenaculum, ditional room of the st Supper, on Mount on. It is part of a four- nth-century structure.

where is the guest-chamber, where I shall eat the Passover with my disciples? And he will shew you a large upper room furnished and prepared: there make ready for us' (Mark xiv). The traditional location of this 'upper room' is on today's Mount Zion. It is called the Coenaculum, which means refectory.

From now on, every move made by Jesus in the final hours of his days on earth was to be commemorated, centuries later, by a shrine. After the ritual meal, he and his disciples go across the Kidron valley to the Mount of Olives, and a little way up the slope come to an enclosed piece of ground called Gethsemane – *Gat-shemanim* is Hebrew for 'oil-press'. Nearby is a cave where they are to rest during the night. Leaving most of them in the cave, Jesus decides to spend his last hours in reflection and prayer under the moon, among the silver olive trees, and takes three disciples with him to witness his Agony. It is from there in the garden of Gethsemane that he is taken on the route which is to lead to the cross.

He is brought first to the 'palace of the high priest' Caiaphas. This is held by modern scholars to have been one of the buildings of the Hasmonean palaces, formerly the site of the Seleucid Akra, the fortress on the south-west hill across the Tyropoeon valley from the Temple compound; but tradition places it close to the Coenaculum.

From there he is led straight to the procurator, Pontius Pilate, at the Praetorium, and taken 'unto the hall of judgement'. The Jews remain outside. There is scholarly controversy as to whether the Praetorium was the Antonia fortress, next to the Temple on the east hill, which housed the bulk of the Roman garrison, or whether the Praetorium, which was any office or residence where the Roman praetor (chief or leader) hung his shield and before which he placed his tribune, was Herod's palace. A unit of Roman troops was stationed there too. The majority hold that it was the latter, and that the trial of Jesus therefore took place on the southwest hill, close to today's Jaffa Gate and Citadel. Tradition, however, has it that the event took place in the Antonia castle.

After Pilate has given judgement – the private part of the trial took place within the castle, the public part in the courtyard open to the populace – 'the soldiers of the governor took Jesus into the common hall . . . and led him away to crucify him'. In the 'common hall', he is scourged and crowned with thorns. He then makes his painful way, his *via dolorosa*, to Golgotha, site of the execution. If the Praetorium were Herod's palace, he would have proceeded along the northern section of the Old City wall, the First Wall, through the Gennath or Garden Gate, roughly midway between Herod's Hippicus Tower and the southwest section of the Temple Mount, and then turned northwards, through a gate in the Second Wall, and out to the west of the northern suburb of Bethesda. If the scene of judgement was Antonia, the sad procession would have come upon Golgotha from the northeast, and would have gone through the same gate in the Second Wall but would not have touched the first. That is the route traditionally accepted, marked by today's Via Dolorosa and the Stations of the Cross. Executions took place outside the city walls, and at the time Golgotha was outside. It became enclosed only a few years later when King Agrippa built his northern or Third Wall.

Jesus, the tablet with his sentence hanging from his neck, reaches the small hillock reserved for capital punishment 'called the place of a skull, which is called in the Hebrew Golgotha'. From this came Calvary, which is the more familiar name for the site. (*Calva* is Latin for 'bald scalp', which is what the hillock looked like.)

Then follows the Passion of Jesus, his sufferings on the cross. At sundown, he 'gave up the ghost' Now come Joseph of Arimathea and Nicodemus who take down the body from the cross 'and wound it in linen clothes with the spices, as the manner of the Jews is to bury'. Nearby is a garden 'and in the garden a new sepulchre', a tomb cut in the rock. 'There laid they Jesus', sealing the entrance with a great round stone.

At the time, a time of tension and conflict, and an atmosphere of rebellion against the rule of imperialist Rome, the death of Jesus caused scarcely a ripple in Jerusalem. His disciples cherished his memory, spoke endlessly of his deeds and goodness, and recounted his miracles, Resurrection and Ascension. But they, too, went unnoticed in Jerusalem. They made their utterances far from the site of the crucifixion, gaining small groups of adherents in the countryside and beyond the borders of Judea. Indeed, for

section of the Via
Dolorosa.

SEPVLCRO DE CHRISTO

SOPRA QVESTA PIETRA CASCO CHRISTO PORTANTE

two hundred years the story of Christianity in the country is obscure, and there was nothing to mark any of the sites in Jerusalem or elsewhere associated with the life of Jesus. The first records mentioning 'Christian' refer to events outside Judea. The very name was coined – as a term of contempt – in a neighbouring land, in the city of Antioch (now in south-eastern Turkey, close to the Syrian border), one of the important cities of the Roman empire. Hellenic influence left it largely Greek-speaking, and followers of Jesus were mocked by the Antiochans as believers in the one they claimed as 'Christos', Greek for 'anointed one', or the Messiah. 'Christians' was the jeering cry they heard when they passed. They accepted the label with pride.

It was a strictly orthodox Jew and rabbinical student, Saul of Tarsus (Tarsus, also in Turkey, is across the Gulf of Alexandretta from Antioch), who did more than anyone else to spread the gospel of Christianity. He is

known to the world as Paul the Apostle. This 'Pharisee of the Pharisees', the most zealous Jewish sect, was converted to Christianity and went round the Middle East and the eastern Mediterranean on fiery missionary journeys, seeking to convert the Jews to the new faith. The doctrines he espoused were largely Hebraic, but he dropped the restrictive and irksome regulations of the Old Testament, and this certainly made his appeal more attractive.

But it made little impact on the Jews of Jerusalem and the Jewish communities outside who did not look for physical ease from their religion nor a release from ritual obligations. In the end, Paul turned his back on his own people, the Jews, gave them up as hopeless, became very bitter towards them, and took his message to the wider non-Jewish world. He found ready ears and thus began the universal spread of the new faith. It is commonly accepted that without the labours of the Jew, Paul, it is unlikely that Christianity would have become a world-wide religion.

In Jerusalem, however, Christianity at first made little headway. (James, 'the Lord's brother', led a small group of followers.) And even when it did, it was several centuries before the Christian leader in the city was given authority over all the Holy Land. That was in AD 451. Up to then, he was the suffragan (assistant) bishop to the metropolitan of Caesarea, who was himself subordinate to the patriarch of Antioch, though from the third century he did enjoy a courtesy eminence.

Jerusalem, in common with other parts of the Roman empire, rose in importance as a Christian centre only in the fourth century when Christianity was adopted by the emperor, Constantine the Great and, more particularly, after his mother, Queen Helena, visited the city. She it was who interested herself in sites associated with the final events in Jesus' life, she who, guided by tradition and her own faith, decided their location, and she who marked them by the erection of shrines. Her visit, too, occasioned the discovery of sacred relics. Thus began the custom followed in succeeding centuries, notably during the Crusades, of building churches, monasteries, convents and hospices in Jerusalem to enshrine the memory of Jesus' last hours, as well as the Resurrection and Ascension. These attracted even more pilgrims. Up to the fourth century – some three hundred years after the death of Jesus – Jerusalem had been the centre of pilgrimage for the Jews alone. Henceforth, it was to be also the centre of Christian pilgrimage.

But much was to happen to this extraordinary city before then.

right: A late fifteenth-century Flemish painting depicting all the importa[events of the life of Jesus Jerusalem, culminating i the Crucifixion (at the to

overleaf: Ancient Jerusalem as conceived by a Russian artist, Moscow, 1894.

With the death of King Agrippa in AD 44, the Romans reverted, as we have said, to rule by procurator. The young son of the king, though sometimes referred to as King Agrippa II, did not in fact rule in Judea but was given some authority in the northern territories. In Jerusalem he was granted the right to supervise the Temple. Real power, however, remained in the hands of the procurator, and one followed another with increasing harshness and repression towards the smouldering Jewish population. The results were inevitable. Outbreaks of violence became endemic.

The people were divided. The official leaders were mostly Sadducees, who, being priests and landowners, preferred a quiet life, even if it lacked independence, and they collaborated with Rome. The priests in any case were appointed by Roman favour, and obviously drawn from those willing to toe the Roman line.

The bulk of the population followed their spiritual guides, who were not the priests but the rabbis, the sages, the learned men, and these were Pharisees. Here, too, there was a division, but for different reasons. The moderates favoured pacifism on the ground that foreign occupation of the country was the Lord's punishment for the nation's waywardness. The activists, equally devout and God-fearing, rejected this approach – and could point to their history to support them: if the Hasmoneans had accepted foreign tyranny as an expression of the Lord's will, they would never have fought for and gained independence. This, the activists urged, was what the Jews should now do. The extreme activists, known as the Zealots, called for the immediate launching of armed resistance. If, in modern parlance, the moderates were 'doves' the activists were 'hawks' and the Zealots positive 'eagles'.

The ranks of the activists began to swell with the arrival on the Judean scene in AD 64 of Gessius Florus as Procurator. His principles, says Josephus, 'were so much more abandoned' than those of his predecessor that the latter 'seemed innocent on the comparison'. And of his predecessor Josephus writes that 'avarice, extortion, corruption and oppression, public and private, were vices equally familiar to him'! The rule of Florus was marked

rt of Herodian tablet in
e Outer Court of the
mple with Latin and
eek inscriptions warning
ntiles against entering
e Inner Temple. Tablet
covered in 1935 and now
the Rockefeller Museum,
usalem.

by massacre and savagery, and reprisals against his soldiers by the people became frequent.

The climax to one such series of incidents occurred after Roman troops at his instigation went on a murderous rampage through Jerusalem. 'The Jews, from the roofs of the houses, assaulted the Romans with such violent showers of stones and darts, that, unable to make any resistance, or press through the crowds of people in the narrow streets, Florus was compelled to retreat to the palace, with the remainder of his troops.' The Jews then fortified themselves in the Inner Temple and cut access to it from the Antonia castle. Florus was unable to dislodge them, and he returned to his headquarters at Caesarea, complaining to his immediate chief, Cestius Gallus, Roman Governor of Syria, about 'the rebelliousness of the Jews'. Gallus was to experience this rebelliousness personally only a short while later.

The Jews were much heartened by this modest, but successful, insurrection, and the arguments of the activists became more compelling. In AD 66 they struck. The 'War of the Jews against the Romans' was to last five years and to end with the destruction of Jerusalem and the Temple in AD 70.

'War of the Jews against the Romans'

It started with the seizure by the Zealots of the Masada fortress. The Roman garrison of this Dead Sea outpost was wiped out and its weapons and supplies captured. The Zealot band, under the leadership of a tough commander named Menahem, then marched on Jerusalem. While they were on their way, revolt broke out in the city, the Jews gaining the upper hand. They captured the Temple area and then assaulted the Roman legionaries in the Antonia castle, taking this stronghold after two days of fighting. The surviving Romans then took refuge in Herod's Palace, in the Upper City, and the Jews put them under siege. When Menahem arrived he took over leadership of the revolt. The Romans eventually surrendered. (Menahem himself was later assassinated.)

On the day the Roman troops were crushed in Jerusalem, almost the entire Jewish community was murdered in Caesarea by the Gentile population, with the enthusiastic approval of Florus. When this news reached the Jews in other cities, they set upon their hostile neighbours and also raided Roman garrisons. Soon, the whole country was a battleground. Roman rule collapsed. In Jerusalem, the Jews established a revolutionary administration.

The principal Roman official in the area, Cestius Gallus, now took personal action. Setting out from Antioch with a large army, he marched southwards on Jerusalem and put it under siege. Josephus says that had Gallus persevered, the besieged would have been forced ultimately to give in. But Gallus failed to realise their desperate position and gave in first. He abandoned the siege and started retiring to the north. He was pursued by lightly armed Jewish groups, less encumbered by equipment and more mobile, who struck at his rear files and harassed his flanks. When he entered the gorge of Beth-Horon, some twenty miles northwest of Jerusalem, the Jews descended upon his forces from the slopes on both sides of the defile and wrought havoc among them. Gallus' retreat became a rout, the Romans fleeing in such confusion that they left behind their equipment,

D·M
L·MAGNIVS
FELIX

one marked 'Leg X
etensis', insignia of the
oman Tenth Legion, which
rrisoned Jerusalem from
t to third century AD.
etensis was the title of this
gion.

'slings, machines and other instruments for battery and attack' which the Jews seized, brought back with them to Jerusalem – and three years later used against their original owners.

This signal success against the Roman army added heart and confidence to the people of Jerusalem – and to the revolutionary government. But they knew that before long there would be another decisive confrontation, tougher and more formidable than anything encountered before, for Rome could not possibly ignore so humiliating a defeat. The government accordingly set about preparing the defences of Jerusalem and the main cities in the country, despatching commanders to take charge of the regional fronts, train the local recruits and organise the fortifications. For the first time since Roman rule by procurator, the Jews again enjoyed independence in the land. Coins were again struck – but now dated 'Year One', the first year of the revolt. There were to be five such dated coin issues, Year Two, Year Three and so on. (At the recent archaeological excavations at Masada, a considerable quantity of these coins were discovered, silver shekels and half-shekels and a large number of bronze coins, ranging through all the years of the revolt, from Year One to the very rare Year Five. 'Jerusalem the Holy' was inscribed on one face of the shekel, and 'Shekel of Israel' on the other.)

While the Jews were making their preparations, the Romans were busy too. Vespasian, their outstanding general, commander of the Second Legion in the conquest of Britain, was sent out to restore Roman rule. By the year 68, after having to fight every inch of the way on his march southwards through Palestine, he had virtually isolated Jerusalem and was ready to put it under siege. As chance would have it, Rome at this time was rocked by political upheaval, and Vespasian decided to await its outcome. Meanwhile, he suspended his campaign. The political upshot was the proclamation of Vespasian as emperor in 69. He appointed his son, Titus, commander of the armies in Judea, entrusting him with the direction of the final operations against the Jews of Jerusalem.

Vespasian's campaign

The Jews had been given a breathing space, but they squandered it on bitter and bloody internal conflict. Lack of unity had sapped their strength, and they revived and sought to compose their differences only when, in the spring of 70, Titus with his vast forces descended upon the city. They consisted of four legions, plus large contingents of auxiliaries. The Twelfth Legion approached Jerusalem from the west; the Fifth and the Fifteenth from the north; and the Tenth from the east. The Tenth set up camp on the Mount of Olives, looking down upon the Temple from the east; the other three encamped on the west, opposite the Upper City, and began to reconnoitre and prepare for the assault. While they were doing so, the Jews sallied forth to attack them, and there were sharp skirmishes which left the Romans confounded. But not for long. Titus eventually managed to move closer to the walls and split his main force into two. He concentrated one slightly north of the present day site of Zion Square, in the town centre – some four hundred yards from the Psephinus Tower, at the northwestern corner of the Third Wall (Agrippa's northern wall). The other was based not far from the site of today's King David Hotel – a similar distance from the Hippicus Tower, adjoining Herod's Palace. The Tenth Legion remained on the Mount of Olives, a magnificent observation point from which to follow all that went on inside the city.

Jewish defence against Titus

The Jewish defenders were led by two Zealot commanders who were former rivals, Simon bar Giora, and the dauntless Yohanan of Gush-Halav in Galilee, better known as John of Gischala, who had fought desperately in the north and had come up to Jerusalem with his small band of survivors. John's sector was the eastern ridge – the Temple and the areas adjoining it to the north and south; Simon was responsible for the western ridge – the Upper City and the area between it and the northern wall.

Titus decided to attack from the northwest. His aim was to breach the least formidable northern wall at points just north of Herod's Palace – Agrippa, it will be recalled, had not been allowed to complete it, and the current defenders had not had time (and had been too busy squabbling) to fortify it to a desirable strength. Once through, Titus planned to attack the second wall, and then send one force southwards to storm the Upper City and another eastwards to assault the Antonia fortress and force his way through to the Temple. The plan made, he set his men to cutting down timber and constructing platforms to serve as embankments reaching up to the base of the wall; over the platforms he would move his battering rams.

Destruction of the
Jerusalem Temple by Titus,
as depicted by a seventeenth-
century Dutch artist.

Spearmen, archers, catapulters and stone-throwers protected the men building the siege works from interference by the defenders, who not only showered them with stones and arrows from the walls, but also dashed out of the city in surprise sorties to engage them in hand to hand combat. The Jews also put into service the weapons they had seized from Cestius Gallus some years earlier.

They could, however, do no more than delay. Eventually, the embankment was completed and the battering rams were ordered up to the walls. The ram was part of a mobile tower which carried on its top platform archers and stone-throwers who forced the defenders on the wall to keep their heads down and allow the ram to batter away without disturbance. Nevertheless, when the battering started on the Third Wall, the defenders rushed to the vulnerable point and despite the enemy missiles flung firebrands against the siege engines and showered their operators with stones and arrows. Bolder groups of Jews sallied forth and tried to overpower the crews of the rams. Titus brought up cavalry and bowmen to shield the engines, beat off the fire-throwers, and neutralise the men hurling missiles from the towers. After stiff fighting the Jews were repulsed. One Jew was taken alive, and Titus ordered him to be crucified before the walls, hoping

– in vain – that the sight would terrify the defenders into surrender.

This was the pattern of fighting for some time. Inevitably, however, the wall was finally breached and the Romans poured through into the northern suburb. Here they established themselves, and began probing attacks against the Second Wall. John of Gischala's men fought from the Antonia fortress and the northern colonnade of the Temple, to defend their section of this wall. Simon's force manned the southwest section which protected the Upper City.

It was in Simon's sector that the Second Wall was eventually breached, and the Romans rushed through, only to be set upon heavily by the defenders (who were more familiar with the narrow alleys), and driven out. It took them four days to crash through the improvised breach-fillings and consolidate their position inside this wall. One wall alone, the First Wall, now lay between them and the beleaguered Jews. The assault proper on the Temple and the Upper City could now begin.

Titus ordered the construction of platforms for his battering rams in front of the Antonia fortress, key to the Temple, and before the monument to Hyrcanus, key to Herod's Palace and the Upper City. (The site of the monument to Hyrcanus, the Hasmonean, also known as the 'Tomb of John', was close, says Josephus, to the Amygdalon Pool, the 'Pool of the Towers'. It is known today as Birket Hammam el Batrak, the Pool of the Patriarchs, and lies between the Jaffa Gate and the Church of the Holy Sepulchre.)

John and Simon well knew that here was their last line of defence, and their men fought most bitterly to prevent the completion of the siege works. They were also aware of the danger of demoralisation among their starving people. So desperate was the food situation that while 'commando' units went out at night on raiding sorties, others issued forth to forage for herbs and roots. Titus soon set cavalry ambushes for them, and any survivors from the ensuing skirmishes were scourged and tortured in other ways and then crucified on the walls. Josephus, who witnessed this great siege of Jerusalem from the Roman side, relates that there were days when more than 500 crucifixions took place, so that after a time there were not enough crosses for the bodies and not enough wall for the crosses.

After seventeen days of continuous toil and battle, the Roman platform near Antonia was completed, and Titus was ready to move up his battering rams. John of Gischala meanwhile had tunnelled under it from within the city, supporting the tunnel with wooden props, and covering the wood with 'a bituminous inflammable matter'. As the rams above were moved into position and about to batter the wall, John's men fired the pillars. As these burned and fell away, the entire tunnel collapsed, and into the crater fell 'the whole fortification with a hideous crash', platform, battering rams and all. 'At first only dust and smoke appeared; but at length the flames bursting forth to view, the Romans were perfectly distracted.' Consternation was followed by despondency. There was no point in trying to put out the flames, for with the platform gone, the wall was inaccessible, and the assault on Antonia was off.

Two days later, Simon's Zealots had their chance. In their sector, two

Roman assault on the Temple

The Temple candelabrum carried in victory procession, shown on the Arc of Titus in Rome.

platforms had been erected and the battering rams were already in operation and already rocking the wall. A breach was imminent. Three of the bravest Zealot officers thereupon dashed out with torches in their hands 'as if', says Josephus, 'towards friends, not massed enemies; they neither hesitated nor shrank back, but charged through the centre of the foe and set the engines on fire. Though opposed by darts and arrows, they resolutely persevered, till the whole erection was in a flame. The Romans used every effort to save the battering rams, the covers of which were by this time consumed; but the Jews advanced even into the flames to prevent them; nor would they let go their hold, though the ironwork was then of a burning heat.' With the fire spreading to the platforms, 'the Romans found that they were encompassed with flames, and retreated to their camp.'

Titus now held a council of war with his principal officers. It was clear to most that conventional weapons would continue to prove ineffective against the besieged when they were in such a fighting mood. They would have to be weakened by starvation, and only thereafter should a fresh assault be mounted. Thus did Titus decide. He insisted, however, that the ring of siege be complete, so that no supplies would reach the beleaguered people, and he accordingly erected a circumvallation, or siege wall, right round the city. It was $4\frac{1}{2}$ miles in length, and it ran from a point on the west somewhere along the Jaffa road of today's Jerusalem; eastwards across the Kidron valley and the Mount of Olives; southwards to Siloam; westwards to about where today's railway station stands; and northwards back to the Jaffa road past 'the sepulchre of Herod' – actually Herod's family tomb next to the King David Hotel.

Titus now applied himself to inflict the final coup. He concentrated on reducing the Antonia fortress and ordered the raising of four platforms against it, bigger and stronger than the ill-fated earlier ones. When they were completed and the rams brought up to the wall, the defenders continued to assail them from the ramparts with torches, arrows and rocks. But the Roman sappers, working under a roof of shields and with covering 'fire' from fellow units, hacked away at the wall, undermining the foundations with hand and crowbar while the rams battered the upper sections. They finally effected a breach. Bloody battles followed within the confines of the Antonia fortress and the Jews were steadily pressed back. They retired and fortified themselves within the adjoining Temple compound.

Titus' call to them to surrender was again spurned, and he therefore ordered his men to flatten Antonia and erect platforms against the Temple ramparts. He then brought up the rams and pounded away at the outer wall of the Temple. Six days of battering and undermining proved ineffective, so solid was the wall. Attempts to scale it with ladders were also fruitless. The Romans then set fire to the gates, the metal melting and exposing the woodwork to the flames. When the fire had abated, picked men of all the cohorts fought their way through the openings and, in hand to hand combat, steadily thrust forward until they were in eventual occupation of the colonnades and Outer Court of the Temple. The Jews fell back to the Inner Temple – the sanctuary itself, the Court of Israel and the Court of the Women – and continued to hold out from there.

Retreat to the Temple Compound

The scene today in the courtyard of the Citadel, site of Herod's Palace, built against the city's western wall.

On the ninth day of the Hebrew month of Ab, the very month and day on which 657 years ealier the Babylonians had sacked the first Temple on this site, the one built by Solomon, the forces of Titus broke into the Inner Temple and set the sanctuary ablaze. 'The flames of fire were so violent and impetuous that the mountain on which the Temple stood resembled one large body of fire, even from its foundations.'

Apart from the soldiers who fell in the fighting, thousands of civilians, priests and laymen, women and children, were butchered as the legionaries charged through the compound, and many thousands more fell victim as the Romans proceeded all the way down along the eastern ridge into the Lower City, as far as Siloam, slaughtering and setting the city aflame as they went.

Simon bar Giora had joined forces with John of Gischala when Titus was delivering his main blow against Antonia and the Temple. Both now managed to escape with decimated remnants of their Zealot followers, crossing from the southwest gates of the Temple esplanade and through the Tyropoeon valley into the Upper City. There they made their last ditch stand, with Herod's Palace as their stronghold. They held out for another month. Then it was all over. Thus ended the great siege of Jerusalem.

Titus ordered the entire city to be razed, except for the three Herodian towers, Phasael, Hippicus and Mariamne, and the western wall, to protect the camp of the Tenth Legion who were to be left as a garrison.

After executing many of the survivors, Titus carried off the rest as slaves – though many of these perished in gladiatorial combat or were thrown to wild beasts at the 'games' held at Caesarea by the Romans to celebrate the victory. Titus then returned to Rome where, together with his father, the emperor Vespasian, he conducted a triumphal procession. Most prominent among the spoils on display were the treasures taken from the Temple in Jerusalem, notably the golden seven-branched candelabrum and the code of Jewish laws.

Also on display and marching in the procession were the Jewish captives brought from Jerusalem. Among them was the surviving Zealot leader who had been taken prisoner, Simon bar Giora. When the procession ended, the dignitaries waited, in accordance with an ancient custom, until news came that the commanding general of the enemy army was dead. Simon bar Giora was dragged forth, a rope round his neck, led to the Forum, and there publicly executed. Titus and Vespasian could now return to the palace to preside over their victory banquet.

To commemorate his capture of Jerusalem, the 'Triumphal Arch of Titus' was erected in the Forum Rome. Its outstanding relief, which may be seen today, shows a float being carried in the Roman victory procession bearing the Temple spoils, the most prominent being a representation of the sanctuary candelabrum.

Despite the destruction of Jerusalem in AD 70, the slaughter of so many of
its inhabitants and the carrying away into captivity of large numbers,
Jewish life in surrounding Judea did not become extinct. The Jewish population there had indeed suffered heavy losses – their war against the Romans
had been countrywide. The survivors were indeed subdued. But they were
at least alive. And gradually they resumed an existence of sullen normality
under Roman rule.

The Roman governor, from his seat at Caesarea, need now pay little
thought to Jerusalem. It was, for him, a garrison town, his men of the Tenth
Legion ensconced within its western wall – though their families probably
lived in the suburbs, for the town, like the Temple, was not allowed to be
rebuilt. As Jews drifted back to the ruins of the city, drawn by its sacred
memories, they could occasion no disturbance and so were unmolested.

With Jerusalem's Jewish leadership dead or exiled, and with Temple
worship no longer possible, Jewry's centre of gravity shifted to its new centre
of learning and Talmudic scholarship at Yavne (Jamnia), on the Mediterranean coast just north of Ashkelon. (It is still a noted seat of Talmudic
learning.) It had been founded shortly before the fall of Jerusalem by the
outstanding scholar, Rabbi Yohanan ben Zakkai. And it was the rabbis
and teachers who soon assumed the leadership of the people in place of the
High Priest – whose office became obsolete with the loss of the Temple.
The Sanhedrin, the supreme Jewish council, was now and henceforth
drawn from the leading Jewish scholars. It was in this period that Jewish
educational patterns were fashioned which were to guide them ever after
to prize scholarship and learning above all things. It was in this period,
too, that the rabbis laid the foundations for the rigid observance of Jewish
religious practice which had such a unifying influence on the scattered
Jewish communities, and prevented their absorption into the Roman
empire – or into any other empire at any other place in any other time.

The synagogue, an institution introduced by the returning Babylonian
exiles some six centuries earlier, which had been a subsidiary place of local
worship throughout the Second Temple period, now took the place of the

Jewish ossuary from the
d of the Second Temple
riod, found in Jerusalem.

Temple – except for sacrifice. Under Jewish law, sacrificial worship was permitted only in the central shrine, so that from now on this practice was discontinued by the Jewish religion.

No matter where the Jewish leadership resided, Jerusalem was still the sacred centre, and still the city of pilgrimage, members of communities elsewhere in Judea and from the Diaspora coming to visit the Temple ruins. The impoverished Jews of Jerusalem were much aided by their brothers outside, and contemporary records show that even some of their synagogues – for they, too, could now worship only in the synagogue – were maintained by Diaspora Jews.

Jerusalem soon resumed its predominantly Jewish character despite the presence of the Roman garrison and other non-Jewish groups. Among these were the Christians, who had left the city at the beginning of the Jewish revolt in AD 66 and moved in a body to Pella, on the other side of the Jordan. With war over, they returned; but they were still not a large community.

For the next sixty years, life in the country proceeded with only small, sporadic insurrections, nothing serious enough to threaten Roman rule, but just enough to remind the authorities that their Jewish subjects had not lost their urge for independence.

Effect of Hadrian's visit to Jerusalem

In the year AD 130, the much-travelled emperor Hadrian paid a visit to this part of his empire, and came to Jerusalem. Here he became aware of Jewish nationalist feeling. Determined to crush it, he later issued a series of anti-Jewish edicts, such as banning the observance of the Sabbath and the rite of circumcision, and he also resolved to convert Jerusalem into a Roman colony and change its name. These acts touched off the last and most desperate Jewish rebellion against Rome, the Jewish War of Freedom, under the heroic figure, Bar Kochba. In the year AD 132, he and his Jewish guerrillas struck, their principal aim being the liberation of Jerusalem from Roman rule and Roman aims. The flame of his insurrection quickly spread, and soon all Judea was ablaze with revolt. Of immeasurable influence was Rabbi Akiba, the greatest scholar of his age, who gave Bar Kochba his wholehearted backing.

The rebellion was initially successful. In savage and bitter fighting, the Jews captured numerous Roman strongholds in Judea, and, after a short time, Jerusalem itself. For the next three years, the Jews again knew independence in their land, with Jerusalem as capital and religious centre. Coins struck by Bar Kochba – some are now in our possession – carry the inscription 'Jerusalem' or 'For the freedom of Jerusalem', to underline the point that they were fighting against the Roman attempt to change the character and name of the capital of the Land of Israel. The coins are dated 'Year One', 'Year Two' or 'Year Three' of the liberation. They do not go beyond the third year.

The Romans employed considerable forces to suppress the Jews. Bar Kochba's men went out to meet them along the approaches to Jerusalem, ambushing them from the slopes, trapping them in tortuous defiles as they made their ascent to the capital. Eventually, Hadrian himself came to the country and brought in a large army together with his successful general, Julius Severus, whom he recalled from Britain and entrusted with the task

A sculptured Hellenistic sarcophagus, found elsewhere but exhibited at the entrance to the Citadel.

of victory. Severus proceeded carefully and systematically to reduce the Jewish outposts one by one. When Jerusalem fell, Bar Kochba and his men took to the nearby hills to continue the bitter struggle. (In 1960, at excavations near the Dead Sea, Professor Yadin made some dramatic discoveries, including fifteen despatches by the Jewish commander written on papyrus, which show him to have been a dynamic leader and scrupulous observer of Jewish religious law. Little had been known about him beyond his meteoric and fateful appearance on the stage of Jewish – and Roman – history, his military genius and the admiration he drew from Rabbi Akiba.)

The end came in 135 at Beth-ther (Beitar, or Battir), a hilltop stronghold only a few miles southwest of Jerusalem, where Bar Kochba made a stubborn last stand. The date it fell is traditionally believed to have been the ninth of Ab, the date on which both the First and Second Temples were destroyed. Bar Kochba was killed in battle. Rabbi Akiba was captured by the Romans and put to death with the utmost cruelty. *The end of the revolt*

It was to take the Jews another 1,813 years to regain their independence.

Hadrian immediately tried to eradicate the name and memory of Jerusalem by wiping out all physical trace of it and erecting upon its site a Roman city called Aelia Capitolina. (Aelius was Hadrian's family name, and Capitoline Jupiter was the chief Roman god.) He destroyed the remnants of the walls and buildings, ploughed over the entire locality, and erected his new city on a smaller and more compact area, following the layout of a Roman camp.

Into this city no Jew was allowed to enter, or even approach within sight of it, on pain of death. Not until two centuries later, in the fourth century AD, was the ban slightly lifted – to the extent of one day a year, the ninth of Ab, when Jews were permitted to visit the site of the Temple and mourn over its ruins. In the following century, the general prohibition was abolished, thanks to the intercession of the Empress Eudocia, widow of Emperor Theodosius II, and Jews could once again settle in the city.

So rigid was the ban in Hadrian's day that even Jews converted to Christianity were forbidden entry. Gentile Christians, however, were free to come. They had left Jerusalem during the Bar Kochba uprising and now returned, and their community grew.

To make final, as Hadrian thought, the eradication of all Jewish association with Jerusalem, he built a temple of Jupiter on the site of the Temple, with an equestrian statue of himself before it. Christian tradition holds that he also built a temple of Venus on the site of Golgotha.

The walls of Aelia Capitolina ran on a course largely followed by those of today's Old City of Jerusalem. They excluded the City of David, on the southern part of the eastern ridge, and also the 'Mount Zion' of today, on the southwest hill. The northern wall was, as today's wall, much drawn in and further south than the Third Wall of Agrippa. The west and east walls were in much the same position as before – bounded as they were by the valleys of Kidron and Hinnom – only they were shorter.

Within the city, as in a Roman camp, two main roads, north-south and east-west, crossed each other, with gates at their terminals. The first one ran roughly between today's Damascus and Zion Gates. The course of the

east-west road was the line of today's David Street and its extension, the Street of the Chain, between Jaffa Gate and the Temple esplanade. Near the intersection stood the Forum (today's Muristan bazaar).

Hadrian also built an aqueduct, a theatre, and the inevitable public baths. The arch (still standing) known as *Ecce Homo*, 'Behold the man!', is not the structure beneath which Pontius Pilate presented Jesus to the populace. It is one of the triumphal arches erected by Hadrian.

Aelia Capitolina

According to Professor Michael Avi-Yonah of the Hebrew University, the two centuries that followed with Jerusalem passing under the pseudonym of Aelia Capitolina, 'were the quietest and least known in its history. Aelia was merely a sleepy little provincial town of no significance to anyone save the Jews, who were not permitted to approach it, and the Christians. The latter, who were subject to no prohibitions, began to come in increasing numbers, for the Church was spreading abroad. More and more Gentiles began to study the life of Jesus, and naturally grew interested in the scene

141

of the crucifixion. From the official Roman point of view, however, the capital of the province Syria Palaestina was Caesarea on the sea, while Aelia was merely one of the many minor cities of the region.'

Throughout this period, then, when there could be no Jewish settlement in Jerusalem and when surrounding Judea was in desolation, its people decimated by slaughter and enslavement at the hands of the conqueror, the physical centre of Jewish life moved from their sacred capital to Galilee in the north. From then until our own day they were to be a minority in their land.

In the third century AD, however, though the ban was still in force, Jewish pilgrims braved the death penalty to visit the site of the Temple. This we learn from Talmudic sources. Such pilgrimages evidently took place during periods when rule was lax and the prohibition was not enforced so rigidly.

It was in the fourth century, with the emergence of Emperor Constantine and his adoption of Christianity, that a veritable gale of change swept Jerusalem. Henceforth, it was to become for the Christians what it had been for the Jews for thirteen centuries – their Holy City; and henceforth, Christians were to adopt the Jewish custom of pilgrimage to Jerusalem, but for them it was a pilgrimage to the sites associated with the last days of Jesus.

The name 'Jerusalem' was restored. 'Aelia Capitolina' was expunged.

Constantine
the Great

Constantine the Great was the first Roman emperor to adopt Christianity. Through his conversion he assured the future of this religion. From a minority sect it became the official religion of the Roman empire.

Constantine started administrative life as ruler of western parts of the empire, with the junior title of caesar, in the year 306. The empire had grown up piecemeal over the centuries, and to streamline unwieldy rule the Emperor Diocletian, who abdicated in 305, had organised it into four large regions, each with its own sovereign. Two held the senior title of emperor; the other two were called caesar. Diocletian took the eastern region, which covered the area of today's Turkey and the Middle East. His capital was Byzantium (which Constantine was to rebuild and rename Constantinople in 330), and Byzantium was to become the name of the eastern empire when the Roman empire split into east and west divisions later in the century.

With Diocletian's departure, there were bitter struggles between the various sovereigns, and after twenty years, Constantine emerged as the sole emperor. He was to retain unrivalled power from 324 until his death in 337. His direct rule now included Jerusalem.

He had by this time become passionately involved with Christianity and, reluctantly, in ecclesiastical controversy, and bishops from all parts of the empire, west and east, began to come to him to judge upon doctrinal differences. Understanding little of theological niceties, he called a kind of ecumenical council of all the churches in Nicaea, near Byzantium, in the year 325. Present with him at this Council of Nicaea was his like-minded mother, pagan turned Christian, the Empress Helena. One of the delegates was Bishop Macarius of Aelia Capitolina, as Jerusalem was still called. He met the Empress and spoke at length with her about the sad state of the sites hallowed by the steps of Jesus. So absorbed did she become in this sorrowful tale of neglect that, when the Council was over, she resolved to visit Jerusalem. She left in 326 with blessings, authority and funds from her son, the emperor.

Her voyage was one of discovery. She and Macarius identified the locations of the crucifixion and burial of Jesus, and of other events associated

left: Church of the Ascension on the Mount Olives, site of the original fourth-century church.

with his last days on earth. They also discovered – or, at least, the discoveries were attributed to Helena later in that century – relics associated with the crucifixion. Such discovery and identification started the traditions of the main Christian sites which are followed to this day. Other locations, adding to the traditions, were marked throughout the period of Byzantine rule which was interrupted with the Persian invasion in 614 and which came to an end with the Moslem conquest in 638.

Constantine decided to erect appropriate shrines on the sacred sites, worthy of the cradle of Christianity; to replace the pagan temples; and to enhance the city hallowed by Jesus. The most magnificent of his monuments, and of immeasureable importance as a sacred site of future Christian pilgrimage, was the one marking the rock held to be Golgotha, the hillock of the crucifixion, and the nearby tomb known as the Anastasis, Greek for the place of the Resurrection. The shrine was the Church of the Holy Sepulchre.

It was then, and in its two major reconstructions in the early seventh and eleventh centuries, a group of buildings within a rectangular architectural framework lying from east to west. The most outstanding, and still the principal feature of this shrine, was the rotunda of the Anastasis, a circular church with the sepulchre in the centre, surrounded by columns and topped by a huge dome. Adjoining it on the east was a cloistered open court; in this court was the traditional rock of Calvary. East of that was the church,

right: Entrance to the Edicule within rotunda of the Church of the Holy Sepulchre.

called the Martyrium, where the services were held. Two rows of pillars on either side of the nave gave the basilica four aisles. The apse was, unusually, at its western end, so that it lay in the direction of the Sepulchre. The church was entered from the east through a covered portico, the atrium, and this in turn was entered also from the east through three portals, reached by steps from the street. In front of the steps were some of the columns lining the *Cardo Maximus*, the main north-south city road of Roman Aelia Capitolina. Beneath the church was a disused cistern which later became, and is called to this day, the Crypt of the Finding of the Cross, commemorating the discovery attributed to Empress Helena of the actual cross on which Jesus had been crucified.

Standing on this site was the temple of Venus which Hadrian had erected. It was this pagan shrine which is said to have led Helena and Macarius to locate the sacred burial place, for it was believed that Hadrian had chosen precisely that spot for pagan worship so as to obliterate all association with the doubly hated Jesus – Jesus the Jew, and Jesus the founder of Christianity. The temple of Venus was the clue. It was torn down. Upon the site whose memory it was to have to effaced rose the Church of the Holy Sepulchre, preserved, in part, to this day. Still to be seen are the foundations of the rotunda and part of the entrance and steps of the church.

The main structure was destroyed by the Persians in 614, but restored on a smaller scale a few years later by the abbot Modestus. In the year 1010 it was again destroyed, this time by the Caliph Hakim of Egypt. It was rebuilt in 1048 by the emperor Constantine Monomachus during the brief period when it came under Byzantine protection. The Crusaders in 1144 were the first to reconstruct the entire shrine so that all was under a single roof, and the present church follows largely their plan. Additions to the earlier churches were a marble covering to the rock of Calvary; a marble enclosure for the sepulchre; a bell-tower; the Stone of Anointing (on which the body was anointed before burial); and sundry chapels and oratories. The dome was rebuilt several times. The existing one is a hundred years old. Constantine's Church of the Holy Sepulchre became the most venerated site in Christendom, and the most powerful focus of pilgrim attraction.

The other outstanding basilica built in Jerusalem by Constantine, or rather by his maternal representative, was the Church of Eleona on the Mount of Olives. The site of Eleona (Greek for 'on Olivet', as the Mount of Olives was known), was marked by Empress Helena as the grotto where Jesus 'revealed to his disciples inscrutable mysteries'. The remains of this church were discovered in 1910 during archaeological excavations and over them now rises the Basilica of the Sacred Heart. It lies close to the Carmelite Convent and Cloister of the Pater Noster, and a short distance south of the Church of the Ascension, believed by the faithful to be the place from which Jesus ascended to heaven.

Incidentally, the original Church of the Ascension was also built in the fourth century, some fifty years after the death of Helena, and also by command of a woman, a pious Roman lady named Pomenia. Its remains, too, may be seen today. It was a round building, open to the sky, and was

Basilica of the Sacred Heart atop the Mount of Olives, on the site of four century Church of Eleon

called the Imbomon, Greek for 'on the hill'. The existing octagonal structure is Crusader.

Basilicas were not the only Christian buildings erected by Constantine, and other wealthy Christians later in the century who followed his example. The growing Christian community, the rising number of monks and nuns and pilgrims called for the construction of monasteries, convents and hospices. Gradually the city began to abound with these structures, and these in turn attracted more and more visitors. By the end of the fourth century, with Jews still barred except for one day a year, Jerusalem became an exclusively Christian city, the only one in the country. The Jewish centres were still in the Galilee.

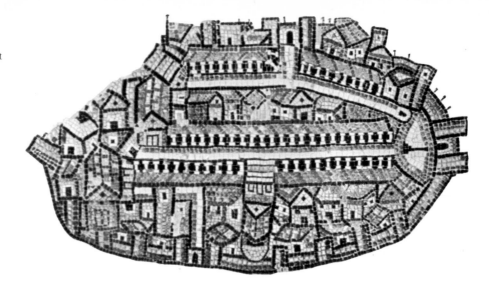

ht: The sixth-century
psaic map of Jerusalem
und at Madeba, southeast
the Dead Sea, in 1897.

The process continued in the fifth century. Contemporary records report the visits and settlement of distinguished Christian families, notably pious – and wealthy – women from Rome and Byzantium who spent their money on buildings and their time in civic service. One, who was also powerful, made a lasting impact on the city. She was the Empress Eudocia, the lady who was responsible for getting the ban lifted on Jewish entry into Jerusalem. Widow of a former emperor and expelled from the court of Byzantium in 438, she found a haven in Jerusalem – as had many aristocrats from Rome with the invasion of that city by the Barbarians. We know that Eudocia built a magnificent palace and we know of at least one church she erected, the Church of St Stephen, in honour of the first Christian martyr. Remains of this church were discovered at excavations just north of today's Damascus Gate. Eudocia is also said to have been responsible for an extension of the city wall so that it now ran further to the south, enclosing within the city once again Mount Zion on the west and Ophel on the east. Archaeological excavations have exposed the remains of this work too.

More Christian shrines were added in the sixth century, the most noted being the Church of St Mary Nova, not far from the Wailing Wall, constructed by the outstanding Byzantine emperor, Justinian I (527–65). Indeed, how crowded the city was with churches and monasteries at this time is clearly seen in a most remarkable 'document' discovered in 1897 in the ruins of a church at Madeba, in Jordan, southeast of the Dead Sea. The 'document' is a pictorial map of the Holy Land, with a special panel for Jerusalem, done in mosaics set in the floor of the church. It gives a bird's eye view plan of the city. Its date is the latter part of the sixth century. It is thus the oldest representation we have of Jerusalem.

*: Part of the original rock
he traditional tomb lies
neath the altar of the
ptic Chapel adjoining the
icule in the Church of the
ly Sepulchre.

The Madeba map shows us the city walls – including Eudocia's enlargement to include Mount Zion. We see Eudocia's palace, the Church of the Holy Sepulchre, Justinian's St Mary Nova, and the Church on Mount Zion. Dividing the map is the north-south road of Hadrian, with pillars on either side, some of them flanking the entrance to Constantine's basilica. Also shown is what forms today's Damascus Gate. Hard by the west gate, the

Jaffa Gate of today, are two of Herod's three original towers, one of them evidently Phaesael whose base is preserved today on the 'Tower of David'. And in amongst the outstanding structures are thick clusters of smaller churches and hospices.

This was the city of Jerusalem at the height of Byzantine glory some fifty years before its fall. In 614, an army of the reborn Persian empire under Chosroes II, overran the country and took Jerusalem after a siege lasting only twenty days. The Persians were much aided by the Jews of Galilee, many of them joining the ranks of the invader as auxiliaries. They had suffered an additional hardship at Byzantine hands only a short time before when the emperor Heraclius had ordered the Jews of the empire to accept baptism, and their sympathies were therefore with the Persians. With the capture of Jerusalem, many Christians were killed and churches destroyed and damaged. The Patriarch Zacharias, thousands of other Christians and the True Cross were taken captive to Persia.

It seems to have been the Jewish hope that Jerusalem would now be turned over to them. But after a few years the Persian attitude changed and local authority was handed to the priest Modestus. He is remembered principally for his rebuilding of some of the ruined churches, notably the Church of the Holy Sepulchre, though on a much reduced scale.

The Persian occupation was shortlived. In 629, Heraclius gained the upper hand; Chosroes II was defeated, and Palestine reverted to the Byzantines. The Patriarch and the True Cross were brought back to Jerusalem. As for the Jews, historians say that while Heraclius was inclined to spare them for having allied themselves with the Persians, he was considerably roused by local accusations against them of having participated in the killing of Christians at the time of the Persian entry. A massacre of the Jews followed, and the survivors were expelled.

The Byzantines may well have thought that they were in for another long spell of rule in the Holy Land. But while Heraclius was celebrating his reconquest, the followers of a new religion in Arabia, headed by its prophet Mohammed, were completing their hold on Mecca. Mohammed died in 632, and his old friend and successor, Abu Bakr, spent the next two years consolidating Moslem authority over the Arabian peninsula. The second caliph, Omar, carried the war to Byzantium and Persia in 634 and two years later entered Palestine. In 638 the Moslems reached Jerusalem and besieged the city. Negotiations followed which resulted in its peaceful surrender. Christians were unmolested and permitted to follow their worship. Jews once again were allowed to return, the caliph Omar overruling the objections of the Christian Patriarch Sophronius. The Moslem occupation had begun.

Part of the west wall of the city which bounds the Citadel, with Mameluke and Ottoman superstructures built on Crusader Herodian and Hasmonean ruins. The minaret is a seventeenth-century addition to the fourteenth-century mosque.

The Persian occupation

The caliph Omar, as we have seen, was careful not to harm Jerusalem. This was because of its special sanctity for the adherents of the new religion of Islam. It was by no means as holy as Mecca, where Mohammed was born, or Medina, which welcomed him after his flight from his home town and where he eventually died. But the Jewish Temple in Jerusalem was the place in the vision of Mohammed to which he was carried from Mecca one night on his legendary steed el-Burak, and from there was caught up through the seven heavens into the presence of the Almighty. The opening verse of the *surah* (chapter) of the Koran on The Children of Israel reads 'Glorified be He who carried His servant by night from the Inviolable Place of Worship (Mecca) to the Far Distant Place of Worship (Jerusalem), the neighbourhood of which We have blessed. . . .'

Small wonder, then, that Jerusalem should have had special significance for the caliph Omar when he entered the city after its surrender. The tradition of special locations holy to Islam only sprang up much later, and possibly for reasons other than religion. There is a medieval story which relates that Omar asked the Christian Patriarch Sophronius to take him directly to the site of the Jewish Temple. Sophronius is said to have been disturbed by this request since the Christians had turned the Temple area into a dunghill and refuse heap. He was somewhat evasive, but Omar was insistent, and, so the story goes, when they reached the site, Omar was so shocked that he made the Patriarch crawl through the muck on his hands and knees as a punishment for Christian abasement of a site venerated by – Moslems!

Omar built a wooden mosque in the Temple compound. The glorious domed building which rises today in the area and which bears his name, the Mosque of Omar, was not in fact built by him. It is more correctly known as the Dome of the Rock, or Mosque of the Dome, and it stands, so Moslems believe, on the spot from where Mohammed made his mystic flight to heaven. The rock within is also believed to have been the improvised altar on which Abraham was commanded to sacrifice his son Isaac, the rock of Mount Moriah, as well as the site of the Holy of Holies in the Jewish Temple.

he Dome of the Rock.
general view from the
uth-west. To its immediate
ght, peeping above the
rizon, is the silver dome
the Mosque of El-Aksa.

This great shrine was built by a later caliph, Abd el-Malik (685–705), of the Umayyad dynasty, and was the work of Byzantine architects and craftsmen of the region. It underwent considerable repairs in the centuries that followed, and received numerous decorative additions; but this magnificent, octagonal, gold-domed building is substantially the same today as it was when completed in the year 691. It stands on the highest point of the Jewish Temple compound, renamed by the Arabs 'Haram esh-Sharif' (Noble Sanctuary), and is approached on all sides by broad flights of steps. Each of the eight outer walls is graced with slender arches. The four doors to the mosque are set at the points of the compass. An inner circle of pillars supports the giant cupola, an outer ring of columns supports the arcade. Immediately beneath the dome is the Rock, 'as-Sakhra' in Arabic.

Abd el-Malik was moved to build this superb Moslem shrine by political, economic and religious considerations. His authority was being challenged by a rival caliph who was in possession of Mecca, and this city, as the birthplace of Mohammed, had powerful political pull. It also attracted considerable revenues from pilgrims – many of whom came from Abd el-Malik's dominions. A shrine in Jerusalem would enhance the political importance of the city, and it would also serve as a substitute for pilgrimage to Mecca, drawing to itself some of the accompanying revenues. Moreover, the presence of so many handsome local churches prompted the caliph's wish to outdo the Christian glory, and the Dome of the Rock was assuredly an admirable instrument for this purpose.

Any Moslem ruler would have been proud to have this fine structure attributed to him, and a later caliph, al-Ma'moon, of the House of Abbas which succeeded the Umayyad dynasty, tried to usurp the honour. The building was in need of repair – it was now 813 – and when the renovations were completed, the masons changed the name of the original plaque, removing Abd el-Malik and substituting the Abbasid al-Ma'moon as 'the servant of God' who had built the mosque. But they left the rest of the inscription – and forgot to change the original date!

[In 1016 the building was gravely damaged by earthquake. It was repaired and strengthened six years later. In 1067, another earthquake struck Jerusalem. The Rock was split, but the structure escaped severe damage.

During the Crusader occupation of Jerusalem (1099–1187), the Dome of the Rock was converted into a Christian church, known as Templum Domini, because of the association of the site with the Jewish Temple. Christian images and paintings were introduced into the sanctuary, and a gold cross was set atop the dome. Early Crusader pilgrims started the practice of chipping off pieces of the Rock and carrying them back home as holy souvenirs. To stop it, the Crusader kings had it covered with marble and erected an iron grille round it. The grille remains to this day. (Incidentally, the religious and military Crusader Order which took over the Temple compound became known as the Order of Templars. When, later, the Order established churches in Europe, they followed the circular design of the Dome of the Rock and were sometimes called Temple Churches. The most celebrated is the Temple Church in London.)

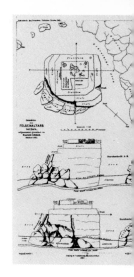

Groundplan and two cross sections of the Rock, from which the Dome of the Rock gets its name, made by a German traveller in October 1883.

Later history of the Dome of the Rock

156

ove: Aerial view of the Temple Compound, from the
uthwest. Dome of the Rock in the centre; Mosque of
-Aksa at right. The Western 'Wailing' Wall is in shadow
 the foreground – in front of the open space cleared
ter the fighting in June 1967. Top right, the Garden
 Gethsemane and the slopes of the Mount of Olives.

overleaf: Looking west from the Russian Tower on the
Mount of Olives. Church of the Ascension (within circular
wall) in the foreground, Old City in the middleground, and
New City in the distance.

157

With the Moslem reconquest of Jerusalem in 1187, Saladin removed all sign of Crusader occupancy (except for the grille round the Rock) and decorated the interior, adding marble facing to the walls and mosaics to the inside of the dome.

The main Mameluke additions in the fourteenth and fifteenth centuries were the marble pulpit, which still stands, and the copper coverings to the doors. (They also had to repair the dome which caught fire in 1448 and collapsed even though, as one writer put it, 'all Jerusalem rushed to save it'.)

Impressive renovations were made in the sixteenth century by the Ottoman sultan, Suleiman the Magnificent (1520–66), notably the replacement of windows in the dome with stained glass of floral design painted in gold, and the facing of sections of the ouside walls with exquisite Kashani tiles. (They were either brought specially from the celebrated tile centre in Persia, or craftsmen from Kashan were brought to Jerusalem to work. Many of the present tiles are inferior nineteenth-century copies of the originals.)

A few years ago, the dull grey cover of lead on the dome was replaced by a layer of gold-plated aluminium. Once again it was the colour of the pure gold with which Abd el-Malik is said to have decorated it (but which he then ordered to be shielded by a covering of hair, wool and leather to protect the gold from the weather). There are few more spectacular sights in the world today than the vision of the golden dome upon the Temple Mount seen at dawn from the Mount of Olives.]

Mosque of El-Aksa

The builder of the Dome of the Rock was long credited with the erection of the nearby silver-domed Mosque of El-Aksa, at the southeastern end of the Temple compound. The original building, however, is now held to have been the work of Abd el-Malik's son, the caliph Waleed, early in the eighth century. Nothing remains of that eighth-century structure beyond a few of the pillars in the colonnade to the east of the dome.

[The silver and gold covering of the original doors were used later in the century to finance a post-earthquake restoration, the first of several in the succeeding years. The most important, however, was the reconstruction carried out in 1034 by the Fatimid caliph Al-Zahir. The dome and seven northern doors of today's rectangular house of worship, large enough to hold five thousand worshippers, are his work. He is said to have used as building materials the columns and capitals of destroyed churches in the area.

During the Crusader period, the mosque became the headquarters building of the Order of Templars, who built additional wings. They called it Palatium Solomonis, the palace of Solomon, considering it to have been the site of the residence Solomon had built just south of the Temple. The vaults beneath the mosque were used as stables by the Crusader knights – they may still be seen – and were accordingly called, and are known to this day, as the 'Stables of Solomon'. They are not, however, Solomonic. They were constructed by Herod to support this southeastern section of the Temple esplanade.

Saladin restored El-Aksa to its former state, decorated the dome with mosaics (which may be seen today), and added a beautiful *mihrab* which is

The dome of the Mosque of El-Aksa, with the twin domes of the Church of the Holy Sepulchre on the left.

still in daily use. (The *mihrab* is the niche reserved for the imam who leads the prayer. It marks the *kibla*, the direction of Mecca.) From Aleppo he brought the handsomely carved cedar-wood pulpit which had been specially made for this Jerusalem mosque by his predecessor who had hoped to be the one to conquer Jerusalem. Saladin also marbled the floor and the walls, decorating the upper parts with mosaics. The northern porch and arches were added early in the thirteenth century.

Today's Mosque of El-Aksa is the building as reconstructed during the period of the British Mandatory Administration in this century. It was completed in 1943. In keeping with the practice of inscribing the names of Moslem rulers and princes who financed repairs or decorations on marble wall-plaques, the last reigning monarch of Egypt, King Farouk, is honoured with this inscription on the wall just west of the main entrance: 'The Supreme Moslem Council has restored the eastern transept, the central aisle, and the front of the northern aisle of this blessed Mosque Al-Aksa. . . The Egyptian Government gave the wooden ceiling in the central aisle [at a cost of 10,000 pounds sterling] in the reign of H.M. the good king, Farouk I. May God preserve him and support his kingdom.'

It was at the entrance to this mosque that King Abdullah of Jordan, grandfather of King Hussein, was assassinated by an Arab extremist in July 1951.]

Jerusalem was never the capital of the Arab empire. Under Abd el-Malik and the rest of the Umayyad caliphs, with one exception, the seat was Damascus. (The exception was Abd el-Malik's second son, Suleiman, who founded the town of Ramla – near today's international airport at Lod. It was the only city in Palestine built by the Moslems.) Abbas al-Saffah, who overthrew the Umayyad caliph in 750 and founded the Abbasid dynasty, moved the capital to Mesopotamia, and his successor established it in the new imperial city of Baghdad which he built.

Under the Umayyads and the early period of the Abbasids, conversions to Islam increased, but Christians and Jews were tolerated and allowed control of their communal affairs. In Jerusalem, monks and pilgrims suffered little interference from the Moslem administration, though desert monasteries were occasionally sacked by Bedouin. The problems of the Jerusalem Christian community were largely internal, caused by the widening breach between the Eastern (Greek Orthodox) and Western (Latin) Churches which has continued to this day. Before the Arab conquest, the Eastern Church was itself torn by schisms, the patriarchate of Jerusalem remaining faithful to the Orthodoxy which, for convenience, is called Greek. Jerusalem shrines, equally venerated by all Christians, became the exclusive possession of one sect, and there was a period when they were closed to other Christians. After the conquest, with Jerusalem now within the Arab dominion, it was cut off from the premier Latin patriarchate of Rome and the principal eastern patriarchate of Constantinople.

Curiously enough, it was during the early Moslem period that the universal character of the Christian Holy Places in Jerusalem came to the fore. The Moslems respected Christian and Jewish shrines, and found pilgrimages profitable. They therefore encouraged pilgrims from all over the west and

Christian Holy Places

Another view of the Citad courtyard showing ruins c various periods.

يكى كشتى قلب درد د لرر سول حضرت بيوردى كه اوس جماعتدن
يكره دورت كشتى كلدى ايتدى بواز ايكى كشتى سز اولدوركز

ددى مر ايكى مسلما ن بر جهودى اولددلر اندلر ابن هشام ايدرا ولتا جركه
حصه بسلمشدى انى اولكون اولددى ردى قرنداش خويصه اول كونك

east. Specific recognition of universal Christian interest in Jerusalem was given by Haroun el-Rashid, most noted of the Abbasid rulers, when he allowed Charlemagne, emperor of the West, to endow and maintain centres for western pilgrims. This understandably irked the Jerusalem Patriarch, and is said to have embittered the factional conflict even more.

Moslem treatment of the Jews

Moslem rule had brought a change of status for the Christians. In the Byzantine period they were the rulers, first class citizens, now they were second class. The Jews were now also second class citizens; but under the Christians they had been less, treated intolerantly at best, but often savagely persecuted. For a time, too, they had not been allowed to settle in Jerusalem. Under the Moslems they were. Returning to the city shortly after Omar's conquest, they lived in the southern quarter close to the 'Wailing' Wall. As they grew in number, they spread to the northern section, near the Damascus Gate. The Pilgrim Festivals, notably the Feast of Succot, again saw numerous visitors from communities elsewhere in Palestine and from the Diaspora.

Not that Islam had suddenly become benign and enlightened towards those of other religions. Inside Arabia, the Jews were treated with little mercy. Their rejection of Islam had been a keen disappointment to Mohammed who had expected them to be attracted by his equal insistence on monotheism (although with Mohammed as the Prophet), his acceptance of the rite of circumcision, and his reverence for the Hebrew patriarchs and for Jerusalem. Neighbouring Jewish tribes were gravely ill-used. But as Arab dominion spread, notably under the caliph Omar, it became good politics not to exterminate or banish all who refused Moslem conversion, as few would be left to people the conquered territories. And so a practical toleration replaced the early bigotry, though the Jews were still subjected to special hardships, some remaining from the restrictions of Christian rule.

At the beginning of the ninth century, the Abbasid caliphs began to rely increasingly on Turkish mercenaries, and these in time assumed more and more power. By the middle of the century, some of the leaders of these hireling groups were governors of provinces, wielding virtually independent control. One of them who started out as aide to the Governor of Egypt in 868 soon made himself Governor and he broke with the court in Baghdad. He was Ahmed ibn-Tulun. In 877 he conquered Palestine and Syria, and Jerusalem became part of an Egyptian province.

Under the Fatimid dynasty in the next century, Jerusalem was to experience both a high and a low point. The Fatimids (claiming descent from Fatima, daughter of Mohammed) conquered Egypt in 969 and founded the new capital – Cairo. A few years later, under caliph Al-Aziz, Fatimid rule was extended to Syria and Palestine. It was during the beneficent reign of Al-Aziz (976–96) that Christians and Jews in Jerusalem enjoyed considerable freedom. It was under his successor, Al-Hakim (996–1021), known as 'the mad caliph', that Jerusalem suffered havoc.

Al-Hakim banned pilgrimages to Jerusalem and ordered the destruction

ohammed ordering the
ecution of members of a
wish tribe. From a
irkish manuscript of
e sixteenth century.

of all churches and synagogues throughout the empire. It was at this time that the Church of the Holy Sepulchre was destroyed, doing more, it is said, than any other single act to pave the way for the Crusades, for here was a shrine venerated throughout Christendom. Al-Hakim's order had another repercussion. When news of the burning down of the sacred church reached the countries of the west, the rumour was circulated that the caliph had acted at the instigation of the Jews, and massacres followed.

After the death of Al-Hakim, the Holy Sepulchre and other churches were rebuilt and pilgrimages were resumed. The next fifty years were comparatively uneventful (except for three earthquakes, one of which gravely damaged the Dome of the Rock).

Then came another army of Turkish invaders. They were the Seljuks, an outlying branch of the Turks who came from the far eastern provinces of Islam, not far from the borders of China. They had been converted to Islam at the end of the tenth century while serving as mercenaries to the Moslem rulers of Persia and northwest India. They, like their earlier counterparts, soon overthrew their masters, and by 1055 were in power in Baghdad. In 1071 they overran most of Syria and Palestine, and held Jerusalem for the next twenty-five years, except for a few months in 1076 when it was re-covered by the Fatimids.

The Seljuks pillaged Jerusalem and followed a policy of persecution of both Christians and Jews. It was their maltreatment of the Christians, stopping of pilgrimage, and abuse of those pilgrims who succeeded in arriving, which gave additional prompting to the counter-offensive of the Christian world – the first Crusade. Shortly before this happened, the Fatimids re-established their authority in Jerusalem. But the western armies were on their way. On 15 July 1099, the Crusaders captured Jerusalem.

Seventh-century map of Jerusalem by the pilgrim Arculf.

Glimpses of Jerusalem during the Moslem occupation are offered by several pilgrim records and, more absorbing, by the account of a knowledge-able and highly literate Moslem geographer. The Christian pilgrims in this period concerned themselves almost exclusively with the holy places with which we are already familiar, and they need not long detain us. The French bishop Arculf in about the year 670, however, notes something of Moslem interest. He saw the temporary mosque put up by Omar, showing clearly that the Dome of the Rock had not yet been built. He says:

Christian pilgrims in the Moslem period

Bishop Arculf

'On the spot where the Temple once stood, near the eastern wall, the Saracens [Arabs or Moslems] have now erected a square house of prayer, in a rough manner, by raising beams and planks upon some remains of old ruins; this is their place of worship, and it is said that it will hold about three thousand men.'

Of Christian sites not before mentioned, Arculf visited Mount Zion where he 'saw a square church, which included the place of our Lord's Supper . . . and the spot where the Virgin Mary died'. Thus, in his day, Mount Zion was already traditionally associated with the Last Supper and with Mary's death. Today's Coenaculum (Latin for refectory), venerated as the scene of Jesus' last Passover meal, is the 'upper room' of a building erected some

centuries later. It still stands on Mount Zion, as does the recently built
Dormition Abbey (Dormitio Sanctae Mariae – the Sleep of Saint Mary)
on the site of the church seen by Arculf.

*Willibald's
narrative*

The Anglo-Saxon pilgrim Willibald, who reached Jerusalem in 721,
makes one observation of special interest after visiting the Church of the
Ascension on the Mount of Olives. It had 'two columns standing within',
and Willibald says 'the man who can creep between the wall and the columns
will have remission of his sins'. This is the first mention of a concept which
was to develop a high importance and to play a considerable role in the
ideology of the Crusades, the concept of pilgrimage to gain remission of sins.

Bernard the Wise

The Breton monk Bernard the Wise arrived in Jerusalem in about 870
and was 'received into the hostel of the most glorious emperor Charles
[Charlemagne, who had been granted, as we have seen, the right to build
such centres by Haroun el-Rashid], where all are admitted who come to
this place for devotional reasons and speak the Roman tongue.'

Bernard is the first to describe the 'Ceremony of the Holy Fire':

'. . . On Holy Saturday, which is the eve of Easter, the office is begun in the morning in this church [of the Holy Sepulchre], and after it is ended the *Kyrie Eleison* is chanted, until an angel comes and lights the lamps that hang above the aforesaid sepulchre. The patriarch gives this fire to the bishops and to the rest of the people, that each may with it light up his own house.'

The 'Holy Fire' was a celebrated miracle in the middle ages, and it is said to have been cited as one of the causes of the persecution of Christians and the destruction of the Church of the Holy Sepulchre by the mad caliph Hakim. An eastern Christian writer Abulfaragius says that

'the author of this persecution was some enemy of the Christians, who told Hakim that, when the Christians assembled in their Temple at Jerusalem, to celebrate Easter, the chaplains of the church, making use of a pious fraud, greased the chain of iron that held the lamp over the tomb with oil of balsam; and that, when the Arab officer had sealed up the door which led to the tomb, they applied a match, through the roof, to the other extremity of the chain, and the fire descended immediately to the wick of the lamp and lighted it. Then the worshippers burst into tears, and cried out *Kyrie Eleison*, supposing it was fire which fell from heaven upon the tomb; and they were thus strengthened in their faith.'

This miracle was probably instituted after the time when so much encouragement was given to the pilgrims under the reign of Charlemagne. It is not mentioned in the works that preceded Bernard, but it is often alluded to by subsequent writers, and continues still to be practised by the Greek Orthodox Church.

Undoubtedly the liveliest of the Jerusalem reports in the period before the Crusades is that of a Moslem, a native of the city, who set down his words towards the end of the tenth century, a few years before the destructive action of the caliph Hakim. He is the geographer known as Mukaddasi – Arabic for 'He who comes from the Holy City' – and he was born in Jerusalem in the year AD 946. Jerusalem has a special place in his narrative of his long and varied journeys.

Mukaddasi's description

'Among provincial towns, [he writes] none is larger than Jerusalem, and many capitals are in fact smaller. . . Neither the cold nor the heat is excessive here, and snow falls but rarely. The Kadi Abu'l Kasim, son of the Kadi of the two Holy Cities, inquired of me once concerning the climate of Jerusalem. I answered, "It is betwixt and between – neither very hot nor very cold." Said he in reply, "Just as is that of Paradise." The buildings of the Holy City are of stone, and you will find nowhere finer or more solid constructions. In no place will you meet with a people more chaste. Provisions are most excellent here, the markets are clean, the mosque is of the largest, and nowhere are holy places more numerous. . . All the year round, never are her streets empty of strangers.'

Mukaddasi now describes the city and its main Moslem shrines.

right: The magnificent fifteenth-century Mamel fountain built by Sultan Qait Bey, on the west of t Temple area, with the Dome of the Rock just visible behind it.

overleaf: The ceiling of th Dome of the Rock, richly decorated in gold and mosaics, and encircled by sixteen stained glass windows, five belonging the fifteenth century. At the edge of the mosaics a inscriptions from the Ko

'Jerusalem is smaller than Mecca and larger than Medina. Over the city is a Castle, one side of which is against the hill-side, while the other is defended by a ditch. Jerusalem has eight iron gates... The Mosque of El-Aksa lies at the southeastern corner of the Holy City. The stones of its foundations, which were laid by David, are ten ells, or a little less in length. They are chiselled, finely faced, and jointed, and of hardest material. . . . This Mosque is even more beautiful than that of Damascus, for during the building of it they had for a rival and as a comparison the great church belonging to the Christians at Jerusalem, and they built this to be even more magnificent than that other.

'In the court of the mosque, on the right-hand side, are colonnades supported by marble pillars and pilasters; and on the further side are halls, vaulted in stone. The centre part of the main building of the mosque is covered by a mighty roof, high pitched and gabled, behind which rises a magnificent dome. The ceiling everywhere, with the exception of that of the halls on the further side of the court, is formed of lead in sheets, but in these halls the ceilings are faced with mosaics studded in.'

Mukaddasi on the Dome of the Rock

Mukaddasi now describes the Dome of the Rock:

'The Court of the Haram Area is paved in all parts; in its centre rises a platform, like that in the mosque at Medina, to which, from all four sides, ascend broad flights of steps. On this platform is the Dome of the Rock, which rises above an octagonal building having four gates, one opposite to each of the flights of steps leading up from the court. . . All these are adorned with gold, and closing each of them is a beautiful door of cedar-wood finely worked in pattern.

'. . . Within the building are three concentric colonnades, with columns of the most beautiful polished marble, and above is a low vaulting. Within these again is the central hall over the Rock; the hall is circular, not octagonal, and is surrounded by columns of polished marble supporting round arches. Built above these, and rising high into the air, is the drum, in which are large openings; and over the drum is the Dome. . . . The Dome, externally, is completely covered with brass plates, gilt, while the building itself, its floor and its walls, and the drum, both within and without, are ornamented with marble and mosaics. . . At the dawn, when the light of the sun first strikes on the cupola, and the drum catches the rays, then is this edifice a marvellous sight to behold, and one such that in all Islam I have never seen its equal.'

Of the Jerusalem in the tenth century, Mukaddasi tells us:

'From Jerusalem comes cheeses, cottons, the celebrated raisins of the species known as Ainuni and Duri, excellent apples, bananas – which same is a fruit of the form of cucumber, but the skin peels off and the interior is not unlike the water-melon, only finer flavoured and more luscious – also pine nuts; . . . also mirrors, lamp-jars and needles.'

And he adds:

'The best honey is that from Jerusalem, where the bees suck the thyme.'

ne of the arcades rrounding the raised atform of the Moslem aram esh-Sharif, iginally the Jewish emple Compound, on hich stands the Dome of e Rock.

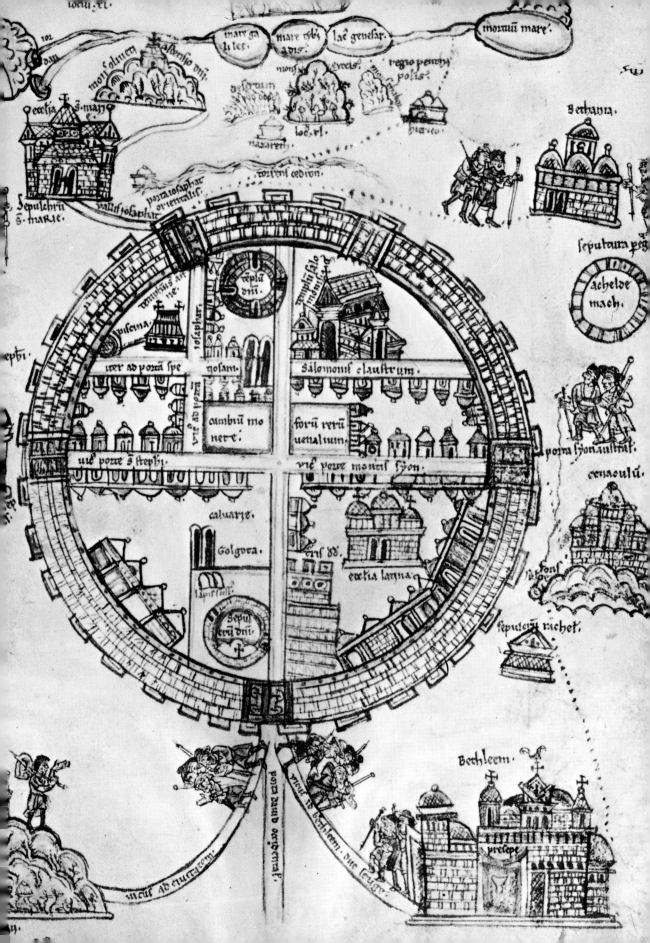

On Friday 15 July 1099 dawn broke over Jerusalem to a fearsome sight and sound. Close to the Gate of Flowers (the present-day Herod's Gate) in the north wall, the soldiers of the Crusader leader Godfrey de Bouillon, Duke of Lorraine, were wheeling a huge siege tower across the ditch to bring it close to the ramparts. It was made of wood and protected by a covering of ox-hide and camel-hide. The Saracen defenders were trying to keep them off with stones and liquid fire ('Greek fire', an inflammable substance projected through tubes, the earliest form of flame-thrower). But the Crusaders were proving more effective with their mangonels – devices for casting stones.

Three hundred yards away, also at the north wall, near the Gate of the Column (today's Damascus Gate), Robert of Flanders, one of Godfrey's commanders, was doing the same thing with his siege tower – putting in a diversionary attack.

At the same time, a third Crusader prince, Raymond of Toulouse, operating from Mount Zion (which was again outside the city), was trying to take the southern wall. He had succeeded on the previous evening in getting his tower up against the wall, but the defences were too fierce for exploitation. Now, with the Crusaders in attacking positions on the north and the south, the defending forces inside the city had to be split to meet the triple threat.

The Crusader assault had been launched a day and a half earlier. It followed a forty-day siege, interspersed with desultory battle, and Friday the fifteenth was the crucial day.

By noon, Godfrey succeeded in bridging the wall from the top of his tower and a few of his men crossed and held it. Scaling ladders were quickly brought up and more men clambered into the city. The defenders in this sector retreated to the nearby Temple area, but before they had time to prepare it for a last ditch stand, the Crusaders were upon them and they surrendered. The Crusader banner was hoisted over the Dome of the Rock and the Mosque of El-Aksa.

The Fatimid governor of the city, Iftikhar, was personally commanding

twelfth-century map of Crusader Jerusalem.

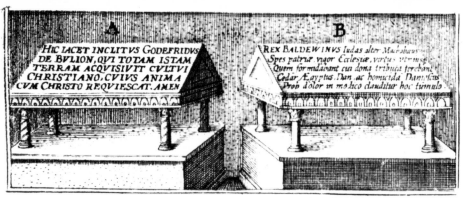

left: Tombs of the Crusac leaders Godfrey de Bouillon and his brother King Baldwin I in the Chu of the Holy Sepulchre. A seventeenth-century Venetian woodcut.

the defences on the southern sector, and keeping Raymond's force at bay. Now there came rushing to him the confused inhabitants and the surviving units who had retreated from the northern wall. He could see the banners with the cross fluttering from the Haram esh-Sharif. He knew it was all over.

Withdrawing into the former Palace of Herod (the citadel near 'David's Tower' at the Jaffa Gate), he offered to surrender to Raymond, promising a large treasure for the lives of himself and his bodyguard. The offer was accepted.

Iftikhar and his men were among the few to survive. The Crusaders went on a rampage through Jerusalem, killing all whom they encountered, Moslems and Jews. (Before the siege, when news of the approach of the Crusaders had reached Iftikhar, he had ordered all Christians to leave.) The remaining Jews sought refuge on this Sabbath eve in their central synagogue. The Crusaders set fire to the building and all perished.

Two days later, the Crusading princes marched in procession through a deserted Jerusalem to the Church of the Holy Sepulchre, there to give thanks to God for their victory. The Christian quarter was, of course, empty and there was no one in the other quarters, for the Moslems and Jews had been slain.

Godfrey de Bouillon became the secular and military ruler, with the title of Defender of the Holy Sepulchre. There was too much rivalry between the Crusader leaders at that time for them to agree that one should hold the title of king. But a year later, with Godfrey's death, his brother Baldwin was offered the throne, and on 11 November 1100 he became King Baldwin I, the first head of the Crusader kingdom of Jerusalem. This kingdom was to last eighty-seven years. Neither Jew nor Moslem was allowed to dwell within the walls of the city.

'Defender of the Holy Sepulchre'

It was the Church Council in Clermont (France) in November 1095 which launched the First Crusade. The Council had been summoned by Pope Urban II, the prime mover in the Crusade, and there he had preached the merit and glory of the deliverance of the Holy Land. What he and the princes planned, and what they eventually carried out, was a carefully directed invasion by picked men. But what immediately followed the Clermont decision was the undisciplined march across Europe of hundreds of thousands of 'thoughtless and needy plebeians', as Gibbon records in *The Decline and Fall of the Roman Empire*, spreading ruin and massacring

right: Crusaders departin for the Holy Land. Illumination from a medieval manuscript.

176

mense decembris. qui subditur et est ad
consumatione et robur hmi libri supra
dicti de ostendendo modum et uiam
quibus recuperari possit terra sca ad dei lau
dem, et ecce sue sce ac uire satatis
honore, quem satere cepi anno dni
nri ihe xpi. M.CCC.vij. mense decembr.
clararie. Incipit liber scdus eiu
stem opis cotinens uias et modos, qb
apte et expedite terra sca recuperari
habens ptes qtuor. Pars prima
continet forma et ordine scdi
exercitus cani, habens cap qtuor.
Cap. pmu ptinet quo unus debe
at preffici capitaneus, et quales
coditiones habere debet, quot etia
in societate sua habere opteat ubi
fat duplicare.

Sit igitur cum ita sit,
q origo et fundamen
tum debilitandi
soldani potentiam
babilonie remo
uendi a multis oc
casionem pticipandi
cu inimicis crucis
e preceptu ecce et
acquirendi terram scam sit pone istud opus
antedictum ad exequti
onem, i tenere fortiter
pressum in tra, eo dictus
.x. galeis uel. vij. in mari
pmodum iam dictu ad hec
ut nichil portaret eis hinc ul
inde afferatur huic pouter cleme
tia ura ordinare ac mandare de
hiis, sicut et qui ponti stalis pru de
tia sco dictante spu puldit ordina
dium. Qd si ea exequtioi mandanda
ura determinauit satis, ad plenam
consumptione eriget si placet satisfa
cmo dno et anno secundo uel tertio post q

sic cursus rex, q fris soldani in inhibi
tione scdm ecce portari solent defecerit,
eligat ut homo diligens, et times deu
bone fame sapies et discretus largus
et liberalis, fortis et constans, diligens et
operans iustitia, qui sit p utilitate toi
comunis xpianitatis et plus diligat
illud, q ipsum habeat beniuolentia
et amicitiam venetor ut possit cum
illis facere facta sua, et in eis consilium
et auxilium inuenire. Huic siquidem
capitaneo opus erit in oibus. v. M
peditum, et ccc. hoies ad equos, ita ut
uno deficiente alius subrogetur loco
eius, omnes ad soldum eor cum naui
giis et uictualibus, et aliis sibi ad bel
lum necessariis ut opteat. Et sit unicus
capitaneus cui comittatur negotius
quia res ordinata unum caput requirit.
Quos omnes dictus capitaneus ducet
sup maritima loca egipti ibiq terram
capiet, et habitationem faciet, iuxta
consilium, q ab expertis datum est fuit
et ostensum. Congregabit ibi etiam
nauigium tam marinum q fluminum ut
possit sup inimicos currere, q et quo
sibi uidebitur, egredi. Cap. scdus
ptinet, q ratio maritima utilior sit
ad huiusmodi expedienda negotia.
q armata dicti capitanei siue ad
miranti de uno loco ubicunq como
dius poterit repleri, assumat, q gere
exercitus galearum, et nauigii in diuisi
ptibus armator congregate, in simul male
sequuntur et male se tollerant, et facile
posset oriri dissensio inter eos, p q to
ta res posset subito deperire, et ulterius
q ista armata pncipaliter debeat fi
venet, p multa. Primo q veneta
gens ita bene attendit id q promittit
sicut aliqua gens de mundo. Secundo q
ibi et in confinibus suis hoies armorum
inueniuntur, et marinarii tam maris

Jews en route. They were roused by such mob orators as Peter the Hermit (Peter of Picardy), a volatile pilgrim who had been maltreated by the Moslems in Jerusalem and who had returned to the west to stir Christendom against the infidel. Flocking behind Peter and others, including 'another fanatic, the monk Godescal', went 300,000, according to Gibbon's estimate, 'the most stupid and savage refuse of the people, who mingled with their devotion a brutal license of rapine, prostitution, and drunkenness.'

As they moved through Europe, says Gibbon, this huge rabble undertook 'the first and most easy warfare . . . against the Jews . . . in the trading cities of the Moselle and the Rhine. . . . At Verdun, Treves, Metz, Worms, many thousands of that unhappy people were pillaged and massacred, nor had they felt a more bloody stroke since the persecution of Hadrian.'

With the Crusader kingdom, Jerusalem again became the capital – for the first time since the Jews were sovereign in the land. For the thousand years that followed its destruction by Titus, Jerusalem had been relegated by its rulers to the status of a provincial town. It was now, under the Crusaders, again the centre, again a fount of international interest.

Crusader administration followed the feudal pattern. Land in the city – and in the entire territory of the kingdom – was allocated to the Church, which inspired the movement, the European knights, who did the fighting, and the merchants, notably of Italy, who supplied the fleets. Later, considerable holdings were granted to the two powerful military orders of Crusaders, the Templars and the Hospitallers (Knights of St John). (There was subsequently a third order, the Teutonic Knights.) The representative of the Pope was the Latin Patriarch, and his power rivalled that of the king.

The shape of the city was much as it was in Roman times, with Mount Zion again outside the walls. Inside, there was a feverish drive to erect ecclesiastical buildings of every kind, churches and hospices, convents and monasteries, and residences for the clergy. The Church of the Holy Sepulchre received prime attention. It was completely rebuilt and given the outline that exists in large part today. The rectangular shape of Constantine's edifice was changed into the form of a cross and the four shrines were united under a single roof, the rotunda of the sepulchre alone following Constantine's design and rising on the original foundations. Further chapels and cloisters were added.

Christian structures sprang up all over the city, crowding in upon each other, but mainly in the 'Patriarch's quarter' – today's 'Christian quarter' – in the northwest and the 'Armenian quarter', as it is still called, in the southwest. Crusader establishments were also erected in what is today known as the 'Jewish quarter', in the southeast. The northeast section, today's 'Moslem quarter', was then called, as we learn from pilgrim records, 'Jewry' or the 'Syrian quarter'. Several churches were built there, the most notable being the Church of St Anne, perhaps the best preserved Crusader church in Jerusalem. In this quarter dwelt the Syrian Christians brought in by King Baldwin to populate Jerusalem, and to them were added other

Christian groups who had come from neighbouring Moslem countries.

What Jerusalem looked like during the Crusader period is known to us largely from the lively report of an unknown pilgrim entitled 'La Citez de Jherusalem'. The city had 'four Master Gates', and he starts his account with the first two, east and west, and the city between. 'The Gate of David is towards the west [today's Jaffa Gate]. And it is exactly opposite the Golden Gate, which is towards the east, behind the Templum Domini.'

This Golden Gate, a magnificent double-arched structure in the east city wall (which is also the east wall of the Temple compound), may still be seen. It may have been the original 'Gate Beautiful' of Herod's time, the sound of the Greek word for beautiful, *oraia*, having been retained in the Latin by *aurea*, which means golden. The present construction is Byzantine. An early Jewish tradition holds that it is through this gate that the Messiah will enter Jerusalem. According to Christian tradition, Jesus came into Jerusalem this way. In Crusader times, it was opened twice a year, on Palm Sunday and on the feast commemorating the 'Finding of the Cross' in the fourth century. Moslems held that this was the gate of judgement referred to in the Koran (Surah 57, verse 13), 'the inner side whereof containeth mercy, while the outer side thereof is toward its doom'. The blocking in of the Golden Gate from the outside – it may still be entered from the Temple compound – is ascribed by some to Saladin in the twelfth century and by others to Suleiman the Magnificent in the sixteenth. Whoever it was did it for security reasons, but it is a Moslem belief that it was done either to prevent the entry of the liberating Jewish Messiah or to ensure that the gate would have no 'outer side . . . toward the doom' on Judgement Day.

The anonymous pilgrim of Crusader days now takes us inside the Gate of David and

> 'when you come to the Exchange where the David street ends there is a street called Mount Zion street, for it goes straight to Mount Zion; and on the left of the Exchange is a covered street, vaulted over, called the Street of Herbs, where they sell all the herbs, and all the fruits of the city, and spices.
>
> 'At the top of this street there is a place where they sell fish. And behind the Market where they sell the fish, is a very large Place on the left hand where cheese, chickens and eggs are sold. On the right hand of this Market are the shops of the Syrian gold-workers. . . . Before the Exchange, close to the Streets of Herbs, is a street which they call Mal-quisinat [bad cooking.] In this street they cooked food for the pilgrims. . . .'

The Via Dolorosa had not yet been given this name when our pilgrim wrote. But we get a clue to its origin in the description of the area, for we learn that what is known today as the Arch of Ecce Homo was called the Gate Dolorous in Crusader times.

Just how thick was the cluster of ecclesiastical buildings in Crusader Jerusalem is indicated in the final words of the pilgrim-author:

> 'Now I have spoken of the abbeys and monasteries of Jerusalem . . . but

A Crusader pilgrim describes the city

I have not named the monasteries and churches of the Syrians, nor of the Greeks, Jacobins, Boamins [Georgians], Nestorians, nor Armenians, nor of the other people who rendered no obeisance to Rome, of whom were many abbeys and churches in the city.'

In the early decades of Crusader rule, the ban on the entry into Jerusalem of a Jew was strictly enforced. By the middle of the twelfth century, there seems to have been a very slight relaxation, a few prominent overseas Jews, like the great Maimonides, being allowed to pay a visit, and a small number of families being permitted to settle – possibly for their needed skill in dyeing. They were seen by Benjamin of Tudela, one of the greatest travellers of the Middle Ages, who visited Jerusalem shortly after the year 1167. This Spanish Jew, usually referred to as Rabbi Benjamin, found Jerusalem 'a small city strongly fortified with three walls. The dyeing house is rented by the year, and the exclusive privilege of dyeing is purchased from the king by the Jews of Jerusalem, two hundred of whom dwell in one corner of the city, under the Tower of David.'

Dyeing seems to have been a major occupation of the decimated Jewish community in Palestine at the time; Rabbi Benjamin came across similar small groups of experts in other centres.

Jewish life in the Crusader period

He makes no mention of any synagogue in Jerusalem. The Jews there worshipped at the Western ('Wailing') Wall, which the visitor said 'is called the Gate of Mercy, and all Jews resort thither to say their prayers.' (Later Jewish pilgrims, describing the Golden Gate, called *that* the Gate of Mercy, and it is still known by this name in Hebrew.)

Small as this Jewish group was, it seems to have dwindled almost as fast as it appeared, for when another Jewish traveller, Rabbi Petachia of Ratisbon (Regensburg, Germany), visited Jerusalem some fifteen years later, he found that 'the only Jew there is Reb Abraham, the dyer, and he pays a heavy tax to the king to be permitted to remain there.'

The Crusaders lost Jerusalem in 1187, after the decisive defeat of their armies at the celebrated battle of the Horns of Hattin, near the Sea of Galilee, by the brilliant military and political leader Salah ad-Din, known to the western world as Saladin.

Defeat by Saladin

Saladin (1138–93), an Armenian Kurd by race and a Moslem by faith, founder of the Ayyubid dynasty, was brought up in Damascus, where his father, Ayyub, was Governor. He was thus educated in what was then the principal centre of Moslem learning, and absorbed the best traditions of Moslem culture. As a young man, he served as aide to his uncle, who had made himself vizier of Egypt. Saladin succeeded him, and within a few years extended his rule over Syria. By the year 1186, he was in control, either by conquest or negotiation, of all the territory which enclosed the Crusader kingdom.

A few months later, an undisciplined Crusader, Reynald of Chatillon, broke a four years' truce which provoked a Moslem reaction. The whole military strength of the Crusaders was then flung into action in Galilee on the foolish order of the inexperienced Crusader king, Guy de Lusignan,

ועיקבעלא אי שלואם עמוזיים עוטקים ומבנקעים כיפא זאן כצר אגן וברי זמנ נרקח
ועבי פירענ ערקענת זב אמאחת שדברי כלתעו ברי כלקבאקנ רבל ויא בעד קרים חפתע
רי שערוים של איש ודרפו לשען זען ועבמו יחול זעיים נצורתב
: זאברמני יי נצורתנ

and on 4 July 1187 was virtually annihilated. The cities and castles of the kingdom lay open to Saladin. On 20 September his forces appeared before the walls of Jerusalem. The city surrendered twelve days later.

Saladin behaved with the utmost chivalry and generosity, granting clemency to the Christian inhabitants and sparing the churches – in stark contrast to the actions of the Crusaders upon their capture of the city eighty-eight years earlier. He did, however, resume possession of the Temple Mount – the Haram esh-Sharif with its Dome of the Rock and Mosque of El-Aksa, which he purified with rose-water and restored to their former state.

The Crusaders had lost Jerusalem, but they still retained a coastal stronghold in the north. This they succeeded in developing by commanding navies, which Saladin lacked. They were thus able to receive reinforcements from the west, and the men of the Third Crusade, under King Philip of France and King Richard the Lion-Heart of England, helped them capture Acre in 1191. From there they were to continue to rule a truncated kingdom for another hundred years.

King Richard, in the fifteen months he spent in the country, took several coastal and other cities, and tried to re-take Jerusalem – even though Saladin continued to allow Christian pilgrimage. But here he was unsuccessful. In September 1192, acknowledging his impotence, the Crusader king signed a treaty with Saladin on the basis of the *status quo*. The coastline was left to the Crusaders as far south as Jaffa; Christians were free to visit Jerusalem's Holy Places; and Moslems and Christians could pass through each other's lands.

Richard returned to Europe, and Saladin to Damascus (where he died in the following spring). For all its holiness, Jerusalem, to Moslem Saladin, was no more than a provincial centre.

Jewish settlement allowed again

With Saladin's conquest, the Jews were once more officially allowed to settle in Jerusalem, and this policy was continued by his successors. Within a short time, there was again a Jewish community in the Holy City, though we have no record of their numbers in the early period. It must have been very small, and as impoverished as the other inhabitants of Jerusalem at the time. There is a brief reference to them in the 'Itinerary' of a certain Rabbi Samuel ben Samson who made the pilgrimage some twenty years later, in 1210. 'We arrived at Jerusalem by the western end of the city, rending our garments on beholding it, as it has been ordained we should do' – as a sign of mourning for the destruction of the Temple. Near the Temple Mount, 'we said our prayers twice with a *minyan* [a religious quorum of at least ten Jews]. . .'

A year later saw the arrival of three hundred rabbis and scholars from France and England who came to settle in the country and greatly enriched Jewish cultural life. The records are thin for the next fifty years, but in 1267 there arrived in Jerusalem one of the most important scholars of his age, a Jew from Spain named Rabbi Moshe ben Nahman, better known as Nachmanides. He it was who revived the Jewish congregation of Jerusalem, established a centre of Jewish learning, and reconstructed a synagogue which bore his name ever after.

In the decades before his arrival, however, there had been several changes in the status of Jerusalem. Forty-two years after the Crusaders had lost the city to Saladin, they recovered it – not by conquest but by gift. Saladin's empire had been divided among his sons, none of whom had inherited his genius, and friction led to frequent conflict between the Syrian and Egyptian branches of the dynasty. Neither was above soliciting Crusader help against the other, and in 1229 the Egyptian sultan al-Kamil, then at war with his nephew al-Nasir of Damascus, offered to the emperor Frederick II of Germany, in return for an alliance, what was a bauble to himself but a glittering prize to the emperor – Jerusalem.

Crusader recovery . . .

Frederick was a brilliant and thoughtful man. Since he was also king of Sicily, he spent most of his time there, and had as many Moslem as Christian friends. He had long resisted the pressure of the Pope to undertake a Crusade, but after marrying the daughter of the titular king of Jerusalem, John of Brienne, he set out for Palestine in 1227. But he quickly turned back, claiming seasickness, and was promptly excommunicated. He left again the following year, still excommunicate, and, in 1229, after little fighting but much diplomacy, concluded the treaty with al-Kamil. Under its terms, which were to run ten years, the Crusaders received Jerusalem, Bethlehem, Nazareth and other places. The Moslems retained the Dome of the Rock and El-Aksa. (The treaty was denounced by the Pope, who considered that the Moslems should be fought, not treated with.) Shortly thereafter, Frederick left, an absentee Holy Roman Emperor.

The Crusader leaders who remained behind were not as wise as he. They quarrelled among themselves and often took opposing sides in the perennial disputes between Cairo and Damascus. In 1244, following one such intervention, an army of nomad Khwarizmian Turks from central Asia, in the pay of Sultan Ayyub (al-Salih) of Egypt captured Jerusalem, pillaged and massacred, and sacked the city. Not for almost seven centuries was it to be governed again by Christians.

. . . *and loss*

Crusaders storming the walls of Jerusalem. From fourteenth-century French manuscript.

Jerusalem was now back under the control of the Egyptian court, but only for a little while longer under the Ayyubids. After the death of Ayyub in 1249, control was seized by Aybak, a Mameluke, and he started a line of sultans who were to rule the region for 267 years.

The Mamelukes were slaves – *mamluk* is Arabic for owned – and they were owned by a sovereign or emir, who was often himself a Mameluke. They were chiefly Turks and Circassians, from Russia, the Caucasus and central Asia, who were brought in by the caliphs of Baghdad to compensate for the military inadequacies of their own people. (The term 'Turks' used here and earlier does not necessarily mean Turks in the ethnic sense, but Turkish-speaking soldier-slaves, which included Kurds, Mongols and others.) As commanders of armies, they wielded the real power, and, as we have seen in earlier instances, often overthrew their masters and usurped political power.

In previous cases, however, as for example with the Abbasids, the Seljuks and Saladin's family, the commander who seized power founded a dynasty. The Mamelukes rejected hereditary succession. They followed a kind of 'survival of the strongest or wiliest' doctrine, recognising from the experience of their own previous masters that genius is not always hereditary.

The dilemma every Mameluke ruler faced was over the choice of commander to defend a distant region. An able man with an adequate army at his disposal would be tempted to rebel and threaten his master's power. An inept commander might fail to repel an invasion. The problem was mostly resolved by appointing two commanders, one to be governor of a district and the other to command the citadel – and to change the governors frequently.

That is what happened to Jerusalem. Since the governor was insecure, and his term of office brief, he usually made the most of it, sometimes for his own pocket, sometimes for the city – and his own glory. Taxation was always heavy, but the proceeds were at times put to good purpose.

The Mamelukes were great builders and patrons of the arts, and though their architectural programmes were applied largely to their main cities,

bil (fountain) in the reet of the Valley, built Suleiman the Mag- icent in 1536.

Jerusalem too felt their influence. They rebuilt the walls of the city, which had been allowed to fall into disrepair, and from a map of 1321 in 'The Book of Secrets for Crusaders concerning the Recovery and Preservation of the Holy Land' prepared by a Venetian, Marino Sanuto, and presented to the Pope, we see that the walls now included Mount Zion. There were, however, also periods when the walls were allowed to crumble. They reconstructed the Citadel (on the site of the old Palace of Herod) in the form with which we are familiar today. And they expanded the city's water supply, repairing an aqueduct which brought water from the Hebron hills, and adding pools.

Moslem architectural improvements

Their main beautification work was directed to Moslem buildings. They built four handsome *Madrasahs* (a combination of mosque and school), hoping to turn Jerusalem into an important seat of Moslem learning, but though these produced a number of pious scholars, Jerusalem never became a centre of Islamic theology. They greatly adorned the Haram esh-Sharif area, adding fountains, arcades, minarets, and small houses of prayer. Some of the present gates are Mameluke. So are several of the buildings at the western end of the area which now contain tombs of Moslem leaders and were originally schools. El-Aksa and the Dome of the Rock were kept in repair and embellished. The Mamelukes furnished the marble pulpit of the Dome, and the graceful arcades at the top of the steps giving entrance to the platform on which the Dome stands.

While Moslem building flourished, church building declined. To build new churches and repair the old required a permit, and bribes to acquire a permit were often beyond the purse of many Christian sects, particularly those belonging to the Eastern Church. In addition, several churches were converted into mosques, the most notable being the Church of St Anne. (It was restored to the Christians in the nineteenth century.)

Nevertheless, the Mamelukes were by and large tolerant of other religions. They were not themselves religious fanatics. Christians and Jews were allowed freedom of worship, though they were subject to such restrictions as the payment of a poll tax and the wearing of distinctive dress – yellow turbans for Jews, blue ones for Christians. Life for them was far from ideal, but the Jews were better off than they had been under the Crusaders, and the Christians fared better than the Moslems had under them.

The Jewish experience during the Mameluke period was one of frequent pilgrimage and of continued settlement in Jerusalem, with the size of the community fluctuating from generation to generation.

The record left in 1331 by the pilgrim Isaac ben Joseph ibn Chelo speaks of a lively, learned and contented congregation.

'The Jewish community in Jerusalem is quite numerous. It is composed of fathers of families from all parts of the world, principally from France. The leading men of the community, as well as the principal rabbis, come from the latter kingdom. . . . They live there in happiness and tranquillity, each according to his condition and fortune, for the royal authority is just and great. . . .

'Among the different members of the holy congregation are many who are engaged in handicrafts, such as dyers, tailors, shoemakers, etc.

racious *minbar*, preaching ¹lpit, near the Mosque of -Aksa, built in 1456 ₃ough ascribed by some to ₃ladin in the twelfth ₃ntury.

191

left: Fifteenth-century sabil (public fountain), right, built by the Mameluke sultan, Qait Bey, and a fourteenth-century minaret over the Gate of the Chain, left, seen through the arcade (Mawazeen) on platform of the Dome of the Rock. *above:* Early Moslem carved panels from the mosque of El-Aksa, now exhibited at the Rockefeller Museum, Jerusalem.

Others carry on a rich commerce in all sorts of things, and have fine shops. Some are devoted to science, as medicine, astronomy, and mathematics. But the greater number of their learned men are working day and night at the study of the Holy Law [the Torah and Talmud] and of the true wisdom, which is the Kabbalah [Jewish oral tradition and mystic interpretation of the biblical texts]. These are maintained out of the coffers of the community, because the study of the law is their only calling.

'There are also at Jerusalem excellent calligraphists, and the copies are sought for by the strangers, who carry them away to their own countries. I have seen a Pentateuch written with so much art that several persons at once wanted to acquire it, and it was only for an excessively high price that the Chief of the Synagogues of Babylon carried it off with him to Baghdad.'

A Jewish pilgrim from Italy, Meshullam ben Menahem, found 'about two hundred and fifty Jewish householders' when he visited Jerusalem in 1481. He lists the names of their notables, the rabbis, judges and warden, and describes how 'all these go every year with the congregation behind them . . . on the ninth of Ab' to pray near the Temple. He then tells of their custom after that service to 'descend to the valley of Jehoshaphat and go upon Mount Olivet, whence they see the whole of the Temple area and mourn for the destruction of the Temple.'

However, it was an impoverished congregation that Rabbi Obadiah da Bertinoro found when he arrived in Jerusalem in 1488, and he stayed to lead it and revive it. Obadiah was the most important Jewish pilgrim of the period, renowned for his great Commentary on the Mishna.

He came when the fortunes of the Mamelukes – and of the inhabitants of Jerusalem – were at a very low point.

'Jersualem is for the most part desolate and in ruins . . . it is not surrounded by walls. Its inhabitants, I am told, number about four thousand families. As for Jews, about seventy families of the poorest class . . . there

is scarcely a family that is not in want of the commonest necessaries; one who has bread for a year is called rich. . . . When I came to Jerusalem there was a dreadful famine in the land. . . I was told that the famine was less severe than it was at the beginning of the year. Many Jews died of hunger. . . . Many lived on grass, going out like stags to look for pasture. . . Now, the wheat harvest being over, the famine is at an end, and there is once more plenty. . . .

'The synagogue here is built on columns; it is long, narrow and dark, the light entering only by the door. There is a fountain in the middle of it. In the court of the synagogue, quite close to it, stands a mosque. The court [also] . . . contains many houses, all of them buildings devoted by the Ashkenasim [the reference here is to western Jews] to charitable purposes, and inhabited by Ashkenasi widows. . .

'The Jews' street and the houses are very large; some of them [Jews] dwell also on [Mount] Zion. At one time they had more houses, but these are now heaps of rubbish and cannot be rebuilt, for the law of the land is that a Jew may not rebuild his ruined house without permission, and the permission often costs more than the whole house is worth. The houses in Jerusalem are of stone, not of wood or plaster.'

This virtual ban on house-repair, with its obvious effects on the life of the community, was not their only hardship. Da Bertinoro mentions the special taxes:

'The Jews in Jerusalem have to pay down every year thirty-two pieces of silver per head. The poor man, as well as the rich, has to pay this tribute as soon as he comes to the age of manhood.

'Everyone is obliged to pay fifty ducats annually to the Niepo, i.e. the Governor of Jerusalem, for permission to make wine, a beverage which

right: A detail of the pulpit shown on page 190.

is an abomination to the Arabs.' (Ritual wine was required for Jewish services.)

He was much impressed by the piety of his fellow Jews:

'I have nowhere seen the daily service conducted in a better manner. The Jews rise an hour or two before day-break, even on the Sabbath, and recite psalms and other songs of praise till the day dawns. Then they repeat the *Kaddish* [prayer of Sanctification]; after which two of the Readers appointed for the purpose chant the Blessings of the Law. . . the "Hear, O Israel" being read on the appearance of the sun's first rays. . .'

The Jews in early times chose a burial site as close as possible to the Temple. Da Bertinoro notes what happened when this was filled: 'At the foot of the slope of the Temple Mount are Jewish graves. The new ones are at the foot of the Mount of Olives, and the valley [of Kidron] runs between the graveyards.' Over the centuries, the Jewish cemetery crept right up the slope of the Mount of Olives, and was the most revered burial site of Jewry. Many pious Jews overseas commanded in their wills that they be laid to rest on this Mount within sight of the Temple compound. Rabbi Obadiah da Bertinoro himself is buried there, having headed an enlarged and revived community in Jerusalem until his death in 1510. (After the Six Day War in June 1967, it was found that this ancient cemetery had been desecrated and the tombstones broken up and removed for use as building materials. Some were discovered in houses built for officers of the Jordan Arab Legion at a nearby camp.)

Such was Jerusalem at the end of the fifteenth century. There had been periods of active Mameluke interest in its welfare, but these had been followed by long periods of indifference and neglect. If conditions were harsh for Christians and Jews, it must not be thought that the lot of the Moslems was much better. The entire country and its people were in decline. Jerusalem became a backwater, with a power of attraction only for Jewish and Christian pilgrims.

Moreover, during the two and a half centuries of Mameluke rule, the country suffered an unusual incidence of natural disasters – famine, drought, plague, earthquake. The Black Death which smote Europe in the middle of the fourteenth century also ravaged Palestine. Buildings shattered by earthquakes remained in ruins. Houses collapsed in exceptionally heavy rains – the records show that more than three hundred tumbled in Jerusalem during the winter of 1473, and da Bertinoro mentions the famine.

With effective government, recovery would have been possible. Under later Mameluke maladministration and indifference, the population dwindled and became impoverished. It has been estimated that Jerusalem numbered forty thousand at the beginning of their rule. At the end, the population had shrunk to ten thousand.

Mameluke dominion over Jerusalem was swept away by the Ottoman Turks in the very last days of 1516, their conquest being marked by the entry into the city of the Turkish sultan, Selim I. For the next four hundred years, Jerusalem was to remain part of the Ottoman empire.

Jerusalem at the end of the fifteenth century

The Lions' Gate, so called because of the heraldic lio[n] on either side of the porta[l] it is also known as St Stephen's Gate. Through this gate, to the immediate left, is the northeastern entrance to the Temple Esplanade. A hundred yards beyond the gate is t[he] start of the Via Dolorosa.

196

The Ottoman star was very much in the ascendant by the time Selim I reached the throne. ('Ottoman' is a corruption of 'Osmanli', the name of the Turkish dynasty founded by the sultan Osman I at the end of the thirteenth century.) Constantinople had fallen to the Ottomans in 1453, and they had overrun what was left of the former great Byzantine empire. By the beginning of the sixteenth century, they already controlled Asia Minor and parts of Europe and the Balkans. Selim I, who reigned from 1512 to 1520, added Syria and Egypt to the Ottoman empire in 1516 and 1517.

Jerusalem – and the rest of the country – fell to him almost without a battle. Selim occupied himself little with the Holy City; he lived only three years after its conquest, and in that time was busy elsewhere on campaigns. The sultan who did, and who left an impressive mark on Jerusalem, was his son, Suleiman I – the Magnificent as he became known in the west, and as the Lawgiver in Turkey. He reigned from 1520 to 1566.

Last of the great sultans, Suleiman was probably the ablest leader of his time, controlling an empire, which he had vastly expanded, with an extremely well-ordered administration. Parts of that empire were given a large measure of self-government; some were allowed semi-independent governors; the rest were ruled from the imperial capital. These latter consisted of twenty-four provinces, called *vilayets*, four in Europe and twenty in Asia and Africa. One of these was the vilayet of Damascus, which included the territory that had been called Palestine.

The governor of a vilayet was a senior ranking pasha who was appointed by the sultan. Each vilayet was subdivided into several districts, called *sanjaks*. The city of Jerusalem was part of a sanjak. To the sultan in Constantinople, therefore, it was a distant place belonging to a district administered by a junior pasha who was answerable to a senior pasha in charge of one of the many vilayets in one of the empire's many territories. Quite unremarkable except that it was one of the places which had become holy to Islam. However, once his interest had been stimulated by the religious associations of Jerusalem, Suleiman the soldier also considered its military value, and he thought it might be useful to have a strong fortress

ew of Jerusalem from the uth, from a fifteenth-ntury manuscript. The ome of the Rock (top) is own between two tall inarets. To its left is the urch of the Holy pulchre, with open dome. ount Zion (with domed ildings) is in the reground.

in the south of Syria. It is this which caused him to restore its ramparts.

The walls surrounding the 'Old City' of Jerusalem which we see today are the very walls, unchanged, which Suleiman rebuilt. Like Hadrian's Aelia Capitolina, the southern wall runs just north of, and thus excludes, Mount Zion. Suleiman's walls have a clean-lined beauty, reflecting artistic taste and fine craftsmanship. They are given a special quality – which must also have been true of the ancient walls – by the natural rose-colour of the local stone. At sunset, the ramparts glow.

The Damascus Gate

Pride of Suleiman's wall structures was the Damascus Gate, which he built anew. (Archaeological excavations brought to light parts of the second century gate on this site, no doubt the one which appears so prominently on the sixth century Madeba map.) This gate, in the centre of the north wall of the city, was – and still is – one of the richest examples of early Ottoman architecture in the region, massive-looking yet graceful. The arched portal is set in a broad façade flanked on each side by a great tower, the entire building topped by pinnacled battlements. The staggered entrance is handsomely vaulted. It all looks powerful enough. Yet the Damascus Gate is more decorative than defensive and seems to have been designed as much to impress the distinguished visitor as the enemy. One curious feature is the rows of bosses above the portal, the lower one adorned with reliefs of flowers and geometric patterns. They appear to be the protruding ends of binding columns running through the wall to strengthen the structure. But they are fake. There are no such columns.

For long, the Damascus Gate was where foreign dignitaries were received, such as the crown prince of Prussia and the emperor Franz Joseph of Austria in 1869. Later the Jaffa Gate was used; it was through here that the German kaiser in 1898 and General Allenby in December 1917 entered the city.

Life under Suleiman

Work on the walls took three years and was completed in about 1540. Earlier, Suleiman had added decorative adornments to the Dome of the Rock, which have been described earlier, and to the Haram esh-Sharif generally. He also improved the water services of the city, repairing the

201

aqueducts, building a number of public fountains (*sabils*), and restoring the dam which forms the ancient Sultan's Pool at the western foot of Mount Zion.

(The aqueducts repaired by the early Ottomans brought water from the 'Pools of Solomon' near Bethlehem. These are three large reservoirs terraced one above the other, and water was carried to the Temple area along an ancient Low Level aqueduct and to the Upper City along another ancient High Level aqueduct. When these structures were built, additional channels were cut from springs in the Hebron hills to the Pools to increase their supply. They were built because over the centuries, with the city's expansion, the waters of the Gihon spring and wells of En-Rogel and others proved insufficient. Scholars disagree on the exact dates of these two aqueducts, but all agree that the High Level is the older, that Herod built one of them in the 1st century BC, and that Pontius Pilate either built or repaired the other in the 1st century AD, having raided the Temple funds to finance the project. But many scholars consider that the first

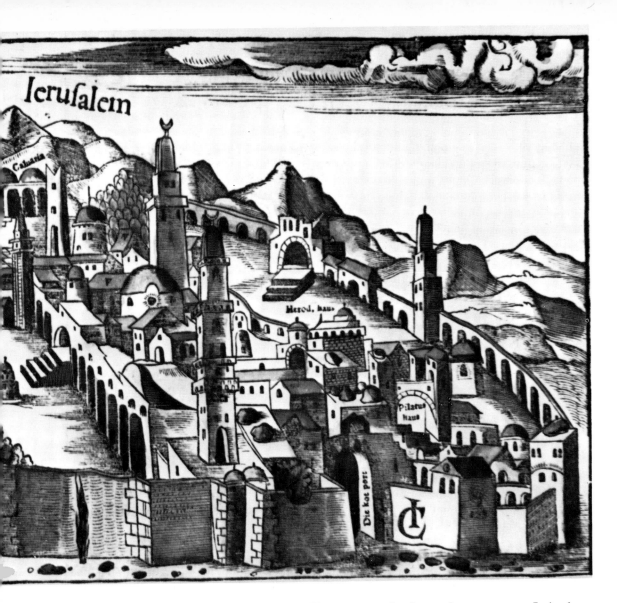

Ierufalem

A map of Jerusalem, looking ~~west~~, published in Basle in ~~1~~544. The Holy Sepulchre ~~at~~ top centre; the Temple ~~co~~mpound is at the right.

aqueduct was built by the Hasmoneans in the 2nd century BC. It is thus most probable that the High Level aqueduct was indeed constructed by the Hasmoneans and *repaired* by Pilate, while Herod built the newer one. Not many scholars credit Solomo with any of this work, despite the name of the Pools. Josephus says that Solomon used to visit the Pools and enjoy the gardens nearby, and this association may have given rise to the name.)

Under Suleiman's efficient rule, Jerusalem prospered modestly. Christians and Jews were subject to the special poll tax which all non-Moslems had to pay, but both were left free to manage their own communal affairs. The Franciscans suffered a blow when in 1551 they were expelled from their church and monastery on Mount Zion adjoining the Coenaculum, traditional site of the Last Supper, but they were provided with alternative ground in the Christian Quarter inside the city walls, where they built the monastery of St Saviour's. It still stands as their headquarters.

Pilgrimage continued, yet visits to the holy sites were as irksome as ever. A Spanish Franciscan friar wrote in 1553:

'Before the entrance to the Holy Sepulchre each pilgrim pays nine castellani ... (the fee extortionate). Then come four or five Turkish officials to open the gate, together with their scribe; and, when they have taken the names of the pilgrims and the countries from which they hail and have increased the amount of the fee, they open the gate with much to do with their keys, taking away the seal. Having entered, we saluted the religious who live therein. .. The Turks then closed and sealed the gate and went away, not returning until the next day or two days after. In the meantime the pilgrims consoled themselves with many visits to the holy places [within this sanctuary].'

Under Suleiman, the Jewish community of Jerusalem fared reasonably well. Indeed, within the wide area of Ottoman rule, they suffered little of the persecution that was their lot notably in Spain, Portugal, Germany and central Europe in the fourteenth and fifteenth centuries. In 1492 had come the great expulsion from Spain and four years later from Portugal. With the French frontier closed, they fled by sea to the nearest refuge, Italy and North Africa, or further, to the Levant. Then came persecution in Italy. But in Palestine under the Ottomans they could practice their religion freely. Many reached the Holy Land in this period, and while most flocked to Safad and Tiberias, centres of Jewish study in Galilee, the community in Jerusalem grew both in numbers and learning.

Decline set in only a few decades after Suleiman's death, and from then until the end of the Ottoman empire more than three centuries later, Palestine was a land in decay, neglected, impoverished, lawless, corrupt.

Decline after Suleiman

Jerusalem and Palestine could never mean as much to a distant imperial emperor as they did to the local population, and his concern for their welfare could be, at best, only secondary. Where it was virtually non-existent and local administration was left to an imperial representative whose sole task was the collection of taxes, the people suffered and any attempt at development was stifled. This is what began to happen to Ottoman Jerusalem and Palestine towards the end of the sixteenth century. It continued to the beginning of the twentieth.

The corruption that crept into Ottoman rule led to the breakdown of a remarkable system of administration which worked brilliantly only so long as the sultan was strong and gifted, like Suleiman and some of his predecessors. When, however, as in the time of Suleiman's grandson, Murad III (1574–95), one of his counsellors could boast openly that he had made a sultan take a bribe for the first time, it was the beginning of the end. Bribery became usual in both the administration and the army. Soon, it was said, every office in the empire was open to the highest bidder.

The impact on Jerusalem and the rest of the country – indeed of the region – was ruinous. Governorships of vilayets and sanjaks were sought after for the revenues they could bring to the pockets of the pashas. All Constantinople demanded of them was that they secure the frontiers, suppress possible rebellion, maintain themselves and the forces allocated to them, and collect the taxes due from their provinces. If they collected more, that was their affair. They could do as little or as much as they

Characteristic window-shutters and stone walls of old Jerusalem.

wished for their subjects. One or two tried to introduce honest and progressive administration into Palestine, notably Mohammed Pasha during his five-year governorship (1620–5). The rest cared for themselves alone. The pasha would tour his province once a year to collect the annual tax. If a farmer was unable to pay, his trees were cut down. Villagers in the same position faced the destruction of their village. The fact that this permanently disabled them from paying taxes did not ruffle the pasha. Over the years, cultivated areas went to waste, attracting the Bedouin whose goats further ravaged the land, while soil erosion completed the process. The settled agricultural population dwindled. The successive pashas remained indifferent.

Jerusalem could not but be affected by the desolation of its hinterland. It was affected more directly by the get-rich-quick aim of its own local ruler. Urban society offered him countless opportunities. A permit to build was a double source of revenue: the bribe extorted to secure the permit, and the official cost of the permit. So was a permit to carry out repairs, or to acquire land. Moreover, a newly installed pasha could repeat the process of double extortion which the victim might already have gone through with his predecessor. The possibilities were endless.

The Christians in Jerusalem were well aware of them, yet their bitter internal rivalries greatly stimulated the practice of exortion. There was the centuries' old hatred between the western and eastern Churches and conflict among the eastern sects themselves. Since each sought to increase its rights in the Holy Places, the Turks were happy to sit back and await the highest bids.

The Christian Holy Places

The Latins had achieved supremacy over the Holy Places during the Crusades. The Greek Orthodox now tried to get their own back. They had more followers among Ottoman subjects than did the westerners, and Greek interpreters at the sultan's court pressed their interests. They soon retrieved rights in Jerusalem's Christian shrines which had hitherto been the exclusive possession of the Roman Catholics. That the Latins were not ousted completely was due to their wealth and political influence. They were protected by European powers with whom the Ottomans wished to remain friendly, notably France. (Towards the end of the eighteenth century, the Greek Orthodox Church countered this by securing the protection of the Russian Czars.)

At the Easter service in the Church of the Holy Sepulchre in 1757, there were clashes between the Greek Orthodox and the Franciscans, and the sultan issued an edict giving the Greeks, among other rights, joint possession with the Latins of parts of the Basilica of the Holy Sepulchre. Despite western appeals, this edict stood. Later, the rights of each community were carefully recorded and have changed little over the years.

Even so, as Professor Avi-Yonah points out in *The Saga of Jerusalem*,

'there remained ample cause for fresh disputes. Thus the Franciscans had the right to clean the steps of the Golgotha Chapel, which descends to the courtyard of the Holy Sepulchre; but the courtyard itself was not included in that right. Now the last riser of the steps was no more than

Beginning of the Via Dolorosa. The domes belong to the Franciscan Convent of the Flagellatio

206

one centimetre high. Was it to be regarded as part of the staircase or as part of the paving of the court? Such and similar problems led to frequent disputes, and sometimes even to bloodshed.'

The British pilgrim Henry Maundrell, who visited Jerusalem in 1697, was scathing about the 'unchristian fury and animosity, especially between the Greeks and Latins', over which 'the several sects [contend for] the command and appropriation of the Holy Sepulchre'. So much so that

'in disputing which party should go into it to celebrate their mass, they have sometimes proceeded to blows and wounds even at the very door of the sepulchre, mingling their own blood with their sacrifices, in evidence of which fury the father guardian showed us a great scar upon his arm, which he told us was the mark of a wound given him by a sturdy Greek priest in one of these unholy wars.'

Maundrell also mentions the loss of rights of the poorer denominations.

'Almost every Christian nation anciently maintained a small society of monks, each society having its proper quarter [in the Church of the Holy Sepulchre] assigned to it by the appointment of the Turks, such as the Latins, Greeks, Syrians, Armenians, Abyssinians, Georgians, Nestorians, Copts, Maronites ... but these have all, except four, forsaken their quarters, not being able to sustain the severe rents and extortions which their Turkish landlords impose upon them.'

No traveller's report during the eighteenth century is free of its reflections upon the run-down state of the country, the indifference of the officials, the widespread corruption. This was the Age of Enlightenment in Europe, which brought a decline in western pilgrimage – and a more rationalist outlook in those who did come. We know from other sources too that Christian pilgrims were now drawn largely from members of the Eastern Church. Jewish pilgrimage – and Jewish settlement – was on the increase. All brought enrichment to the Turkish officials.

A Swedish botanist and doctor, Frederick Hasselquist, left these figures after a visit in 1751. On his arrival, he was visited by

'a clerk of the customs who . . . came to receive the twenty-two piastres which every Frank is obliged to pay . . . for the privilege of coming on shore and travelling in the country. . . . As 4,000 persons arrive yearly, besides as many Jews, who come from all quarters of the world, this may be esteemed a considerable revenue for the Turks; and indeed they receive no other from this uncultivated and almost uninhabited country.'

Uncultivated and almost uninhabited – this is what the 'land flowing with milk and honey' had come to.

It grew worse; and with the country impoverished, the local Ottoman administrators exploited the religious communities even more. Instead of uniting them, it had the reverse effect. Writing thirty-four years later, the Comte de Volney observed that while the most important source of Turkish income was still 'the visits of the pilgrims', the Turks gained extra sums through 'the follies of the Christian inhabitants'. He explained these 'follies':

manuscript illumination owing pilgrims paying lls after landing at Jaffa their way to Jerusalem.

209

'The different communions . . . Greeks, Armenians, Copts, Abyssinians and Franks, mutually envying each other the possessions of the holy places, are continually endeavouring to outbid one another in the price they offer for them to the Turkish Governors. They are constantly aiming to obtain some privilege for themselves, or to take it from their rivals; and each sect is perpetually informing against the other for irregularities.'

Incidentally, it was during the Ottoman period that the tradition of the Stations of the Cross developed, the path of the Via Dolorosa running to Calvary (in the Church of the Holy Sepulchre) from the northwest of the Temple esplanade, site of the Antonia fortress. This was based on the belief that the Antonia, and not Herod's palace, was the Praetorium, where Jesus was condemned. The tradition of the Stations is thus a comparatively recent one. It owes its full development largely to pilgrims.

From faint beginnings at the end of the thirteenth and beginning of the fourteenth centuries – when pilgrims would be led along the 'Way of the Cross' – the custom of marking specific events associated with Jesus' progress from the Praetorium to Golgotha became firmly established by the end of the sixteenth century. (It was in the middle of that century that the term Via Dolorosa came into use.) But the events selected for commemoration, and the locations where they were believed to have happened, varied from period to period. In the fifteenth century, for example, the scene of today's Third Station was located somewhere near the end of the route, and in the same century pilgrims record only seven Stations. Only as late as the second half of the sixteenth century are there records of fourteen Stations, not necessarily the ones now familiar to us. Indeed, not until the middle of the nineteenth century, more than eighteen hundred years after the crucifixion, were the subjects and sites standardised into the Fourteen Stations commemorated today.

Nine of the incidents are referred to in the Gospels; five have been handed down by tradition. The first two are placed in Antonia, the next seven along the route, and the last five within the Church of the Holy Sepulchre. Each is now marked by a church, a chapel, a piece of column, or just a sign, and today one moves from one to the other through the narrow, winding, cobbled alleyways of the markets in the Old City, whose present level is very much higher than the pavement level in the time of Jesus. (Incidentally, the term 'Station' is ascribed to an English pilgrim, William Wey, said to have been one of the original fellows of Eton, who was in Jerusalem in the 1450s and recorded the list of what he called 'Stations' visited on the 'Holy Circuit'.)

The First marks the spot where Jesus was sentenced to death. By relatively recent custom, this Station is the site of the hall inside Antonia where the private part of the trial took place, and upon it stands the courtyard of a Turkish barracks, now serving as the Umariya boys' school, about 300 yards from the Lions' Gate. Actually, if Antonia was the Praetorium, sentence would have been passed by Pilate in the open court below the palace known as the Lithostrotos (which means 'paved' in Greek) or Gabbatha (which means 'raised' in Aramaic). Parts of what are believed to be the Lithostrotos may be seen in the nearby Chapel of the Condemnation and the Convent of the Sisters of Zion. The paving is striated, and carved on the flagstones are traces of games played by the Roman soldiers.

The Franciscan Order, which did much to promote the tradition of the Stations of the Cross, has a fine museum in the neighbouring Convent of the Flagellation, which also stands on part of the Antonia fortress.

The second Station, in the street outside the Chapel of the Condemnation, marks the spot where Jesus is said to have received the Cross.

The Third, commemorating Jesus' first fall – not mentioned in the Gospels – is reached after passing under the arch built by Hadrian which has been known since the sixteenth century as the 'Ecce Homo' Arch. This Station is shown by a broken column, now part of a renovated chapel which was formerly the entrance to a bath-house.

The Via Dolorosa then turns sharp left, or south, for a short distance, and a few yards from the corner is the Fourth Station, the traditional site where Jesus met his fainting mother. It is marked by a small oratory over the door of the Armenian Catholic Church of Our Lady of the Spasm.

Some twenty yards beyond, the Via turns sharply right, or west, and leads uphill to Calvary. An oratory at the first building on the left marks the Fifth Station, where the Cross was laid upon Simon of Cyrene.

The Sixth Station, where Veronica wiped the face of Jesus, is indicated by a fragment of a column inserted into the wall on the traditional site of her house. A Greek Orthodox chapel stands there today. An opening in one wall of the chapel leads to an ancient grotto, about ten feet below the level of the road. It was part of a pre-Roman Jewish building.

The Seventh, where Jesus fell the second time, is now a Franciscan chapel. It is said to be close to the old gate through which Jesus passed to reach the crucifixion site which was then outside the city walls.

The Eighth Station, where Jesus spoke to the compassionate daughters of Jerusalem, is marked by a cross set in the wall of the Greek Orthodox convent of St Charalambos, adjoining the German Lutheran Hospice of St John.

The Via Dolorosa ends here as a street; the rest of the original route is now enclosed by buildings, so that the Ninth Station, where Jesus fell the third time, is reached by retracing one's steps and proceeding up a long flight of steps to the Coptic Church. It is marked by a pillar in the door. The nearby terrace, which is level with the ground of the Church of the Holy Sepulchre, is actually the roof of the Chapel of St Helen, commemorating the 'Finding of the Cross'.

The remaining five Stations are within the Church of the Holy Sepulchre. The Tenth, where Jesus was stripped of his garments, is the Latin chapel on Calvary, to the immediate right, through the main entrance of the Basilica. The Eleventh, where Jesus was nailed to the cross, is the altar of that chapel. The Twelfth, where the cross was fixed and where Jesus died, is the altar in the Greek Orthodox chapel, adjoining the Latin chapel. The Thirteenth, commemorating the taking down of the body from the cross, is marked by the Latin 'altar of the Stabat Mater', between the Eleventh and Twelfth Stations. The Fourteenth, where Jesus was laid to rest, is the Holy Sepulchre itself.

right: The crypt of the Dormition Church on Mount Zion, with the figure of Mary in eternal sleep.

overleaf: The Holy Places of Jerusalem, described and illustrated in a Serbian manuscript of 1662. The language in which the manuscript is written is old Slavonic.

дасе миръ. иже пероидше ѿпрадфии
ипдаиѣоше пдцрпта дюбное :⁓·
ѡси црıсо пелиıса ипсрдпдю жⷠ
сдтрди стдд еıедıмⷬпıи црд ıсоⷪт
дтııпдоıдмⷮтⷡ ̃те чдⷮт ии
тро̃ · иголтафд · ⁓:⁓ ⁓⁓ ⁓⁓⁓

ДОМЬ ДѢДѢЬ

The Jews under
Ottoman rule

One of the most remarkable phenomena of Ottoman Jerusalem was the survival – and eventual growth – of the Jewish community. We have seen how the Jews, in common with all the inhabitants of the city, fared quite well under Suleiman I at the beginning of Ottoman rule. We have also seen what started happening to the land and the people later in the sixteenth century, and how it kept growing worse. Once the administration started to decay, all suffered. The Jews fared worst of all. The Christians had their protectors – the Latins in the west, the Greeks in Constantinople and Moscow. The Jews had none. Their fate was determined by the whim of the pasha – or of his underlings, or of the Moslem in the street. Persecution was their normal lot – disabilities, restrictions, extortion, humiliation; murder or physical injury were frequent hazards. But still they came, as pilgrims and as settlers, to their beloved Jerusalem.

Gone were the days when Ottoman tolerance could attract to its provinces Jews fleeing from Christian persecution in Europe. In the 1580s, the local pasha could seize the chief synagogue in Jerusalem of the Sephardim (Spanish Jews), the thirteenth-century synagogue of Nachmanides (the Ramban), and declare that it would be used as a mosque – thereby making it inalienable Moslem religious property and denying it permanently to Jews. (During the recent Mandatory and Jordanian periods it was used as a food-processing factory.) Still, the Jews could, and did, with painful effort and bribery, establish another synagogue shortly afterwards – on the traditional site of the synagogue of the first century's celebrated Rabbi Yohanan ben Zakkai. This in our own day was the oldest synagogue in Jerusalem, and in continuous use from the sixteenth century until 1948 when it was destroyed by the Jordanians.

Jerusalem had a brief spell of fair administration from 1620 to 1625 under the governorship of Mohammed Pasha, and this is reflected in the following record written a few years later by a Jerusalem Jew who had lived through the period:

'The City of God contained more of our people than at any time since the Jews were banished from their country. Many Jews came daily to live in the City, apart from those coming to pray at the Western Wall. . . . Moreover, they brought with them bountiful gifts of money to strengthen the Jews of Jerusalem. It was reported in all countries that we were dwelling in peace and security. Many of us bought houses and fields and rebuilt the ruins, and aged men and women sat in the streets of Jerusalem, and the thoroughfares of the City were thronged with boys and girls. . . . The teaching of the Holy Law (the Torah) prospered, and many houses of study stood open to all who sought to engage in the labour of Heaven. The leaders of the community provided the students with their daily needs. All the poor were relieved of their wants. . . .'

The Greek Orthodox
Chapel of Calvary in the
Church of the Holy
Sepulchre, with the Altar
of the Cross positioned
above the traditional site
of the crucifixion.

The idyll was short-lived. The next pasha of Jerusalem, Mohammed ibn-Farouk, who had bought the governorship from the senior pasha in control of the vilayet of Damascus, arrived in the city with three hundred mercenaries intent on multiplying his investment. One method was to surround the synagogues on the Sabbath, seize the leading figures among

Above: A Moslem dignitary in the seventeenth century.

Left: A lithograph of the Jewish Quarter in the Old City, made by a French artist in 1802.

Below: A seventeenth-century French engraving of 'A Jew in the Holy Land'.

IVIF DE LA TERRE SAINTE.

the worshippers, and hold them for high ransom. When this was paid, and the community was just about recovering from the financial blow, the pasha would order a synagogue to be impounded and converted to stores – unless a large payment was forthcoming to prevent the sacrilege. On one occasion, when two congregants were grabbed and the impoverished community was finding it difficult to raise the money for their release, the victims were brought to the synagogue and tortured before the eyes of the congregation. Household chattels were sold or pledged to speed the payment.

The day after ibn-Farouk completed his term and left the city, the Jews 'assembled and rendered thanks to the Almighty in the synagogue, and we praised His name . . . for all His goodness to us in removing strange worship from our land and driving away from us the wicked foe, ibn-Farouk. Some of the sages and leaders of the community went round the city and collected food and gifts for the poor; and there was light and joy for the Jews'. But they had been reduced to penury, and most of their possessions had been pledged to meet the arbitrary extortions of the ruler. 'Today', says the narrator of this record, 'we are mortgaged – men, women and children – to the Ishmaelite dwellers of this land.'

The city 'contained more of our people', the Jerusalem Jew had written, than at any time since the exile. He was writing in the early part of the seventeenth century when the total population of Jerusalem was about ten thousand and the Jews numbered only a few hundred. Two hundred years later, the general population still stood at the same figure, but the Jewish community had grown to three thousand. Despite the misery and the suffering, there were always groups in the Diaspora who were prepared to brave life, however hard, in the Holy Land. By the third quarter of the nineteenth century, the Jewish population of Jerusalem had grown to some eleven thousand and they constituted the majority – for the first time since their independence – a majority they were to retain to this day, when they number nearly two hundred thousand.

They showed an astonishing persistence in the days when they were a very small minority, considering how fragile was their shell of security. It could be punctured at any time by the pasha and his officials, and also, in the general atmosphere of lawlessness, by hooligans, robbers or more dangerous criminals. Moreover, any Moslem could make sport of them, attack, rob or simply dun them for money. They had no redress. If they were unwise enough to dispute a Moslem claim for a non-existent debt, their testimony could never stand up to the word of a True Believer.

But it was from the local administration that the community as a whole had most to fear. In 1720, twenty years after the arrival of Rabbi Yehuda He'Hassid with a thousand Jews from Poland and their erection of an Ashkenasi synagogue, 'the Ishmaelites [Arabs or Moslems] suddenly came and burned down the large synagogue with fire . . . and they drove out the Ashkenasim.' (Ashkenasi means a Jew from central or eastern Europe.)

Rabbi Yehuda had come with his large group during a brief period of lenient administration 'and bought a house in the holy enclosure of the synagogue of the Ashkenasi community . . . . The enclosure had several buildings within it, about forty houses and also a study hall ... a ritual bath ... and a house for the poor.' (The quotation is from the record left by Rabbi Gedalia, one of Rabbi Yehuda's immigrant companions.) The site was in the Jewish Quarter not far from the Western Wall, and it had been Rabbi Yehuda's plan to enlarge the synagogue and study hall and settle his group in and around the compound. He himself died shortly after his arrival, but his friends proceeded with his plan, 'and very large sums have been spent on the synagogue with the holy enclosure and all the living quarters within it. And many bribes as well. . . . For such are the ways of the kingdom of the Ishmaelites.'

But shortly afterwards, 'the leaders of the Ishmaelites imposed on the members of the group heavy taxes which they could not pay', and so they set the synagogue on fire, looted the silver vessels, and tore up adjoining buildings in the search for hidden treasure. The shell of the synagogue remained, for it was built of stone, and it was known ever after as the Hurva Synagogue – 'Hurva' is Hebrew for 'ruin' – or, by its full title, 'Hurvat Rabbi Yehuda He'Hassid'. (He'Hassid means 'the Pious'.)

The Ashkenasim were expelled from Jerusalem, both the new arrivals and the few hundred who had been living there before, and most of them took refuge in Safed, Tiberias or Hebron, the three other 'holy cities' of learned Jewish communities in Palestine. Some managed to remain in Jerusalem by disguising themselves as Sephardi Jews. Though Sephardi means Spanish – Spain was one of the early centres of exile from Palestine – the term covers Jews from southern Europe and the Near East to which the Jews fled from Spanish persecution. They wore distinctive eastern dress. The Ashkenasim wore the familiar dress of the Jews of eastern Europe, which may still be seen in the ultra-orthodox quarter of Jerusalem known as Mea She'arim. The Turks, after destroying the synagogue for non-payment of 'debt', held all Ashkenasim responsible, and would not allow them to return until extortionate sums of money were forthcoming. This was the official reason. The real reason was probably the almost continuous military conflict between Constantinople and the countries from which the Ashkenasim came.

While there were Ashkenasi communities elsewhere in the country, they were kept out of Jerusalem for about a century, though overseas pilgrims still came in openly. Ashkenasim from other cities in Palestine who ventured in on pilgrimage thought it safest to be attired as Sephardim. For Sephardi Jews were allowed to stay. The Ashkenasi community re-established itself in Jerusalem in the 1820s, and from then on their numbers kept growing. Their restoration followed an Ottoman decree of remission of old debts. They soon set about preparing a temporary house of prayer and religious school from some of the buildings of the Hurva compound, but the local Turkish administration was in no mood to give up so valuable a source of extortion. It took years of steady pressure, the expenditure of large sums, and finally the intercession by various Jewish and Gentile European dignitaries in Constantinople, before the property was turned over to the community and they were able to re-establish their theological seminary, religious schools, religious court, ritual bath and study hall. The rebuilding

right: The ancient Jewish cemetery on the Mount of Olives, desecrated by the Jordanians during their 1948–67 occupation.

below: A Jewish doctor. Illustration in a 1586 travel book by the Geographer Royal to the king of France

S⚬ Medicin Iuif.

: The noted synagogue
d *yeshiva* (theological
ademy) Etz Chaim, one
the fifty-eight religious
titutions in the Jewish
uarter of the Old City
stematically ruined by
e Jordanians after its fall
1948, now being rebuilt.

of the synagogue itself was completed in 1864, and a most handsome edifice it was, its dome rising above the rooftops of the city. This Hurva synagogue, 'the glory of the Old City' as it was called, was destroyed by the Jordanian Arab Legion in 1948.

That some progress, however plodding, was made during the nineteenth century in the protection of Christian and Jewish rights in Jerusalem, was due largely to the renewed interest in Palestine by the western powers. This interest was prompted only slightly by sentiment and religion – though religion was often the official reason for intervention. Their primary purpose was to safeguard and develop their political and commercial interests with India, China, and other parts of the Far East and Australasia which had been vastly expanded in the eighteenth century by conquest and colonisation. The bridge to these regions was the area of Palestine.

Napoleon had tried to wrest it from the Ottomans, capturing Egypt in 1798 and moving into Palestine in 1799. He proceeded right up the coastal plain, by-passing Jerusalem, and encamping outside Acre. But he failed to take it. The British navy came to Turkey's rescue, and Napoleon eventually withdrew. From then on, while France and Britain continued their rivalry, each seeking to extend its influence in Palestine, both joined in preventing the third great interested power, Russia, from toppling Turkey, though they were unable to stem Russia's considerable expansion southwards. The result was a growing presence in Jerusalem of Britain, France and Russia and, towards the end of the century, Germany.

This process was aided, because it shook and weakened local Turkish rule, by the capture of Jerusalem and the whole of Palestine by the pasha of Egypt, Mohammed Ali, who rebelled against the sultan in 1831 and sent an army under his son, Ibrahim, to take the country. For the next ten years, Jerusalem was governed by Ibrahim, but in 1841, again with naval help from Britain, Ottoman rule was restored and Mohammed Ali had to content himself with the hereditary pashalik of Egypt.

The ten years of Ibrahim's rule saw a great improvement in the lot of Jerusalemites. True, there was grumbling at his introduction of conscription and high taxation. But his administration was reasonably efficient, and, at least in the beginning, there was security. He 'wrought fearful judgements upon all wicked men', wrote Yaacov Shaul Eliashar, who later became Sephardi Chief Rabbi, 'and caused such fear and trembling that a small girl could walk in the streets carrying gold coins in her hand and no one would molest her.' It was possible, indeed, to travel throughout the land in comparative safety, and the country was opened to western visitors.

It was during this period, in 1838, that the first consulate was opened in Jerusalem – the consulate of Great Britain. This set the pattern. Five years later, two years after the Ottoman return, France and Prussia sent a consul, and they were followed a few years later by Austria and Spain. Russia had a consul in Beirut and sent an agent to Jerusalem. By agreement worked out in Constantinople, these consuls in Jerusalem were given special rights and privileges, such as the running of their own postal services; but most important was the right to extend their protection to certain minority

ow: The 'Hurva'
nagogue of the
shkenasim in the Jewish
uarter of the Old City as
looked in 1870. It was
stroyed in 1948.

communities. The Christians turned for aid to the French or Russian officials – though in the 1840s an English bishop and a Latin patriarch were allowed to be installed in Jerusalem, just as a rabbi was given authority over Jews who were Austrian or Russian subjects. The other Jews came under the protection of the British – Jews who were Ottoman subjects and Jewish residents who had no other protector.

Special role of British consul in mid-nineteenth century

The British consul was in fact specifically instructed by his government to make it his official duty to care for the welfare of the Jews, and this delicate task occupied much of the energies of the first two consuls. The second, James Finn, who served from 1845 to 1862, was a most remarkable man who did a great deal to benefit the Jewish community in Jerusalem. The return of Turkish rule had brought with it a return to corrupt and extortionate practice, and recourse to the protection of the British consul was unfortunately frequent.

James Finn was an outstanding member of a rising group of English intellectuals who believed in Zionism, though that term did not come into popular use until several decades later. They were appalled by the persecution of the Jews in so many countries, and felt that this was the result of their long exile, their homelessness. They were particularly saddened by the Christian rôle in Jewish suffering, Christians oppressing them in the name of Christianity, and they thought it a Christian duty to help in the restoration of Palestine to the Jews. There were others in England who were equally concerned in helping the Jews – but in a different way. They thought persecution was due to the Jews' unwillingness to adopt Christianity, and they conceived it their mission to bring salvation to them by converting those who lived at the fount of Jewry, Jerusalem.

One of these was Lady Egerton, who came out in 1840. Arrived in Jerusalem, she made straight for the Jewish Quarter, first visiting the Western Wall with its

'prodigious stones and beauty of chiselling, [where] every Friday, the Jews come and weep for the desolation of their people and city, as of old. . . . Being the Jewish Sabbath, they were all in their best attire, and their houses are luxurious, clean and even comfortable to a great degree, their rooms are fitted round with divans of a pleasant shape, and they possess the most agreeable studies, well filled with books. The women, too, unlike the natives of the Mohammedan persuasion, live together with their male relatives. . . . They received us admirably, insisting upon our partaking of sherbet and sweetmeats. We went into several synagogues. . . . The appearance of these Jews certainly does not yield an impression of decadence. . . .'

There is a good picture of the Jewish mood of the period in the record of an American traveller, John Lloyd Stephens, who visited Jerusalem in 1835, after seeing something of Jewish persecution in other lands:

'I had already seen a great deal of the Jews. I had seen them in the cities of Italy, everywhere more or less oppressed; at Rome, shut up every night in their miserable quarters as if they were noxious beasts; in Turkey,

Jews at prayer in a synagogue in Jerusalem. An 1836 engraving.

persecuted and oppressed; along the shores of the Black Sea in the heart of Russia, looked down upon by the serfs of that great empire of vassalage; and, for the climax of misery, I had seen them contemned and spat upon even by the ignorant and enslaved boors of Poland. I had seen them scattered abroad among all the nations . . . everywhere a separate and peculiar people; and everywhere under poverty, wretchedness and oppression, waiting for, and anxiously expecting, the coming of the Messiah, to call together their scattered tribes, and restore them to the kingdom of their fathers; and all this the better fitted me for the more interesting spectacle of the Jews in the holy city.

'In all changes and revolutions, from the day when the kingdom of Solomon passed into the hands of strangers, under the Assyrian, the Roman, the Arab and the Turk, a remnant of that once-favoured people has always hovered around the holy city; and now, as in the days of David, old men may be seen at the foot of Mount Zion, teaching their children to read from that mysterious book on which they have ever fondly built their hopes of a temporal and eternal kingdom. . . .

An illustrated map of Israel, with Jerusalem in the centre, drawn by a Safad rabbi in 1875.

'They took me to what they call a part of the wall of Solomon's Temple. It forms part of the . . . wall of the mosque of Omar, and is evidently older than the rest, the stones being much larger. . . . And I saw that day, as other travellers may still see every Friday in the year, all the Jews clothed in their best raiment, winding through the narrow streets of their quarter; and under this hallowed wall, with the sacred volume in their hands, singing in the language in which they were written, the Songs of Solomon and the Psalms of David. White-bearded old men and smooth-cheeked boys were leaning over the same book; and Jewish maidens, in their long white robes, were standing with their faces against the wall, and praying through cracks and crevices. . . .

'Now, as the Moslem lords it over the place where the Temple stood, *and the Jews are not permitted to enter*, they endeavour to insinuate their prayers through the crevices in the wall, that thus they may rise from the interior to the Throne of Grace. The tradition is characteristic, and serves to illustrate the devoted constancy with which the Israelites adhere to the externals of their faith.'

The Temple Mount was, as Stephens wrote, out of bounds to Jews. The Moslems also barred it to Christians, but midway through the century when European influence was more marked, the heir to the Belgian throne on a visit to Jerusalem was given special permission to enter the area with his party. Thereafter the ban was less harshly enforced and it was eventually abolished – as far as Christians were concerned. But it continued to be rigidly applied to Jews – even after the fall of the Ottoman empire and its supersession by the British Mandatory Administration. Only after its capture on 7 June 1967 were Jews once again, after many centuries, freely able to visit their Temple Mount.

Up to 1860, almost no one lived outside the walls of the city, because it was too dangerous. In the desolate and neglected countryside, particularly

A scene in 1900 at the Western 'Wailing' Wall.

at night, the robber and marauder were king. The Turkish garrison closed the gates at eventide and opened them in the morning. No citizen went out in the dark.

Up to then, the bulk of the Jewish community lived their lives at Jerusalem in study and learning, and were supported by the philanthropy of Jews from overseas. But there were a few Jews, particularly Yosef Rivlin and David Yellin, who dreamed of establishing Jewish quarters outside the walls, and encouraging the training of Jewish artisans who would live there. This idea was given practical realisation by the renowned Anglo-Jewish benefactor, Sir Moses Montefiore, who began visiting Jerusalem in 1836 and made seven extended trips in his lifetime, the last, in 1875, at the age of ninety-one! In 1855, en route to the Holy Land, he stopped off in Constantinople, saw the sultan, and received from him the right to acquire land outside the walls of Jerusalem, as well as the right to repair the Tomb of

First Jewish quarters outside the walls

left: A lane in Nachlat Shiva, the first settled Jewish suburb in the New City, founded in 1869.

right: The Western Wall on a seal used by the Austro-Hungarian Jewish community in Jerusalem, Hebron, Safad and Tiberias in the last century.

Rachel, the Jewish holy place in Bethlehem. Two years later, he built the windmill which still stands (although without its head which was blown off by a Jordanian shell in 1948) just south of the King David Hotel, and in 1860 he started construction of the nearby Yemin Moshe quarter to house Jewish artisans. The buildings were first used as a weaving factory. But this project failed, and a hospital was established instead. This, too, was unsuccessful, since the site was considered unsafe for helpless patients. The houses were then used as small workshops during the day, the artisans returning to the Old City each night. It was another fifteen years, during which time the Jewish population doubled, before Yemin Moshe was lived in.

The first Jew who is credited with settling – and actually spending the night! – outside Jerusalem's walls was Yosef Rivlin, whose obsession to found a new quarter pre-dated Montefiore's project. However, it took him several years to achieve his plan, and not until 1869 were the first two houses completed. Though his friends thought him mad, Rivlin resolved to move into one of them immediately, without waiting until homes were ready for all the members of the founding group. As related by his distant cousin, the noted orientalist, Professor Yosef Yoel Rivlin, his relatives would anxiously rush through the city gate each morning as soon as it was opened to find out if Yosef was still alive! Eventually, his group being reassured by his survival, Nachlat Shiva, as this quarter was later called, became the first settled Jewish outpost in the New City of Jerusalem. It was followed shortly afterwards by Mea She'arim, still the suburb of the ultra-orthodox community.

By now, with Jews already a majority in the city and beginning to extend their settlement outside and to the west of the walls, they began to receive a fresh influx of immigrants. This was the period of the spirited resurgence of the 'Return to Zion' movement in central and eastern Europe. Throughout their nineteen centuries of exile, there had always been some Jews from some community somewhere in the world who, as we have seen, not only made the pilgrimage to Jerusalem but went there to settle. The bulk, however, remained where they were, most of them too impoverished to journey

even beyond their village, and having to content themselves with the regular synagogue prayer 'Next Year in Jerusalem'.

Now, however, that prayer was taking on the urgent validity of a travel directive. In eastern Europe the Jews were living in abject conditions, the target of severe persecution. And these were the very times when intellectuals and writers and social reformers were uttering the great cry for liberty. Among the Jews, this theme emerged in an outpouring of Hebrew prose and poetry filled with the 'Love of Zion', and 'Lovers of Zion' societies sprang up in town and ghetto devoted to the revival of Jewish nationhood in its own land. Jews had had enough of wandering, enough of persecution, enough of escaping from one hell to a new land, only to find themselves confronted there by a new tyranny ten, fifty or one hundred years later. They would go to Palestine, desolate after centuries of neglect, and rebuild it with their own hands.

And so, in the last quarter of the nineteenth century, they began coming. The pioneers, of course, went out to clear swamp and revive desert. But the centre of their movement was Jerusalem. And many others, unfit for hard physical labour, settled in the city. By 1897, the resurgent mood among the Jews was such that they could hold an international conference in Basle, that turned out to be historic, and create the World Zionist Movement which gave a political and organised shape to their yearnings for independence. The key figure at the conference was Theodor Herzl, father of modern political Zionism. Fifty-one years later, the Jewish State was established.

While the Jewish population grew, the Christain community in Jerusalem remained relatively static. But with the sustained interest in Palestine of the western powers, and the presence in Jerusalem of their protective consuls, Christian interests were advanced, each denomination secure in its

A view of Jerusalem, painted by Edward Lear during his travels in the Middle East during the latter half of the nineteenth century.

right: 'Hebrew women reading the Scriptures at Jerusalem', a lithograph made by Wilkie in 1841.

below: The Western Wall, a scene early in the present century shown on a stamp issued by the Jewish National Fund.

David Wilkie f.^t 1841

Hebrew Women reading the Scriptures at Jerusalem

he Prussian Crown Prince,
riedrich Wilhelm,
ntering Jerusalem on a
sit in 1869.

political backing. France was still behind the Latin Church, Russia the Orthodox, their conflicts over the Holy Places being settled by the Turkish sultan in a *status quo* edict issued in 1852. Despite the defeat of Russia by England, France and Turkey in the Crimean war, Russian influence in Jerusalem remained unaffected, and in the latter part of the century, the huge Russian compound was erected outside the city walls consisting of a cathedral, hospital and hostels for pilgrims. It is still known as the Russian compound today.

Germany appeared as a fourth political influence on the religious scene of Jerusalem at the end of the century, the sultan, Abdul Hamid, grasping the friendship of this new European great power to check the influence in his empire of the other three. When Kaiser Wilhelm II paid a state visit to the Holy Land in 1898, the walls of Jerusalem were breached at the Jaffa Gate to make possible his entry in mounted procession. Almost immediately the Germans started working on buildings, some of which dominate the skyline today. On the nearest available site to the Church of the Holy Sepulchre rose a German Lutheran church. On Mount Zion, above the old Franciscan buildings, was erected the German Benedictine Abbey of the Dormition. And between the Mount of Olives and Mount Scopus rose the castle-like palace, hostel and hospital which was named after the Empress Augusta Victoria.

Incidentally, as a result of the increasing European interest and the increasing flow of European Jewish immigrants, Jerusalem in 1889 was designated an independent sanjak with a pasha appointed directly by Constantinople, and outside the control of the Syrian vilayet. The Jerusalem sanjak covered the city and a considerable area around it.

The end of Ottoman control

Ottoman control of Jerusalem came to an end in 1917 when the city fell without resistance to the British commander, General Allenby. Turkey had joined Germany against the Allied Powers a month after the outbreak of World War One, and her army in Palestine had been seriously engaged by British forces two and a half years later. After being routed in the south in November 1917, the Turks retired to a line from Jerusalem westwards to Jaffa. Allenby took Jaffa and then marched on Jerusalem. He captured the nearby height of Nebi Samuel on 21 November, thus threatening the Jerusalem–Nablus highway north of the city, the main line of communications left to the Turks, and hoping thereby to avoid combat in Jerusalem itself. The plan worked. On 9 December, the city surrendered.

Some five weeks earlier, on 2 November 1917, the British Government had issued the 'Balfour Declaration', viewing 'with favour the establishment of a national home for the Jewish people . . .', and this was incorporated into a League of Nations Mandate in 1922 which was vested in Britain. For the first time since the Crusades, the country was to be governed by a Christian power. And, also for the first time since then, its seat of local administration was to be Jerusalem. Britain was to remain in control until 14 May 1948 when the State of Israel was proclaimed.

he windmill, built by
r Moses Montefiore in
357 in the new Jewish
uarter outside the city
alls.

With the departure of the Ottomans, Jerusalem began to live again. British army control was followed in July 1920 with the inauguration of a civil administration headed by the outstanding British Jew, Sir Herbert (later Viscount) Samuel, as Britain's first High Commissioner. 'Government House' was established in Jerusalem, in the Augusta Victoria complex of buildings. (It was moved some years later to an imposing new building on one of the city's southern ridges traditionally known as the 'Hill of Evil Counsel'. With the subsequent administrative deterioration, it was cynically observed that the location had been aptly chosen.) Jerusalem also became the headquarters of all the major institutions in the country, including the Zionist Organisation and the Jewish Agency Executive, representing world Jewry, and the Jewish National Assembly representing the Jews of Palestine.

The stage was set for the dynamic revival of this ancient city. Hopes were high. Two years earlier, in the spring of 1918, four months after the capture of Jerusalem, the Zionist Commission led by Dr Chaim Weizmann had come out under the auspices of the British Government to begin implementing the Balfour Declaration and organise the basis of Jewish development. As a first step, Dr Weizmann, who later became first President of the State of Israel, laid the foundation stone of the Hebrew University on the summit of Mount Scopus, where it was inaugurated seven years later.

Little conflict between Jew and Arab was envisaged at the outset. After all, as a result of the victory of Allied arms – and with minimal effort on the Arab part – the Arabs of the Middle East were eventually to receive independence in territories covering more than a million square miles. Palestine, home of the Jews, was but a few thousand square miles, only a 'small notch', as Balfour called it. Moreover, Dr Weizmann had had a cordial meeting in 1918 in Transjordan with the Emir Feisal (later king of Iraq), and in March 1919 in Paris, Feisal, who headed the Arab delegation to the Peace Conference, went on record with these words: 'The Arabs, especially the educated among us, look with deepest sympathy on the Zionist Movement'. Referring to the future – Arab independence in the

General Allenby on his way to the Jaffa Gate, where he dismounted and entered the Old City after the Turkish surrender, December 1917.

Crowds waiting for the arrival of the Zionist Commission, on the Mount of Olives April 1918.

Middle East and Jewish development in Palestine – he wrote: 'I think that neither can be a real success without the other.'

But events rapidly moved the other way, and Arab hostility to the idea of the Jewish National Home soon made itself felt. This was not without its effect on the British Government – and particularly on those who had reservations about Zionism and who considered that British interests would be better served by indulging the more numerous Arabs. Thus, despite the Balfour commitment, the British Mandatory Administration in Palestine was to see its task not primarily as that of assisting the revolutionary development of the country – which was now possible with Jewish pioneering effort and resources – but of appearing to maintain an even balance between Jew and Arab.

However, at the technical level, the British administration brought a radical change to Jerusalem and to the country. Gone was the crude corruption and somnolent indifference of the Ottomans. Gone was chaos and lawlessness – at first. New roads were built. Jerusalem was provided with a new water supply, served by a pipeline from the Rosh Ha'ayin springs on the coastal plain. Though the diameter of the pipe was modest, and the flow not over-abundant, this was the greatest water project Jerusalem had ever known. The supply from Solomon's Pools was also increased by the installation of a pumping station. Attempts were made to improve the sanitation in the Old City. Public health services were provided for the Arabs. Some public schools were established, supplementing missionary schools, for the Arabs. The British claimed that the Jews could and did look after themselves, establishing their own educational, health and social services, whereas the Arabs needed help.

In the light of this approach, the Jews expected that they would at least be allowed, if not encouraged, by the authorities freely to proceed with the challenging development tasks they had set themselves – to rebuild the impoverished and underpopulated country, to turn swamp into cultivable land, bring fruitfulness to the desert, raise new cities and farm villages on the ancient sites, and restore the splendour of Jerusalem. They were to do all these things, but they were to encounter frequent obstruction from the Mandatory Administration.

Nevertheless, Jerusalem became a vibrant and cosmopolitan city during the period of British rule, attracting pilgrims and ordinary visitors from all over the world, for international travel was now easier, and local travel was safe. The historic sites of Jerusalem were high on tourist itineraries. At any time, sightseers from every country could be seen strolling through the colourful bazaars in the vaulted alleyways, visiting the Church of the Holy Sepulchre, the Western Wall, the Haram esh-Sharif, and moving beyond the walls to the spacious modern city of stone that was springing up to the west. For there had been a great expansion outside the Old City, largely by the Jews, and soon the Jewish population in these western suburbs outgrew the numbers in the Jewish Quarter of the walled city.

The quarters founded in the latter part of the nineteenth century were

ft: The Bezalel Museum and Art School, founded in the New City in 1906 by Professor Boris Schatz, as it was in 1910. The building is now the Jerusalem Artists' Centre.

ft: On the steps leading to the Damascus Gate.

ght: An immigrant craftsman from Morocco.

237

no longer alone. Adjoining them grew up commercial, manufacturing and residential suburbs, with Ashkenasi Jews from eastern, central and western Europe, and Sephardi communities from the Mediterranean, the Near East, the Middle East, from the Yemen and Morocco, and from such distant places as Bukhara, near Samarkand, in Uzbekistan, the east Asian part of Russia. The Bukharan community was the wealthiest and most exotic of these groups, and theirs was the first prosperous suburb in western Jerusalem. The first members had settled in the Holy Land in the 1880s.

The Jews also developed Mount Scopus, with its glorious view of the Temple Mount, the Old City and the new suburbs stretching away to the west, the Dead Sea to the southeast, and the plain of Jericho to the northeast. After the inauguration of the Hebrew University in 1925 came the construction of the Jewish National Library and, some years later, the Hadassah Hospital–University Medical School, the most modern medical centre in the Middle East.

Inside the Old City, the Jews lived in as crowded conditions as ever, cheek by jowl with the equally crowded Moslem Quarter. The Jewish inhabitants mostly belonged to the ultra-orthodox communities who were largely engaged in Talmudic study. In this confined area near the Western Wall, there were no less than fifty-eight synagogues, religious schools and theological academies.

By administrative arrangement, the mayor of Jerusalem was an Arab, but there was an overall Jewish majority in the city, as there had been for more than half a century, and it kept growing throughout the Mandatory period: in 1922, when the first census was taken, there were 34,000 Jews out of the City's population of 62,500. The 1931 census showed that in nine years the figures had risen to 51,000 Jews out of a total of 90,500. In 1947,

on the eve of the British departure, the population of the City had grown to
157,000. Of these, 97,000 were Jews. It was a far cry from Mameluke and
Ottoman days!

The Arabs also started moving outside the walls and established handsome residential suburbs, particularly to the north. In 1929, the generosity
of the Rockefeller family gave their area one of its finest buildings, and
certainly the most important cultural centre – the Palestine Archaeological
Museum. Its superb architecture well matches the treasures it houses,
treasures of ancient Jerusalem and Palestine. It stands just across the way
from the northeast corner of the walled city, its octagonal tower soaring
above the Kidron valley.

*Religious
rights under
the British*

In religious matters the British, on the whole, maintained the *status quo.*
There was freedom of access to the holy places of the three creeds, although
the Moslem ban on Jews entering the Haram esh-Sharif, which stood on the
site of the Jewish Temple Mount, was maintained. Christians, however,
were allowed to enter.

The churches and the Christian community were, for the first time, as
free as they had been in the Crusader period, and no longer feared being
molested by the ruling authorities. Nevertheless, some Christian leaders
felt that the special Christian relationship to the Holy Land demanded
some special action to restore 'churches and convents which still lay in
ruins, or had been turned into mosques, dwelling houses and stables by
the intolerance of Islam.' But the administration had no desire to arouse
Moslem resentment by restoring churches or synagogues which Islam had
taken over.

There was one notable occasion when the administration abandoned the religious *status quo*. The shofar, the ram's horn, was traditionally blown at the Western Wall to mark the end of the fast on Yom Kippur, the Day of Atonement, the most solemn day in the Jewish religious calendar. In 1929 this touched off a violent Arab demonstration, which spread through the country and led to massacres, the ancient Jewish communities at Hebron and Safad being almost wiped out. The riots took the British by surprise and there was extensive loss of life before order was restored. One of the recommendations of the British Commission appointed to investigate the causes, was to ban the blowing of the shofar at the 'Wailing' Wall. (This was the least of the restrictions on Jews which the Commission advised and the Government adopted.) However despite the ban, enforced by arrest and imprisonment, the sound of the shofar continued to be heard each year. It became a matter of national honour, as much a political as a religious act, to defy the British order. (On 14 October 1967, at the close of the first Yom Kippur after Jerusalem was reunited, the shofar was blown freely and openly at the Western Wall before ten thousand worshippers.)

right: The Russian Church of St Mary Magdalene on the slopes of the Mount of Olives, just above Gethsemane. Built in 1885–8 by Czar Alexander III. The architectural style is that of Moscow in the sixteenth–seventeenth centuries.

One of the effects of the violence in 1929 was to strengthen the Haganah, the underground Jewish defence force, since the Jews realised that in time of trouble, they would have to rely on themselves alone; they could not depend on the security forces of the administration. This saved many lives in Jerusalem, as elsewhere in the country, when the Arab-Jewish conflict erupted into severe disturbances in 1933 and virtual civil war between 1936 and 1939. As a result of these troubles, a British Royal Commission recommended that the country be partitioned into Jewish and Arab States, but the proposal was shelved. Then came World War Two and with it an uneasy truce between the Jews and the Arabs. It was broken soon after war ended, and for the next three years Palestine was a land of violence. Those three years also saw the collapse of the Mandatory Administration.

British recommendation of partition into Jewish and Arab States

In 1947 the British Government informed the United Nations that it could no longer govern the country and would terminate the Mandate in May 1948. On 29 November 1947, the United Nations General Assembly adopted, by a two-thirds majority, its celebrated Partition resolution whereby two separate states would be created out of Mandatory Palestine. one Jewish, one Arab. They recommended an international status for Jerusalem.

The Arabs vehemently rejected this solution to what had become 'the Palestine problem', and next day they launched a country-wide attack on the Jews. Throughout the land the two communities fought each other. The local Arabs were in an advantageous military position for they could receive arms and heavy equipment – as well as armed reinforcements – from the Arab states bordering on Palestine. The Jews had to rely on sporadic arrivals of small arms brought in clandestinely from overseas – for the British were still in power, and the Haganah was still illegal – and from primitive home-made armaments, such as a crude 6-inch mortar which had small lethal effect but which made a frightening noise.

overleaf: Buildings of the New City just outside the old walls. Left foreground, the Convent and Church of the Sisters of the Rosary Top right, the tower of the YMCA. To its left, the King David Hotel, in the process of adding another storey.

In Jerusalem, buildings were dynamited, bombs exploded, bullets flew, people were killed and maimed. Most serious of all, the Jewish parts of the

city were cut off from the Jewish centres of strength on the coastal plain. The highway from Tel-Aviv became almost impassable by the beginning of 1948. The ascent to Jerusalem through the steep, heavily wooded slopes of the Judean hills was a slow tortuous climb. The narrow, twisting road skirted by deep ditches, was so very vulnerable to ambush as the villages on both ridges commanding the defile were held by the Arabs. The losses to Jewish supply trucks, buses and other vehicles were heavy. Nevertheless they kept trying to press through, and those who managed to reach Jerusalem brought modest relief to the city's dwindling supplies.

Travelling in the buses and trucks as military escort were young boys and girls of the Haganah – the girls hiding under their robes the dismantled parts of sub-machine guns and pistols, hand grenades and ammunition, for there were frequent spot checks by British patrols and the possession of arms, even in circumstances of such danger, could carry the death penalty. By the third week in March, however, the toll of life and vehicles was too punishing, and traffic had to be halted. Jewish Jerusalem was under full siege.

Under the emergency – and superb – control of Dr Dov Joseph, a member of the Jewish Agency Executive (he was appointed Military Governor of Jerusalem with the proclamation of Israel's statehood and the start of the 'official' war), food rationing was promptly put into effect. The allocation was below subsistence level, and young mothers, between spells of armed duty, went foraging in the less dangerous fields for something green to cook for their children. The water pipeline ran through Arab territory, so all cisterns in private houses were sealed and marked and an equal water ration distributed to all.

On 1 April 1948, David Ben Gurion, head of the Jewish Agency Executive – which had moved its headquarters to more convenient Tel Aviv – ordered the Haganah to open the road to Jerusalem at least long enough to get a few food and ammunition convoys through. This meant capturing the Arab villages commanding the road and holding them for a few days.

There were not enough Haganah men – or weapons – to hold them for longer. As this was thickly populated Arab territory the Arabs would undoubtedly bring up massive reinforcements to regain them. Moreover, the Haganah men assigned to the operation would have to be drawn from other sectors in the country, which were already thinly held, and they would need to get back fast. So the Haganah Command resolved to do something they had never done before, mobilise a brigade of 1,500 men for this single task, and do so within hours. Up to then, being a clandestine force, the Haganah had never operated beyond company level.

The attack went in after sundown on 5 April. Meanwhile, close to the start of the defile, a relatively small test convoy of trucks with food, fuel, weapons and ammunition awaited the signal to move. It came at midnight and the convoy started up the mountain road. The Haganah units had cleared the western end though battles were still continuing above the section nearest Jerusalem. It took ten hours for the convoy to cover a stretch that normally took half an hour, but it got through, bringing joy to the beleaguered. Off-loading was fast and the empty vehicles were about to return when the Arabs counter-attacked a key height and the road was blocked while the battle raged. It was re-opened three days later and the trucks returned to the plains.

The success of this test convoy showed that the operational plan was feasible, and preparations were made to assemble large convoys and push them through. On 13 April, 175 trucks reached Jerusalem in seven hours and returned the same afternoon. On the seventeenth, more than 250 vehicles got through in four and half hours, bringing in arms, ammunition and one thousand tons of food. The largest convoy of all – 294 trucks – was on the twentieth. This was a special Passover convoy, bringing, in addition to the normal supplies, unleavened bread (matzah) for the Jewish festival. But this one had a rough time. By now, the Arabs had concentrated large forces and they launched a heavy attack on the tail-end of the convoy, destroying thirty-six trucks and killing and wounding a number of drivers. The rest, however, got through.

Thereafter, the road to Jerusalem was completely shut and the ring of siege was complete. But the three convoys had provided the Jews of the city with the means to hold out until the siege was lifted.

On 14 May 1948 the British Mandate ended and the State of Israel was established. A few hours after the proclamation of independence, the regular armies of six neighbouring Arab countries attacked the new-born State. They were Lebanon, Syria, Iraq, Transjordan, Egypt and Saudi Arabia (which sent a formation to fight under Egyptian command).

Units of the Arab Legion of Transjordan (now the kingdom of Jordan) had been in the country for some time, brought in by the British as part of the regular security forces of the administration. They had greatly aided the Arabs of Palestine in the 'unofficial' fighting against the Jews, notably in the Jerusalem sector. The war was now 'official', and when the British departed from Jerusalem on 14 May, the Arab Legion stayed – together with the standard heavy equipment and weapons of a regular army unit. These were then turned upon the hungry, ill-equipped Jews of Jerusalem.

The Jews had to hold a long, ragged and exposed line largely with spirited but poorly trained civilians, men and women of all ages, stiffened by the comparatively few trained Haganah units which the High Command could spare. Women and old men built fortifications, dug ditches, filled sand-bags, while children served as runners. The younger middle-aged inhabitants became static troops, holding positions as they were captured by the Haganah, enabling the fighters to go on to battle for new positions. The inventory of arms was pitifully small, and as one group would come out of the line, another group would take over its weapons and go into action. The Jews had no artillery beyond two 2-pounder cannon; about ten machine-guns; twenty-five 2-inch mortars with a limited number of shells; and only five 3-inch mortars. Three primitive, home-made 6-inch mortars, known affectionately as 'Davidke', and small home-made bombs, rounded out their arsenal. These weapons were switched from front to front as the fighting progressed.

The enemy they faced consisted of the Arab Legion, equipped with artillery, heavy machine-guns and armoured cars; irregular Egyptian forces with artillery which had come up through Beersheba and Hebron and attacked Jerusalem's southern sector; and the local Arabs.

As soon as the British left, the Arab armies intensified their shelling of Jewish Jerusalem, knowing that the Jews had no artillery, and hoping that they would thus be forced to surrender. From the Legion came 25-pounder shells (their artillery units were commanded by British officers who had been seconded to them, as was their commander, General [Sir John Bagot] Glubb Pasha). From the Egyptians came 4.2-inch shells and 120–1 mm mortar bombs thrown in from a hill near Bethlehem. And from positions close to the Israeli lines – some were only ten yards away – hand grenades and mortar bombs were flung into Jewish houses and streets. From time to time, enemy planes flew over the city dropping incendiaries. Altogether more than ten thousand Arab shells hit the New City in the three weeks following 14 May, taking a heavy toll of civilian life. The only retaliation open to the Jews was the firing of their Davidkes, their bark doing more damage to Arab morale than their bite did to Arab positions. Despite all the destruction pounded into the New City, the Arabs were not allowed to advance an inch, and in the fierce fighting for key front-line buildings, the small Haganah units gained the upper hand. At no point where entry was possible into the New City were the Arabs able to break through, despite their superiority in numbers and fire-power.

Civilian morale in beleaguered Jerusalem remained high despite the constant shelling. Each day the brave water-carriers would appear in the streets to distribute the meagre ration and the women would queue in a disciplined line near the water points. These groups were among the hardest hit, and not a day passed without casualties. But the daily water parade was a constant feature of those times.

The weak spot was the Jewish Quarter of the Old City. The Jews here were surrounded by Arabs and Arab Legion forces. They were mostly old folk with their families, and they had been joined by some eighty members of the Haganah, some of whom had been there for months and others who had fought their way through the walled city to help the resistance. Out-numbered by thirty to one, with few weapons and little ammunition, they were systematically driven back from house to house as each was destroyed by the crushing weight of the Arabs' attack. During the fighting in this crowded quarter, the Arabs destroyed twenty-seven synagogues. (Later all the remaining synagogues and religious academies were systematically razed – a total of fifty-eight.)

On 28 May, with most Haganah officers and NCOs killed or wounded and civilian casualties high, with larders empty and ammunition spent, mortared and shelled from all sides, the Jewish Quarter fell.

It was the blackest event in Israel's War of Independence. Elsewhere, the invading armies were held back in every sector, and by the time the first United Nations truce came into effect, on 11 June, the new state was still intact. In further fighting between the various truces that year, on the northern, central and southern fronts, the Arab armies were not only held but pushed back behind their own frontiers. (Israel in the meantime, had been able to acquire more weapons.) War ended with the signing of Armistice Agreements in the first half of 1949 – with Egypt in February, Lebanon in March, with Transjordan in April and Syria in July.

The aftermath of the siege of Jerusalem. The Jaffa Road in 1949.

'No-man's Land', opposite the Citadel and the Jaffa Gate.

Looking across 'No-man's Land' towards the Mandelbaum Gate.

These agreements froze the armistice lines broadly at the cease fire positions. In Jerusalem, the line ran roughly north to south, just skirting the west wall of the Old City; everything west of it, namely the whole of the New City, as well as Mount Zion, was Israeli Jerusalem. Israel's territory also included Mount Scopus, for the Arab army had failed to dislodge the Israeli troops from there. Apart from Scopus, everything east of the armistice line, including the Old City, was Jordanian Jerusalem.

Under the terms of the Agreement, Jews were to have access to the Western Wall of the Temple Mount to pray at their most sacred holy place, and access to Mount Scopus, which was now an Israeli enclave within Arab Jerusalem. The Arabs were to have access to Bethlehem – part of the Jerusalem–Bethlehem road now ran through Israel-held territory. Neither side was allowed to bring in heavy weapons. The truce was to be supervised by UN observers and the UN Truce Supervision Organisation took over Government House as their headquarters.

Jerusalem became the divided city.

Despite the Agreement, Jews were denied access to the Western Wall. They were also denied the use of the Hebrew University and Hadassah Hospital on Mount Scopus. All the Arabs would agree to, under pressure, was the maintenance there of Israeli guards and caretakers, to be relieved fortnightly by convoy under United Nations escort. The Arabs freed themselves from counter-measures by building a new road to Bethlehem through their own territory.

It had been Israel's hope that armistice would before long be converted into peace, and Jerusalem joined into a single city available to both peoples. But this was not to be, and for the next eighteen years the two halves of the city led independent lives, with the watchful sand-bagged positions of the opposing forces facing each other across the narrow demarcation line. Exchange of fire was sporadic over the years, and Israel was driven to build concrete anti-sniping walls along exposed parts of the border; but on the whole the period was trouble-free. There were sections of the frontier where Arab and Jewish families were virtual neighbours, their children at play in the streets or backyards being separated only by a wall or a barbed wire fence.

Diplomatic, consular and UN personnel, and VIPs, could pass freely from one Jerusalem to the other through what became known as the Mandelbaum Gate. This was not like a city gate. It was simply a road barrier near a building which had belonged to a Mr Mandelbaum, with an Israeli police hut on one side and a Jordanian hut on the other at the positions the opposing forces had held at the time of the cease-fire. Israel allowed all pilgrims and tourists to cross into Jewish Jerusalem, but the Jordanians were less flexible, reluctantly permitting them to cross from Jordan into Israel, but not the other way.

On each side of the dividing line, each country began to develop its Jerusalem. The Jordanians did a good deal, expanding their suburbs beyond the city walls, again mostly in the north, and improving the conditions of the bazaars in the Old City. Sanitation, though, still remained a

The floodlit Monastery of the Cross at left, and, middle right, the pavilion of the Israel Museum.

Early pottery and glass vessels found at archaeological excavation in and around Jerusalem, in the collection of the Israel Museum. The pottery dates from the eleventh to seventh centuries BC, and the glass from the first to fifth centuries AD.

problem, and the water services were somewhat limited. With the exception of the Coenaculum and the Tomb of David on Mount Zion, all the holy places, Christian, Moslem and Jewish were now under their control, and Christian pilgrimage and tourism served as the country's principal source of revenue. This, perhaps, was the key importance of Jerusalem for Jordan. Amman, not Jerusalem, was its capital, though when the UN resolved that Jerusalem should be internationalised, Jordan joined with Israel in rejecting the idea as impractical and stagnating.

Development of Israeli Jerusalem

The development of Israeli Jerusalem was infinitely greater – largely because the need was greater. With the gates of independent Israel flung wide open to homeless Jews – and to all Jews who wished to come – there was a vast influx of immigrants into the country. A considerable number settled in Jerusalem, and a complex of residential suburbs soon sprang up, spreading ever westwards, while light industry was served by special zones prepared near the northern outskirts. Jerusalem was proclaimed the capital of Israel and thousands of officials moved in. New government buildings were constructed. The Knesset (parliament) met in temporary premises until they could move into their handsome new building, the gift of the late James de Rothschild of Britain, in 1966.

When it became clear that the Jordanians would not relent on the use of the Mount Scopus buildings, a new Hebrew University campus was constructed on high ground across the way from the area marked off for the government buildings and the Knesset. Though nothing can match the old Mount Scopus site, with its unrivalled view of the surrounding countryside, the present campus is a handsome series of well-landscaped terraced structures, each housing its own faculty. One of the largest buildings is that of the National Library, probably the most impressive library in the Middle East. A huge stadium for sports and pageants was constructed in the shallow valley at the foot of the campus.

A recent addition of architectural beauty and cultural importance to the area of campus, Knesset and ministerial offices is the Israel Museum, with its fine archaeological wing, art pavilions, open air sculpture garden and Shrine of the Book, housing the Dead Sea Scrolls and other ancient manuscripts. Below the Museum is the Byzantine Monastry of the Cross, rebuilt by the Crusaders and later by Georgian monks, a building of massive beauty housing fine ancient frescoes and mosaics.

The Hadassah Hospital on Scopus, like the old University, could not be used, so a huge new Hadassah Hospital complete with nursing school and medical faculty buildings, was constructed on the western outskirts of Jerusalem, above the village of Ein Karem, birthplace of John the Baptist.

The New City of Jerusalem grew and grew. Its water problem, more acute than ever because of the vastly expanded population, was solved by linking the city with Israel's National Water Carrier through huge pipelines. New housing estates appeared on the skyline, schools, clinics, shopping centres, hotels, swimming pools, theatres and a huge concert hall, all of varied architecture but all built of or faced with Jerusalem stone – following an old Mandatory regulation which the Jerusalem Municipality was wise enough to retain.

The lower floor of the Shrine of the Book, in the Israel Museum, which houses the Dead Sea Scrolls and other ancient manuscripts. Exhibited here are artefacts found in caves where the documents were discovered.

Request for 'modesty of
dress' to visitors entering
the orthodox quarter of
Mea She'arim.

The new Knesset building,
Israel's parliament.

This ancient city with modern facilities became the pride of Israel, seat of government, parliament and supreme court of justice, centre of learning and scientific research, a city of international congresses, of parks and pine woods, of concerts and art exhibitions, of football and folk-dance – and above all, a city of beauty. But it was a divided city. In its westward growth, buildings which were formerly in the heart of Jerusalem were now at its eastern edge, hard by the border which split it in two. One of these buildings was City Hall.

'One of my first tasks on being elected Mayor of Jerusalem at the end of 1965 [writes co-author Kollek] was to scrap a project I found to build a new City Hall further to the west. After all, we were building apartment houses for new immigrants right up to the border, not only because this afforded the best protection but also in the hope that people living and children playing on the frontier would lead to its elimination and bring peace nearer.

'The existing municipal offices were fifty yards from the frontier, and that is where I decided they should remain – hoping that this site would again become the centre once the city became re-united.

'I confess that when I took office I had not imagined that my hope would be fulfilled so soon, and in so dramatic a fashion.'

A few minutes after eight o'clock in the morning of 5 June 1967, the warning sirens wailed in Jewish Jerusalem, and people wondered whether or not to rush to the shelters. (Those who had shelters, that is; most of the houses had none, although those of stone were considered safe enough.)

Three weeks before, on 15 May, Israel had celebrated the anniversary of its independence, and that year the military parade – modest because of the armistice restrictions – was held in Jerusalem. At night, the streets were bright with coloured lights and bunting, and thronged with dancing and singing crowds. The festivities were capped by the annual Music Festival whose highlight – which had the audience clamouring for encore after encore – was the presentation of a haunting new song, 'Jerusalem the Golden'. Next morning, the newspapers carried enthusiastic reports of the festivities. But also on the front page was an item of news on sudden Egyptian troop concentrations in Sinai.

The days that followed were days of partial mobilisation, then of an increased call-up, coupled with civil defence preparations and the testing of emergency services. Youngsters and those over-age, scouts and bearded rabbis, busied themselves with filling sandbags and digging trenches. Windows were blacked out and crisscrossed with anti-splinter adhesive strips.

On this first Monday morning in June, Jerusalemites already knew that the threat of attack on the country was real enough. The latest reports had said that the Egyptians had now moved 80,000 troops and 800 tanks into Sinai (the true figures proved to be nearer 100,000 men and 950 tanks) and the Straits of Tiran had been blocked. The siren may thus have been the signal that war had broken out and attack was imminent. But many people were still sceptical of any serious trouble in Jerusalem. True, five days earlier King Hussein had flown to Cairo and he and Nasser had made a compact. But Jordan would hardly dare attack homes in Jewish Jerusalem. It would only invite retaliation against Jordanian Jerusalem. And so the sirens wailed and Jerusalemites proceeded about their business. Children went to school and infants to kindergarten.

Chief Army Chaplain Rabbi Goren (soft officer's cap) leads a prayer service at the Western Wall with the soldiers who captured it.

None of the civilians knew at that moment that the war had indeed started, nor that with the first clashes with the Egyptians in the south, the Israel Government had sent messages to King Hussein through the UN and other intermediaries telling him that if Jordan stayed out of the war, the Israel–Jordan frontier would remain silent. If she went to war, she could expect the strongest reaction from Israel.

At 9 a.m. word reached Israel's Foreign Ministry that the Jordanian king had received the message. His reply came at 10.45 – with the hurling of Jordanian mortar bombs into densely peopled Jewish Jerusalem. For the next fifty hours, the indiscriminate mortaring and shelling of the New City was to continue without let-up. (The Knesset, the Israel Museum, the residences of the President and Prime Minister and the City's hospitals were among the buildings hit.)

Israel did not retaliate by mortaring the Old City, as she could easily have done. This would have offered emotional satisfaction but nothing of strategic value. It was resolved to wait and see whether Jordan meant business, whether in fact she had decided to join forces with Egypt in a major confrontation with the Israel Army. If she did, what was required was not 'getting one's own back' by destroying Jordanian homes but moves which would put the Jordanian army out of action.

Israel did not have to wait long for signs of Jordan's intentions. Jordanian artillery opened up all along the frontier, and a little while later put in a ground operation. A unit of the Arab Legion moved up through the Arab approach to Government House and seized it, over the ineffective remonstrances of its United Nations occupants. Holding this key height gravely threatened the southern suburbs of Jewish Jerusalem. Within less than an hour, a lightly armed infantry unit of Israel's Jerusalem Brigade, a reserve holding brigade, moved up to dislodge an enemy now entrenched behind the thick stone walls of the large building and deployed on the high ground of its extensive compound. They approached in broad daylight, without cover and without heavy weapons – these had been banned under the now shattered Armistice Agreement. After brisk fighting for an hour and twenty minutes, Government House, its compound and Arab Legion positions to its rear, were in Israeli hands.

Up to midday on the Monday morning, the Israeli positions in the whole of the Jerusalem sector were thinly manned by this lone Jerusalem Brigade of somewhat elderly reservists who had been called up a few days earlier and were expected to do no more than maintain a holding operation. (In the next two and a half days, they were to see as much fighting as regular assault troops.) It was now clear that the Jordanians had opened the second front – and the means they had were very threatening. Into the West Bank they had moved an infantry brigade, an armoured brigade and an additional tank battalion. They could deploy another eight infantry brigades, a second armoured brigade and another tank battalion. Moreover, an Iraqi infantry division with powerful armoured support had crossed into Jordan and stood ready to ford the river into the West Bank.

Israel's Army GHQ quickly decided to switch forces to deal with the new situation. A paratroop brigade, mostly composed of young reservists,

dispersed near an airfield waiting to emplane for an operational jump in
Sinai, was ordered to Jerusalem instead; and a mechanised brigade, completely reservist from the commander downwards, which was being held
in the coastal plain to block a Jordanian attack there, was ordered to a
point some ten miles west of Jerusalem.

The plan was for the mechanised brigade to punch through the Jordanian
positions west of Jerusalem, move north, then wheel east and cut the road
out of Jerusalem to Ramallah and Nablus. The main force of the brigade
was then to swing south and come at Jordanian Jerusalem from the north.
The Jerusalem Brigade would exploit the Arab defeat at Government
House, engage further Arab Legion units in the southern sector, and
also work their way round to seize enemy positions in the east. While
Jordanian Jerusalem was thus being encircled, it would be the task of the
paratroop brigade to do the tough fighting inside Jerusalem itself.

On Monday afternoon, at 5.30, the mechanised brigade stormed the
first strongly fortified Jordanian hill position west of Jerusalem. Its approaches were heavily mined; behind the minefields were concrete bunkers,
machine-gun posts and artillery positions; behind these were tanks. The
Israeli brigade were bent on speed, even at the cost of heavier casualties.
They had no flailer tanks to crash through the minefields – these were all
in Sinai – so their sappers simply cleared the mines by hand with prod and
knife. Operating in daylight and under fire from the enemy on high ground,
they suffered forty casualties in less minutes from enemy fire and exploding
mines. But enough of a track was cleared for the tanks and half-tracks to

261

steamroller their way through to the Arab Legion position and capture it. They did the same with the other enemy positions along their axis, battling uphill all the way. Fighting and advancing through the night, they reached the northeastern outskirts of Jerusalem early next morning, captured the residential suburb of Shu'afat, fought a bitter battle with the Arab Legion for the key 'Hill of the Pass' overlooking Jerusalem, took it, lost it, attacked it again and re-gained it after heavy casualties, while at the same time another company took the adjacent French Hill. It was there that, at mid-day on Tuesday 6 June, the men of this mechanised brigade met up with the surviving remnant of the paratroop battalion who had successfully, but at very great cost, fought their way from Jewish Jerusalem through the northern suburbs of Jordanian Jerusalem.

This paratroop brigade experienced some of the heaviest fighting in the Six Day War, and probably suffered the highest casualties. They had arrived after dark the previous evening, in a Jerusalem that was being heavily shelled and mortared, to be greeted by the civilians in the neighbourhood of their improvised headquarters who had emerged into the gunfire from trench and shelter to welcome and serve them as telephone operators, tea-makers and messengers. To almost the entire brigade, the ground they would soon be fighting over was unfamiliar, and there had been no time for a thorough briefing on the new battle target. Only the battalion commanders and a few others had been able to rush up to Jerusalem as soon as the Sinai jump had been called off, in order to get a glimpse of the terrain. As for the rest, they had managed only a hurried inspection of air photos and maps and intelligence diagrams of the Arab Legion positions. They would be going into action virtually blind, attacking a built-up area – the hardest of military tasks – stiffly protected by stout perimeter fortifications.

Tuesday 6 June

They launched their assault at 2 a.m. The immediate objective was the district north of the Old City walls. This would bring them alongside the north wall in position to launch the second phase – the breakthrough into the Old City, which it was hoped to effect through Herod's Gate.

One battalion started from the border tenement building just in front of the Jordanian Police School, its aim being to take the high ground of the school and the adjacent Ammunition Hill which dominate the northern sector. The other two battalions went in a few hundred yards to the south, just north of the Mandelbaum Gate. One was to push straight across to the east through the American Colony and swing south to the Rockefeller Museum, hard by the northeast corner of the walls. The other was to wheel south almost to the Damascus Gate and then turn east, parallel with the north wall, to link up with the second battalion at the Museum.

The first battalion had the most gruelling time. The Jordanians were well aware that the Police School hill and Ammunition Hill were the key to the Old City from the north, and they had fortified them with the utmost strength. Both were honeycombed with deep, concreted trenches and firing posts, while well-sheltered bunkers scooped out of the hillsides commanded all the approaches.

Eighty yards in front of them, to the north, ran the Israeli first line

The battle for the Police Training School.

holding positions, manned by a unit of the Jerusalem Brigade. This unit had gone into the line at eleven in the morning, just after the Jordanians had started shelling the city. Twenty minutes later they had come under a barrage of 25-pounders, recoilless guns, mortars and machine-guns, fired at point-blank range from well-entrenched positions, while the only cover they enjoyed was afforded by a low sandbagged wall and a shallow slit trench. All they had were small arms. For the next six hours they were pinned, suffering casualties all the time, and only with darkness could artillery, mortars and rockets be brought up to counter the enemy fire. But the effect of this Israeli fire on the Jordanians was minimal. Their positions were not even dented. They could be taken only by direct frontal assault (for there was no way of getting round them quickly). This the paratroopers were now about to do.

Jumping into action, they raced boldly towards the Police School, fully exposed, their forms well silhouetted in the brilliant flashes of gunfire. Many were mown down in the eighty yards dash towards the enemy minefields, and more fell victim to the mines. The surviving wounded were hurriedly evacuated in daring rescue operations. The rest pressed on, aided now by their own artillery and fire from support tanks in the rear, which could not yet manoeuvre any closer because of minefields. Enemy fire became more intense, but the paratroopers did what they had to do – blast their way through five barbed wire fences protected by mines before they could get at the first row of fortified Arab Legion positions which had them in full view.

These first line posts were reached, and stormed, some paratroopers pushing on to the buildings themselves, others jumping into the network of slit trenches, and for the next few hours there was bitter hand-to-hand fighting, in the trenches, the rooms, the bunkers, on the roofs, everywhere. There was no way of by-passing a single fortified post. Each had to be fought for.

This was the bloody pattern of fighting in the sector which went on until 7 a.m., until the Police School compound and Ammunition Hill were in Israeli hands. The officers were in the thick of the battles, the first to jump into the enemy trenches. They wasted no time radioing back reports, they just pressed on with the job, not counting the cost, knowing that they held the key to the liberation of Jerusalem. One company emerged with only four men unscathed, another was left with seven. This was only discovered later. During the fighting, asked by rear HQ how they were getting on, they had replied 'We'll be okay soon'. They had requested no reinforcements, no help. The dead were beyond help; the wounded were well tended by doctors and medics who were with them in enemy trench and bunker; and the fighting fit were fighting.

The unit that exploited their success and went through to take Sheikh Jarrah, the main northern suburb lying athwart the road to Mount Scopus, encountered the same obstacles and the same type of action – casualties before they began; evacuation of the wounded; blasting through fence after fence and bangaloring their way through minefields; breaking into concrete enemy posts; and hand-to-hand fighting. They, too, ended up with only a few unwounded – but with Sheikh Jarrah in their hands.

In these engagements, the Arab Legion fought extremely well.

The other units which had jumped off near the Mandelbaum Gate had also had a tough time, losing many men in the initial breakthrough of the perimeter defences and in the built-up districts through which they had to fight their way to reach the north wall of the Old City. By first light, when the brigade commander arrived at their advance post to join them in the move towards Herod's Gate, many of these units were either dead or on their way to hospitals in the rear.

From their various positions in the northern suburbs, the brigade now pressed their advance on the Old City. Some Arab legionaries who had managed to escape took up positions in buildings and tried to hold up the Israelis by sniping and hurling grenades from the windows. Casualties mounted, and the going was slow, marked by severe house-to-house fighting. However, tanks were soon brought into action and they operated along the main streets right up to the Rockefeller Museum. The tanks were there only because while fighting was going on in the Police School, paratroop sappers were clearing a path through the minefield alongside the school compound. It took them several pre-dawn hours, for they were under continuous and accurate shellfire, mostly from 81-mm guns, and mine-clearing had to be done by hand between salvos. They would rush out from cover during the brief lulls, clear a few mines, and then race back as the rounds came over.

By 10 a.m., the suburbs outside the north wall of the Old City were more or less cleared, and the remains of the brigade was ready for the next and final stage: breaking into the Old City. This would have to be done with infantry alone. The alleys were too narrow for tanks, and in any case the order was not to damage the holy places. But getting to the city gates was a problem. The huge, thick, stone walls of Suleiman the Magnificent were still in the hands of the Arab Legion and were heavily defended. They dominated every approach, and every Israeli soldier who ventured towards them was hit.

This was also the case with the Arab-held Augusta Victoria ridge, between the Arab-held Mount of Olives and Israeli-held Mount Scopus. With its commanding position above the city, it could sweep with fire the space the paratroopers would have to cross to reach the north or east wall. It was evident that Augusta Victoria and the walls themselves would need to be neutralised before entry could be made into the Old City. It was resolved to delay the assault on both until dark. But even then little progress was made, beyond the capture of a few intermediate Arab positions. The lead tanks and several reconnaissance jeeps were hit right away at the foot of the wall near the Lions' Gate, and began burning. There were heavy casualties, made more heavy by the suicidal efforts of their comrades to save the wounded. At the same time the Augusta Victoria attack was called off when intelligence was received that a Jordanian squadron of Patton tanks was only an hour away and racing to Jerusalem. There was no point in engaging Augusta until the Pattons had been dealt with. So the assault was put off until morning. Meanwhile, the mechanised brigade and the Jerusalem Brigade had been encircling the city, blocking the Jordanian tanks, capturing key heights, and neutralising Jordanian action against the paratroopers.

By dawn on Wednesday 7 June, Jerusalem was virtually surrounded (except for Augusta Victoria and the Mount of Olives) by Israeli forces, and this had already affected Jordanian morale. It was made lower by the air and artillery bombardment of the Augusta Victoria ridge which began at 6 a.m. Sensing that the enemy spirit was cracking, the brigade decided on an all-out frontal charge of their positions. At 8.30 a.m., one battalion sped through newly captured Sheikh Jarrah to Mount Scopus, to attack Augusta Victoria from the north. A second battalion dashed straight up the mountain road directly towards Augusta's main entrance, fighting uphill, driving right into the teeth of the enemy, their backs to Arab snipers holding the city walls. The third battalion battled for the north wall, making for Herod's Gate.

Wednesday 7 June

The sheer brazenness of the operation worked – coupled of course with the collapse of Jordanian morale. The battles were brisk; tanks were knocked out by mines; the paratroopers suffered casualties. But in a short while, the Augusta Victoria ridge and the Mount of Olives were theirs. Spread below them was the magnificent esplanade on the Temple Mount, the gold and silver domes of the two mosques gleaming in the morning sun, and just visible at its southwestern edge was the top of the Western Wall. Beyond was the cupola of the Church of the Holy Sepulchre. Clus-

The Dome of the Rock and Mount Scopus beyond.

tered within the city walls they could see the crowded quarters, 'Jewish', 'Moslem', 'Armenian' and 'Christian'. And, stretching away to the west, was the New City.

The brigade commander took it all in as he stood beside his command half-track in front of the Inter-Continental Hotel atop the Mount of Olives. There before him lay the two halves of Jerusalem, in his eyes already joined. Taking the signals' microphone into his hand, the transmitter set to network, he gave 'all battalion commanders' the final objective: 'the Temple Mount, the Western Wall, the Old City. For two thousand years our people have prayed for this moment. Let us go forward – to victory'.

All converged on the Old City, each battalion racing to be the first inside. The sections of the wall near Herod's and the Lions' Gates were subjected to artillery fire, and then the tanks and recoilless guns took over. They steered clear of the holy places, and none was hit.

The brigade commander was also in the race. Jumping into his half-track and ordering his heavily-built young driver to slam his foot hard down on the accelerator and leave it there, he dashed down the mountain towards the walls, all the while signalling his tanks and infantry to go faster. Overtaking the tanks near the bridge below the Lions' Gate, and passing the burnt-out hulks of his tanks and jeeps and comrades' bodies from the night's engagement, he roared up the approach alley to the Gate. In front of the Lions' arch was a burning vehicle, but there was just enough room to scrape through. He manoeuvred past the flaming vehicle, shattered the half-closed door, crunched over the stones and rubble that had fallen from above, stifled the thought of possible grenades being hurled from the top of the wall, ignored an Arab soldier who was too dazed to fire, sped a few yards towards the start of the Via Dolorosa, then turned smartly left towards another gate, rumbled over a motor cycle that straddled it, was relieved to find that it was not booby-trapped, drove through this gate – and found himself at the entrance to the Temple Mount. The time was 9.50 on the morning of Wednesday 7 June 1967.

The tanks could not come this far, but the infantry could – and did. Soon the esplanade was filled with paratroopers. The brigade commander signalled GHQ: 'The Temple Mount is ours. Repeat: The Temple Mount is ours.'

Through the narrow alleys of the city moved the battalions, suffering further casualties as they tried to deal with snipers (sniping continued throughout this and the next day) and clear Arab Legion positions that had not yet fallen or been abandoned. But the fight had gone out of the Jordanians and white flags went up everywhere.

Another paratroop unit made straight for the Western Wall. Near the entrance stood Arab legionaries, their hands raised in surrender. The first soldier through gave a great shout: 'The Western Wall! I can see the Wall', and then the rest rushed through to touch and kiss the hallowed stones. Tough paratroopers, who had fought hard and non-stop for thirty-two hours, wept at the Temple wall over which their people had wailed for so many centuries. But theirs was no wail, no lament, except for their fallen comrades. With this sadness was mingled the ineffable joy of men who

'The Temple Mount is ours'

268

Minister of Defence
General Moshe Dayan,
flanked by Chief of Staff
General Yitzhak Rabin and
GOC Central Command
Brig.-General Uzi Narkiss,
enters the Old City shortly
after its capture. Between
Dayan and Rabin is Moshe
Pearlman, co-author of
this book.

had won back for their nation their most sacred site – and who were alive
to savour the historic privilege.

At 10.15, a jeep bearing the Chief Chaplain to the Forces, Brigadier-
General Rabbi Shlomo Goren, came flying through the Lions' Gate and
across the Temple Mount, oblivious of sniper's bullets, and stopped near
the southwest corner. The Rabbi jumped off and rushed down the lane
which brought him to the Western Wall. There he offered a Hebrew
prayer, and, drawing forth a shofar, normally sounded only on the most
solemn of Jewish Holy Days, he blew a long and powerful blast. Shortly
afterwards came General Moshe Dayan, the Minister of Defence, and
General Yitzhak Rabin, Chief of Staff, who had come by helicopter from
another of the fronts. And then came the Prime Minister, Levi Eshkol,
followed by other members of the Cabinet.

Pilgrims at the Festival of
Shavuot after the June wa

Battles were still raging elsewhere in the country, for this was only the
third day of war. But every Jew, both in Israel and overseas, must have felt
this to be a day of liberation. The city of Jerusalem was again united, and
again, in its entirety, the Capital of Israel.

That evening, the mayor of Jerusalem announced that the municipal
administration were prepared to restore essential services to the former
Arab sector which had completely broken down. 'We are ready to undertake arrangements for water, sewage, sanitation, garbage collection, elec-
tricity, food distribution, as soon as we are asked to do so.'

Next morning they started, together with the army, and the pace of the
restoration of normality was so rapid that within days the municipality's
provision of milk and bread to children was rendered superfluous as shops
and offices were re-opened and people started going about their regular
business. The only unusual background noise was the sound of detonations
as army sappers systematically cleared minefields in and around the city,
a background sound that continued for weeks. At the same time, they
began tearing down the anti-sniper walls and destroying the barricades,
anti-tank obstacles and barbed wire fences that had been erected on both
sides of the now non-existent border. They also started laying new roads
between the two sectors, paving old ones that had fallen into disuse, and
bulldozing the ruins of abandoned houses in no-man's land. Once again
the old and new parts of the city were linked and visible to each other.

The Jewish pilgrim festival of Shavuot, the Feast of Weeks, occurred
that year on Wednesday 14 June, exactly one week after Jerusalem was
united, and while the city still bore grim signs of the fighting. On that day,
a quarter of a million Jews from all parts of the country came to the capital
in a mass pilgrimage, entered through the Dung Gate in the southern wall,
past notices 'Danger: Mines', and paid homage at the Western Wall. It
was the largest pilgrimage to the relic of the Second Temple since the great
dispersion nineteen centuries before, though it is doubtful whether so many
had ever thronged the forecourt of this hallowed site in a single day.

Soon after the fighting, the Government of Israel announced that persons

Part of the shell of the nove
synagogue of the Hebrew
University. The new
building of the Knesset,
Israel's parliament, is in
the centre background. At
right, the ceramic tiled
dome of the Shrine of the
Book, part of the Israel
Museum.

The view from the Mount
f Olives. The Temple
splanade and Dome of
ne Rock are in the centre.
eyond is the New City.

of all three faiths, Christian, Moslem, Jewish, would have free access to their holy places. On Friday 23 June, thousands of Moslem Arabs from Israel came to the Haram esh-Sharif for the first time in nineteen years, visited the Dome of the Rock and joined in prayer at the Mosque of El-Aksa with families and friends from whom they had been separated by the Israel-Jordan frontier. Two days later, on Sunday the twenty-fifth, Arab Christians from both areas were free to worship together at the Church of the Holy Sepulchre. Again, during Jordanian rule, Arab Christians from Israel had been banned from regular Sunday services at this holy site. Only twice a year, at Christmas and Easter, were some permitted to attend services there, crossing through the Mandelbaum Gate. These Friday and Sunday religious gatherings are part of normal life in today's Jerusalem.

Official
reunification

On 27 June, Israel's Knesset passed three enabling bills which made possible the official reunion of the two halves of Jerusalem. At noon next day, the Old City and its environs and Israeli Jerusalem became one. The capital was now a city of some 270,000 – 200,000 Jews and 70,000 Arabs (Moslems and Christians). The army relinquished control to City Hall. The last barriers came down, and access to all parts of Jerusalem was free to everyone.

It was a bold step by the authorities; and the day, for Jerusalemites, was unforgettable. There were no clashes, no incidents, no trouble – beyond traffic jams. Few had believed that only a few days after a bitter war in which both sides suffered heavy casualties, and after nineteen years of intense hatred on one side and anxiety on the other, the two communities would be allowed, and would find themselves able, to mingle with each other, and would do so with such ease. A few tentative souls started crossing into formerly prohibited territory. Others joined them. They were followed by hundreds, then by thousands. Within a week, the numbers crossing from one part to the other were in the tens of thousands.

At first the two communities eyed each other with reserve, then with shy smiles. They soon became more expansive, each taking in the world of the other. Jerusalem's Arabs came outside the walls to walk the broad avenues and boulevards of the New City; to stop, with amusement and surprise, at traffic lights; to gaze in fashionable shops; to take in the unusual buildings of the University campus, the Knesset, the Israel Museum, the Convention Centre, the Kennedy Memorial; above all to sense the throb of a thriving modern city that had grown up on their doorstep.

Later, they brought their families to the Hadassah and other hospitals of the New City for specialist treatment; and young mothers flocked to the infant welfare and ante-natal clincs – until the municipal health department established similar clinics in their neighbourhoods. (Whatever they had heard in their radio propaganda about the Israelis, they seemed to know about the standard of their health services.) The young people came to the New City's cafés, parks and cinemas, YMCA gymnasium and open-air swimming pools. And in the first few days, camels and donkeys, their panniers high with vegetables, appeared in the streets of the New City's residential suburbs, until municipal food inspectors explained to the

The stadium and new
ampus buildings of the
Hebrew University.

273

bewildered hawkers that selling vegetables this way was against regulations.

The Israelis in their turn moved through the vaulted bazaars and market alleys of the Old City, colourful, crowded, noisy; visited the holy sites that had been denied to them for so long; walked the flagstoned esplanade of the Temple Mount from which they had been banned since it had been theirs; crossed the ancient valley of Kidron and ascended the Mount of Olives, saddened by the desecration of their ancient cemetery; and came again and again to this Mount to see the Old City, its history and beauty, laid out below them, to see what pilgrims and visitors throughout the ages had journeyed to behold – perhaps the most absorbing sight in the world.

Jerusalem's problems are still great; but the successes already registered justify optimism for the future.

On the morning of 28 June, there was a modest ceremony in the office of Israel's Minister of the Interior, Moshe Haim Shapiro, at which he officially handed the Mayor the administrative order, which had just been gazetted, enlarging the Capital's city limits.

The Minister said: 'To Mr Kollek has fallen the privilege of presiding over a great united Jerusalem. Let us ensure that peace and mutual understanding shall prevail among all the city's residents, and that all may enjoy the great and sacred things which the city contains.'

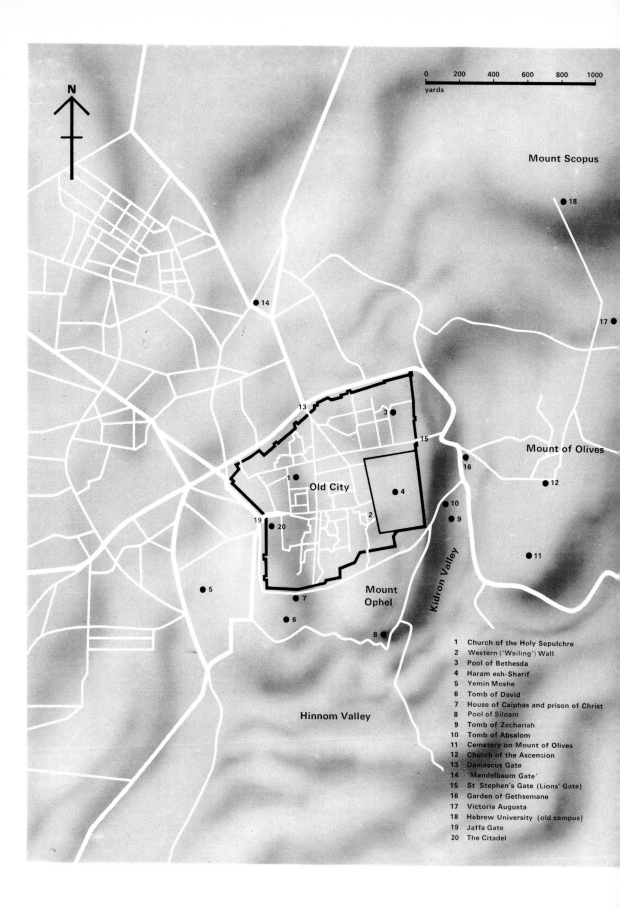

N

Mount Scopus

● 18

● 17

Mount of Olives

13

3 ●

15

● 16

● 12

1 ●

Old City

● 4

● 10

2

● 9

19

20

Kidron Valley

● 11

Mount
Ophel

● 5

● 7

● 6

Hinnom Valley

8 ●

1   Church of the Holy Sepulchre
2   Western ('Wailing') Wall
3   Pool of Bethesda
4   Haram esh-Sharif
5   Yemin Moshe
6   Tomb of David
7   House of Caiphas and prison of Christ
8   Pool of Siloam
9   Tomb of Zechariah
10   Tomb of Absalom
11   Cemetery on Mount of Olives
12   Church of the Ascension
13   Damascus Gate
14   'Mandelbaum Gate'
15   St Stephen's Gate (Lions' Gate)
16   Garden of Gethsemane
17   Victoria Augusta
18   Hebrew University (old campus)
19   Jaffa Gate
20   The Citadel

● 14

0   200   400   600   800   1000
yards

Main Events in the History of Jerusalem

c	19th century	Jerusalem listed in Execration Texts – first recorded mention of the city
	18th–mid 16th century	*The Hyksos period*
	14th century	Letters by local ruler of Jerusalem in Tel el-Amarna archives
	1000–961 (reign)	King David establishes Jerusalem as Capital of United Kingdom of Israel
	961–922 (reign)	King Solomon – building of the First Temple
	922	Division of Kingdom into Israel and Judah
	837–800 (reign)	Joash, king of Judah, carries out first extensive repairs to Temple
	715–687 (reign)	Hezekiah, king of Judah – tunnels conduit from Gihon spring to Siloam pool
	701	Hezekiah successfully withstands Sennacherib's assault on Jerusalem
	587	Destruction of Jerusalem and of the Temple by Nebuchadnezzar, and exile of Jews to Babylon
	537–332	*The Persian period*
	537	Return of the Jews from Babylon
	515	Completion of Second Temple
	about 440	Nehemiah arrives from Babylon and rebuilds the walls of Jerusalem
	about 435	Ezra the Scribe comes from Babylon and joins Nehemiah in rebuilding the community and city of Jerusalem

Map of Jerusalem, showing principal places of interest.

The façade of the Temple shown on a shekel struck during the Bar Kochba revolt.

BC	*332–167*	*The Hellenistic period*
	332	Alexander the Great visits Jerusalem
	312–198	Rule of the Ptolemies
	198–167	Rule of the Seleucids
	169	Seleucid king, Antiochus IV Epiphanes (175–163) plunders Temple
	167–63 and 40–37	*The Hasmoneans (Maccabees)*
	167–141	Maccabean War of Liberation
	164	Re-conquest of Temple Mount and re-dedication of Temple
		The first Hasmonean leaders, sons of Mattathias:
	166–160	Judah the Maccabee
	160–143	Jonathan
	143–135	Simon
	63 BC – AD 324	*The Roman period*
	63	Pompey captures Jerusalem
	40–37 (reign)	Romans ousted briefly by Hasmonean king, Mattathias Antigonus aided by Parthians
	37–4 (reign)	King Herod the Great – builds Antonia fortress, palace and three towers and starts rebuilding the Temple
AD	26–36	Pontius Pilate, Roman procurator of Judea
	33	Crucifixion of Jesus
	41–44	Agrippa, king of Judea, builds new city wall (The 'Third Wall')
	66–70	The Great Revolt – The War of the Jews against the Romans

Jerusalem depicted in a fourth-century mosaic in Rome.

AD 70	Fall of Jerusalem and destruction of the Second Temple by Titus
132–5	Bar Kochba's war of freedom – Jerusalem again the Jewish Capital
135	Emperor Hadrian's total destruction of Jerusalem and building of new walls and new city renamed Aelia Capitolina
324–638	*The Byzantine period*
326	Queen Helena, mother of Emperor Constantine the Great, visits Jerusalem, determines locations of events associated with last days of Jesus, and causes churches to be built to commemorate them, notably the Church of the Holy Sepulchre
end of 6th century	Madeba map of Jerusalem
614	Persian conquest of Jerusalem
629	Recaptured by Byzantines
638–1099	*The Moslem period*
638	The caliph Omar enters Jerusalem
691	Dome of the Rock completed
1099–1187	*The Crusader Kingdom*
1099	Crusader capture of Jerusalem
latter part of 11th century	Visit of Rabbi Moshe Ben Maimon (Maimonides)
1173	Visit of Benjamin of Tudela
1187	Saladin captures Jerusalem from Crusaders

279

right: A Moslem leader, depicted in a sixteenth-century manuscript.

far right: Lord Balfour and Dr Weizmann, 1925.

AD	*1250–1517*	*The Mameluke period*
	1267	Rabbi Moshe Ben Nahman (Nachmanides) arrives from Spain, revives the Jewish congregation and establishes synagogue and centre of learning bearing his name
	1488	Rabbi Obadiah da Bertinoro settles in Jerusalem and leads the community
	1517–1917	*The Ottoman Turkish period*
	1517	Ottoman conquest of Jerusalem
	1538–40	Sultan Suleiman I ('The Magnificent') rebuilds the city walls
	1700	Rabbi Yehuda He'Hassid arrives, starts building 'Hurva' Synagogue
	1836	First visit of Sir Moses Montefiore
	1838	First consulate (British) opened in Jerusalem
	1860	First Jewish settlement outside walls of the city
	1898	Visit by Dr Theodor Herzl, founder of World Zionist Organisation
	1917–48	*The British Occupation and Mandatory period*
	1917	British conquest and General Allenby's entry into Jerusalem
	1918	Dr Chaim Weizmann lays foundation stone of Hebrew University on Mount Scopus
	1920	Sir Herbert Samuel appointed first British High Commissioner and 'Government House' established in Jerusalem
	1925	Hebrew University buildings inaugurated
	1947	United Nations Resolution recommending the partition of Palestine into Arab and Jewish States

No-man's Land', the last
days of the Mandate.

AD	*1948–67*	*The Divided City*
	14 May 1948	British Mandate ends and State of Israel proclaimed
	May 1948–Jan 1949	Israel's War of Liberation
	28 May 1948	New City of Jerusalem remains intact but Jewish Quarter in Old City falls
	April 1949	Israel-Transjordan Armistice Agreement signed, whereby Jerusalem divided between the two countries
	13 December 1949	New City of Jerusalem declared Capital of the State of Israel
	5 June 1967	Jordan shells and mortars New City on opening day of the Six Day War
	7 June 1967	Israeli troops capture Old City and Jerusalem reunited
	14 June 1967	Mass Jewish pilgrimage to Western Wall of Temple Mount on Feast of Shavuot (Feast of Weeks)
	23 June 1967	Moslems and Christians again given access to their Holy Places

A Jewish rabbi and two
Greek Orthodox priests,
each of whom can worship
freely in the reunited city.

Acknowledgements

The authors express their warmest thanks to John Curtis of Weidenfeld and Nicolson, their London publishers, who was responsible for selecting the illustrations and seeing the book through the press.

The authors would also like to thank Eliyahu Mizrahi, of the State Archives, Jerusalem, for his help in research.

The majority of the pictures were taken for this book by Ronald Sheridan.

Pictures from the collection of Teddy Kollek, taken by Ronald Sheridan, are: 24, 34, 38, 42, 44, 46, 47, 50, 93, 102, 114, 118, 122, 129, 134, 166, 176, 179, 201, 202, 219, 220, 223 and 225.

Other pictures taken by Ronald Sheridan appear by courtesy of the following: *Bamakhane*, the Israeli Army Weekly, 200 and 265; Holyland Hotel, Jerusalem, 94, 104 and 109; Israel Department of Antiquities and Museums, 124, 127, 193, 253 and 254; Israel Museum, Jerusalem, 99, 115, 136, 218 and 233; Central Zionist Archives, Jerusalem, 238; Jewish National and University Library, Jerusalem, 3, 23 and 214.

The remaining pictures are reproduced by permission of: Aldus Books, 35, 53, 72, 84, 101, 164 and 208; *Bamakhane*, 258, 261, 263, 265, 269, 274 and 275; Ben Zvi Institute, Jewish National and University Library, 156 and 237; Bibliothèque de l'Arsenal, Paris, 84; Bibliothèque Nationale, Paris, 60, 75, 90, 101, 187, 198 and 280; Bibliothèque Royal, Brussels, 174; Bodleian Library, Oxford, 77; Bollinger Foundation, New York, 151; Trustees of the British Museum, London, 36, 58, 177 and 208; Chester Beatty Library, Dublin, 53 and 164; Dr Moshe Dothan, 136; H.Erel, 267; Felix Gluck, 182; David Harris, 14, 33, 69, 88, 192, 240, 244, 253, 256 and by courtesy of the Israel Museum, 26, 80, 81, 82, 87 and 88; Hebrew Union Library, New York, 72; Imperial War Museum (Central Zionist Archives), 234; Israeli Air Force, 157; Jewish Agency, 41, 228, 234, 239, 245, 246, 247 and 280; Jewish National Fund, 230; Kadman Numismatic Museum, Tel-Aviv, 278; Behram Kapadia, 143 and 231; H. Kneller, (courtesy of Israel Deapartment of Antiquities and Museums), 48; Fritz Kohn (Government Press Officer), 35; Editions Robert Laffont, Paris, 100; Mansell Collection, London, 12, 131 and 279; Maritime Museum, Haifa, 227; Novaes, Lisbon, 121; Rhenisches Bildarchiv, 49 and 50; Cecil Roth Collection, Jerusalem, 187; Rubens Collection, London, 231; Trustees of the Victoria and Albert Museum, London, 230; Dr Z. Vilnay, *The Holyland in old Prints and Maps*, 229; A. Volk, 13, 71, 197, 205, 236, and 257; Central Zionist Archives, 234, 238, 248, 250 and 281.

Maps by Tom Stalker-Miller.

Endpapers by courtesy of Daniel Doron, New York.

The text of the Authorised Version of the Bible is Crown copyright and the extracts used herein are reproduced by permission.

Index

Abbad al-Saffah, 162

Abijah, king of Judah, 56

Abd el-Malik, 156, 161–2

Abdu-Heba, ruler of Jerusalem, 20–1

Abraham, 17, 47, 155

Abu Bakr, successor to Mohammed, 152

Abu Ghosh, 34

Abulfragius, early Christian writer, 168

Acre, 185, 223

Aelia Capitolina, 140–1, 142, 145, 201

Agrippa, king of Judea, 98, 106–8, 111, 117, 125, 128

Agrippa II, king of Judea, 125

Ahab, king of Israel, 56

Ahaz, king of Judah, 59, 61

Akiba, Rabbi, 138, 140

Alexander, son of Aristobulus, 93, 95

Alexander the Great, king of Macedonia, 79

Alexandria, 79
   Jewish community, 79–80

Allenby, General, 201, 233

Amaziah, king of Judah, 56–7

Amenhotep III and IV, pharaohs of Egypt, 20

Amos, 58

Antigonus, Mattathias, 93, 95–7

Antioch, city of, 79, 118, 126; patriarch of, 120

Antiochus III, king of the Seleucids, 85

Antiochus IV Epiphanes, 85–6, 88

Antipater, Idumean counsellor, 92, 95

Antony, Mark, 95, 96, 99

Apollonius, Seleucid general, 87

Aqaba, Gulf of, 34, 43

Arabia, 152
   Jews in, 165

Arabs: and British Mandate, 235–7, 240; life in Jerusalem, 239; civil war with Jews, 240; reject UN partition resolution, 240; attack Jerusalem, 240, 245–6; and Israel War of Independence, 249–50; armistice agreements, 250–2; Six Day War, 259–68
   see also Jordan

Archelaus, king of Judah, 106

Arculf, Bishop, 166–7

Aretas, king of the Nabateans, 92

Aristobolus, Hasmonean king, 91

Aristobolus II, Hasmonean king, 91–5

Ark of the Law, 34, 40–1, 43, 47, 50, 105

Armistice agreements, 250–2, 260

Artaxerxes, Persian emperor, 74

Asa, king of Judah, 56

Ashdod, 89

Ashkelon, 17, 89, 91, 137

Ashkenasi Jews, 194, 219, 220, 238

Assyria and Assyrians, 11, 15, 59, 62, 65, 67, 68, 73

Atonement, Day of, 105, 240, 269

Avi-Yonah, Professor Michael, 141, 206

Babylonian empire, 11, 20, 34, 68, 70, 73, 79; and Jewish exiles, 68, 70, 73–4

Baldwin, king of Crusader Kingdom of Jerusalem, 176, 179

Balfour Declaration, 233, 235

bar Giora, Simon, Zealot commander, 128, 130, 135

Bar Kochba, 138, 140

Beersheba, 68, 249

Ben Gurion, David, 245

Benjamin of Tudela, 184

ben Menahem, Meshullam, 193

ben Nahman, Rabbi Moshe Nachmanides, 186

ben Samson, Rabbi Samuel, 186

ben Zakkai, Rabbi Yohanan, 137; synagogue of, 217

Bernard the Wise, Breton monk, 167–8

Bethlehem, 46, 229, 250, 252

Bible and Biblical quotations: 43, 56, 58, 62, 65, 67, 100, 113, 120; *Old Testament:* Genesis, 17; Deuteronomy, 67; Joshua, 17, 22; Judges, 22; Samuel, 27–8, 34, 47, 61; I Kings, 46–7, 50, 52; II Kings, 62; I Chronicles, 28; II Chronicles, 57, 62; Ezra, 74; Nehemiah, 74, 75, 76; Psalms, 70; Isaiah, 15, 58–9, 61; Hosea, 58; Amos, 58; Maccabees, 86–8; *Septuagint*, 80; *New Testament:* Mark, 114; Luke, 111

Birket Hammam el Batrak, Pool of the Patriarchs, 130

Boghaz-Koy, Hittite capital, 28, 30

British Royal Commission, 240

Bukharan Jewish community, 238

Byzantine empire, 98, 145–6, 148, 151–2, 199;
   architecture, 156
   see also Jerusalem – Byzantine

Caesar, Julius, 95

Caesarea, 97, 111, 120, 135, 137

Caiaphas, High Priest, 114

Cambyses, king of Persia, 74

Canaan, 15, 17, 20, 22
   see also Israel

Channukah, festival of, 87–8

Charlemagne, Emperor, 165, 167

Chatillon, Reynald of, 184

Christians: early, 117–20; at Jerusalem, 120, 138; at Aelia Capitolina, 140, 141; Constantine, Council of Nicaea, 145; churches and shrines, Queen Helena, 145–8; under Byzantine rule, 148–9, 151; Persian massacre, Byzantine return, 152; under Moslems, 152, 162, 165–6; churches destroyed, 166; Seljuk persecution of, 166; First Crusade, Kingdom of Jerusalem, 175, 179; Syrian, 179; and Saladin, 184–6; under Mamelukes, 191, 196; under Ottoman empire, 203–4, 206, 209, 211–2, 217, 223, 226, 230, 233; denominations, 209–11; access to Temple Mount, 226; under British rule, 239; under Israel and Jordan, 273
   see also Byzantine empire; Crusades; Jerusalem – Byzantine, Crusader

Chosroes II, Persian emperor, 152

Coins, 89, 127, 138

Constantine the Great, 120, 142, 145, 146, 148, 149, 151

Constantine, Monomachus, Byzantine emperor, 148

Crusades: reasons for, 166; origins in Europe, Council of Clermont, 176; conquest of Jerusalem, 175–6; Crusader Kingdom of Jerusalem, 179; Saladin's conquests, 184; Third Crusade, capture of Acre, 185; treaty with Saladin, 185; Frederick II's treaty with Moslems, 186

Cyrus, Persian emperor, 73–4

da Bertinoro, Rabbi Obadiah, 193–4, 196
Damascus, 34, 57, 92, 162, 173, 184, 185, 186, 199, 217; Sultan al-Nasir of, 186
  see also Syria
David, king of Israel, 11, 22, 27–41, 43, 47, 52, 55, 56, 61, 65, 98, 173; Tomb, 255
Dayan, General Moshe, 269
Dead Sea, 91, 126, 140, 151, 238; scrolls, 255
de Bouillon, Godfrey, duke of Lorraine, 175, 176
de Lusignan, Guy, king of Crusader Kingdom, 184
Demetrius, king of Seleucids, 89
Demetrius III, king of Seleucids, 91
Diaspora Jewry, 77, 80, 89, 105, 111, 138, 165, 204, 226, 229–30, 238, 255
  see also names of individual communities

Edomites see Idumeans
Egypt, 34, 70, 73; conquest of Jerusalem, 11; rule over Canaan, 15–7, 20–1; and Solomon, 43; exodus from, 68, 76; Ptolomaic rule of Judah, 79–80, 85
  see also Execration Texts
  sultans and caliphs, Fatimid dynasty, 161, 165; Ahmed ibn-Tulun, 165; Al-Aziz, 165; Al-Hakim, 148, 165–6; Al-Kamil, 186; Al Zahir, 161; Ayyub (al-Salih), 186, 189; Iftikhar, governor of Jerusalem, 175, 176
Elath, 57
Eliashar, Yaacov Shaul, Sephardi Chief Rabbi, 223
Eshkol, Levi, Prime Minister of Israel, 269
Eudocia, Byzantine empress, 140, 151
Euphrates, river, 17, 34
Execration Texts, 15, 17
Ezra the Scribe, 74, 77, 91

Feisal, king of Iraq, 235
Finn, James, British Consul, 224
Flanders, Robert of, 175
Florus, Gessius, procurator, 125–6
France, 185, 191, 204, 223, 233
Frederick II, Holy Roman Emperor and king of Sicily, 186

Galilee, 91, 113; Jewish community, 142, 149, 152, 204

Gallus, Cestius, Governor of Syria, 126–7
Gehenna, 67
Germany, 186, 201, 223, 233; Lutheran Church, 212, 233
Gischala, John of, 128–30, 135
Glubb 'Pasha', General Sir John Bagot, 250
Godescal, crusader monk, 179
Goren, Brigadier-General Rabbi Shlomo, 269
Great Britain: Napoleonic wars, 223; Consulate in Jerusalem, 223–4; missionaries from, 224; Balfour Declaration, 233–5; policy of Mandatory Administration, 236–7, 239; British Royal Commission recommends partition of Palestine, 240; Mandate ends, 240, 249
  see also Jerusalem – British Mandate
Greek Orthodox Church, 162, 168, 191, 206, 209, 212, 217, 233
Gush-Halav, Yohanan of, see Gischala, John of,
Greeks see Hellenism

Hadrian, Roman emperor, 108, 138, 140–1, 201, 212
Haganah, 240, 245–6, 249–50
Haram esh-Sharif, 156, 176, 185, 191, 201, 237, 273
Haroun el-Rashid, 165
Hasmonean dynasty, 86–91, 95–7, 114, 125, 130
Hasselquist, Frederick, 209
Hebron, 27, 32, 46; hills of, 191, 249; Jewish community, 220, 240
He'Hassid, Rabbi Yehuda, 219–20
Helena, Empress, 120, 145–8
Hellenism, 79, 85, 99, 118
  see also Ptolemys; Seleucids
Herod the Great, king of Judea, 89, 92, 95–100, 105–8
Herzl, Theodor, 230
Hezekiah, king of Judah, 59, 61–5, 67, 68
Hiram, king of Tyre, 37, 43
Hittites, 28–31
Hosea, 58
Hospitallers, Crusader order, see St John, Knights of,
Hussein, king of Jordan, 259
Hyksos, 17, 20
Hyrcanus, John, son of Simon, 89, 91
Hyrcanus, son of King Alexander Jannai, 91–3, 95–7, 130

ibn Chelo, Isaac ben Joseph, 191
Idumeans, 56, 57, 89, 92, 96
Immigration see Diaspora Jewry
Iraq, 235, 249, 260

Isaac, 47, 155
Isaiah, 11, 15, 58, 59, 61–2, 65, 67
  see also Bible
Islam see Mohammed and Mohammedanism
Israel: conquest of Canaan by Joshua, 22; Philistines, 22; war with Judah, 59; Assyrian conquest and Jewish exile, 59
  see also Canaan; David; Jerusalem – Biblical; Judah; Saul; Solomon
Israel, State of, 11; Balfour Declaration, 233, 235; Arab views on, 235–6; UN resolution, 240; established, 249; Arabs attack throughout, 240, 245–6; War of Independence, 249–50; Six Day War, 259–69; Jerusalem reunited, 273–4
  see also Diaspora; Jerusalem – Israeli; Palestine
Italy, Jewish community, 204

Jaffa, 89
James the Apostle, 120
Jamnia, Jewish community, 137
Jannai, Alexander, Hasmonean king, 91
Jebusites, 22, 27–8, 30–1, 47
Jehoiachin, king of Judah, 68, 73
Jehoshaphat, king of Judah, 56
Jeremiah, 11, 67, 70
Jericho, 92; plains of, 70
Jerusalem – ancient and Roman: 1, 15–7, 20–2; David, 27–8, 31–4, 37–8, 40–1, 76, 140; Solomon, 43, 46, 50, 52; capital of Judah, 55–8; Israel, wars against, 59; sole national capital, 59; Isaiah and Hezekiah, 61–2; Assyrian attack, 65; religious revival, 67; Judah and Israel reunited, 68; Babylonian conquest and exile, 68, 70; Persian conquest, 73; restoration, Nehemiah, exiles return, 73–7; under Ptolemys, 79–80; Seleucids, 85–9; Maccabees' revolt, 87–8; Maccabees' rule, 89; Nabatean invasion, 92; Roman invasion and conquest, 92–3; Parthians help Hasmonean revolt, 95–6; Antipater, 95; Phasael, 95; independent, 96; Roman conquest, 96; Herod, 96–100, 105–6; procurators, 106, 111, 125; Jesus, 111–7, 118; St Paul, effects on Christianity, 120; early Christian leaders, 120; Agrippa's rule, 106, 108, 125; Zealot rebellion, Romans defeated, 125–6; Roman siege and destruction, 128–30, 132, 135; Christian community, 138; Bar Kochba rebellion, 138, 140; city becomes

Aelia Capitolina, 140

Jerusalem – *Byzantine:* 142; Constantine, 120, 145; Queen Helena, churches and shrines, 120, 145, 146, 148–9; Byzantine rule, 148–9, 151; ban lifted on Jews, 151; Persian occupation, 152; Byzantine return, massacre and expulsion of Jews, 152

Jerusalem – *Moslem:* Moslems occupy city, 152, 155; Christians under, 152, 162–3, 165–6; Jews return, 152, 162, 165; religious significance, 156; Turkish Egyptian conquest, 165; Fatimid rule, 165–6, 175, 176; products, 173; Mukaddasi's description, 168, 173 for rulers *see* Moslem empire, caliphs; Egypt, sultans

Jerusalem – *Crusader:* First Crusade, 179; conquest of Jerusalem, 175–6; Kingdom of Jerusalem, Godfrey de Bouillon, 175, 176; Baldwin, 176, 179; description, 179, 180; Patriarch of, 179; destruction of synagogues, 176; Jewish community, 179–80, 184; Saladin's conquest, 185; treaty with Moslems, 186
see also St John, Knights of; Templars, Order of; Teutonic Knights

Jerusalem – *Mameluke:* buildings, 189–91; centre of Moslem theology, 191; religious toleration, 191; Jews under, 191, 193–4, 196; Ottoman conquest, 196, 199
see also Mamelukes

Jerusalem – *Ottoman:* conquest, 196, 199; Suleiman's rule, 201–4; under Ottoman empire, 202–4, 206, 209, 211–2, 217, 219–20, 223, 224, 226, 233; European presence and influence, 223–4, 233; Egyptian conquest, Ottoman rule restored, 223; contemporary description, 225–6; Christians allowed in Temple Mount, 226, 228; Jews settle outside city walls, 229; immigrants, 230; German influence, 223, 233; fall of empire, 233
see also Ottoman empire

Jerusalem – *British Mandate:* 217, 233; Government, 235; British improvements, 236–7; city under British, 237–8; immigration, 237–8; Jewish life in, 237–8; religious rights, 239; Christians in, 239; Arabs in, 239; Arab massacre of Jews, civil war, 240; Haganah, 240; Mandate ends, 249
see also Great Britain

Jerusalem – *Jordanian:* improvements, 252, 255; control of Holy Places, 252; importance to Jordan, 255; Israelis capture in Six Day War, 261–4, 266, 268
see also Jordan

Jerusalem – *Israeli:* United Nations recommendations, 240, 255; Arabs attack, 240, 245–6; Israel proclaimed, 249; War of Independence, 249–50; Armistice agreements, 250–2; city divided, 252; immigrants, 255; growth of, 255, 257; Six Day War: mobilisation, 259; Jordan attacks city, 260; capture of Jordanian Jerusalem, 261–4, 266, 268–9; services restored, 270; city reunited, 273; freedom of worship, 273; co-existence of Jews and Arabs, 273

Jerusalem – *Pilgrimages:* Christian, 142, 146, 149, 162, 165–8, 185, 203, 209; Jewish, 68, 111, 138, 142, 162, 165–8, 186, 193, 270; Moslem, 156

Jerusalem – *Sites:*

Amygdalon Pool, 'Pool of the Towers', 130

Anastasis, tomb, 146

Akra Citadel, 87, 88–9, 114

Antonia Fortress, 99, 117, 126, 128, 130, 132, 135, 211–2

Armenian quarter, 179; Church, 212

Ascension, Church of the, 148, 167

Augusta Victoria, palace and ridge, 233, 266

Baris, fortress, 99

Bethesda, suburb of Jerusalem, 106–8, 117

Calvary (Golgotha), 117, 140, 146, 148, 212
see also Anastasis, tomb of; Holy Sepulchre, Church of the

Christian quarter, 179, 203, 268

Cemeteries, 196, 274

Citadel, 117, 191

Coenaculum, 114, 166–7, 255

Condemnation, Chapel of the, 212

Coptic Church, 212

Cross, Monastery of the, 255

Dome of the Rock *see* Omar, Mosque of

Dormition Abbey, 167, 233

Ecce Homo Arch, 141, 180, 212

El-Aksa, Mosque of, 161–2, 173, 175, 185, 191, 273

Eleona, Church of, 148

En-Rogel 'spring', 38

Flagellation, Convent of the, 212

Gates: Damascus, 140, 151, 165, 175, 201; Golden, 180, 184; Herod's, 175, 262; Jaffa, 98, 117, 130, 152, 179, 201, 233; Lions', 211, 266, 268, 269; Zion, 140

Gethsemane, 114

Gihon, spring of, 28, 38, 62, 76

Hadassah hospital, 238, 252; new building, 255, 273

Hebrew university, 141, 235, 238, 252; new building, 255, 273

Herod's Palace, 98, 117, 128, 130, 135; Herod's towers: Corner, 108; David's, 98, 152, 184; Hippicus, 98, 108, 117, 135; Mariamne, 98, 135; Phasael, 98, 135, 152; Psephinus, 98, 107, 128; Women's, 107

Herod's family tomb, 132

Hinnom, valley of, 38, 67, 140

Holy Sepulchre, Church of the, 130, 146, 148, 151–2, 166, 168, 179, 206, 209, 211, 212, 217, 233, 237, 266

Hurva Synagogue, 220, 223

Israel Museum, 255, 260, 273

Jewish National Library, 238, 255

Jewish quarter, 179, 237, 250, 266

Kidron, valley of, 38, 106, 108, 114, 132, 140, 196, 239, 274

Knesset, 255, 260, 273

Lithostrotos court, 211–2

Mea She'arim quarter, 229

Millo, 40, 52, 65

Moriah, Mount, 47, 155

Moslem quarter, 179, 238, 268

Muristan bazaar, 141

Nachlat Shiva, 229

Nachmanides Synagogue, 217

New City, 229, 250, 252, 255, 260, 268, 273

Old City, 38, 201, 211, 229, 237, 250, 252, 260, 262, 264, 266, 268, 274

Olives, Mount of, 113–4, 128, 132, 148, 161, 167, 196, 266, 268, 274

Omar, Mosque of, 155–6, 161, 166, 173, 175, 185, 191, 201, 226, 273

Ophel, Mount, 40, 50, 76, 151

Our Lady of the Spasm, Church of, 212

Palestine Archaeological Museum, 239, 262, 264

Police School, 262–4

Praetorium, 117, 211

Rephaim, valley of, 61

Robinson's Arch, 106

Rockefeller Museum, *see* Palestine Archaeological Museum

Russian Compound, 106, 233

St Anne, Church of, 179, 191

St Charalambos, Convent of, 212

St Helen, Chapel of, 212

St John, Hospice of, 212

St Mary Nova, Church of, 151

St Stephen, Church of, 151

Scopus, Mount, 233, 235, 252, 255, 266

see also Hadassah hospital; Hebrew university

Sheikh Jarrah, suburb, 264

Sisters of Zion, Convent of, 212

Solomon, royal buildings, 50, 52, 70, 161

Stations of the Cross, 117, 211–2

Synagogues, 11, 137–8, 176, 193, 217, 220, 223, 238–9, 250

Temple: Solomon's, description of, 46–7, 50, 52, 61, 74, 105; mentioned, 55, 58, 62, 65, 67–8, 155; destruction by Babylonians, 70, 135

Second Temple: description, 74, 76, 80; desecrated by Seleucids, 85, 87; rededicated by Maccabees, 87, 89; Sadducees and Pharisees, 91; Nabatean threat, 92; Roman invasion and conquest, 92–3, 96

Herod's reconstruction, description, 99–100, 105–6, 161; Jesus, 111, 113; Agrippa II, 125; Zealots rebellion, 126; Romans destroy, 128–30, 132, 135, 140; Aelia Capitolina and Jews, 140; Jupiter's temple, 140; under Byzantine rule, 155; Mamelukes, 193; after Six Day War, 274

see also Holy Sepulchre, church of Omar, Mosque of; Western Wall

Temple Mount, 76, 79, 85, 87–8, 92, 98, 100, 105–6, 117, 266, 268–9, 274

Upper City, 98, 106, 126, 128, 130, 135

Via Dolorosa, 117, 180, 211, 212, 268–9

Wailing Wall see Western Wall

Walls, 140, 184; Hadrian's, 108, 140; Nehemiah's 75–6; Old city, 52, 57, 75, 98, 117, 130; Ophel, 58; Second, 117, 130; Third (Agrippa's), 106, 108, 117, 128, 129, 140; Suleiman's, 201–2, 266

Western 'Wailing' Wall, 105, 151, 165, 184, 217, 220, 226, 237–8, 240, 252, 268–9, 270

Wilson's Arch, 106

Yemin Moshe quarter, 229

Zion, Mount, 50, 114, 140, 151, 166–7, 175, 179, 180, 191, 194, 201, 202, 226, 233, 252, 255

Zion Square, 128

Jerusalem – Physical features: climate, 12, 15; topography, 38; earthquakes, 156, 166, 196; water supply, 12, 28, 38, 59, 62, 75, 98, 191, 202, 236, 245, 255

Jesus, 11, 99, 111–7, 118, 120, 145, 146, 211–2; disciples, 113, 117

Jewish Agency, 235, 245

Jews, national and religious life, Biblical, 17, 65, 67–8, 77, 79–80, 85, 87–8, 111, 137–8, 140, 142; under Moslems, 162, 165–6; Seljuks, 166; Crusades, 179–80, 184; Saladin, 185–6; Mamelukes, 191, 193, 196; Ottomans, 203–4, 217, 219, 223, 225–6, 229–30; British Mandate, 237–40; Six Day War, 268–9; afterwards, 273–4; Monotheism, 15, 50, 68, 165; religious identity, 77, 80

Joab, 28, 31

Joash, king of Judah, 56

Jonathan, the High Priest, 89, 91

Jordan and Jordanians, 89, 91–2, 138, 162, 201, 249–50, 255, 260, 262, 263, 268

see also Arabs; Jerusalem – Jordanian

Joseph of Arimathea, 117

Joseph, Dr Dov, 245

Josephus, 28, 86, 91–2, 96, 98, 106, 125–6, 130, 132

Joshua, 17, 22

Josiah, king of Judah, 67–8

Jotham, king of Judah, 58–9

Judah, Kingdom of, 27; separate State, 55–6; war with Israel, 59; Assyrian conquest, 65, 67; Babylonian conquest, 68, 70; Persian conquest, 73; return of Babylonian exiles, 73–4; restoration under Persia, 73, 79; Hellenist influence, 79; Ptolemys, 79–80; Seleucids, 85–6; Maccabees' revolt, 86–7; Hasmonean rule, 89, 91–3; Pharisees and Sadducees, 91; Nabatean invasion, 92; Roman conquest, 92–3, 96; Hasmonean independence briefly restored, 95–6; Herod's conquest and rule, 96–7, 106; Agrippa, 106; Procurators, 106–7, 111, 117, 125; Pilate, 111, 113–4; pharisees and sadducees, 125; Zealot's rebellion, 125–30; destruction of Jerusalem, 132, 135, 137; Bar Kochba rebellion, 138, 140

see also Israel; Jerusalem – Biblical; Palestine

Judea see Judah

Kabbalah, the, 193

Latin Church, 162, 206, 209, 212, 217, 233

League of Nations, 233

Lebanon, 11, 52, 249–50

see also Tyre

Levites, 55, 68, 77

Maccabees, the: Mattathias, Johanan, Simon, Judah, Eleazar, Jonathan, 86–9 see also Hasmonean dynasty

Macarius, Bishop, 145

Madeba Map of Holy Land, 151, 201

Maimonides, 184

Mamelukes, 189, 191, 193–4, 196; Mameluke Sultan Aybak, 189

see also Jerusalem – Mameluke

Manasseh, king of Judah, 67

Mandelbaum Gate, 252, 262, 264, 273

Mariamne, wife of Herod, 97

Masada, fortress, 97, 126–7

Maundrell, Henry, 209

Mecca, 152, 155–6, 162, 173

Medina, 155, 173

Melchi-zedek, king of Salem, 17

Menahem, leader of Zealots, 126

Mesopotamia, 20, 59, 68

'Miracle of the Oil', 88

Missionaries, 225–6

Modestus, Abbot, 152

Modin, village of, 86–7

Mohammed and Mohammedanism, 11, 152, 155, 165, 180, 226, 239, 273

see also Jerusalem – Moslem; Moslem empire

Montefiore, Sir Moses, 228–9

Moslem empire: 11; Mohammedanism, 152; conquest of Palestine, 155; capitals of, 162; Turkish mercenaries, 166; Fatimid dynasty, 165–6; Seljuks, 166; Crusader Kingdom of Jerusalem expels Moslems, 175–9; Saladin's conquest, 184; empire divided, treaty with Frederick II, 186; Mameluke occupation, 189

see also Jerusalem – Moslem; Mohammed and Mohammedanism

Moslem empire: caliphs; Abu Bakr, 152; Omar, 152, 155, 165; Umayyad dynasty, 156, 162; Abd el-Malik, 156, 161–2; Waleed, 161; Suleiman, 162; Abbasid dynasty, 156, 162, 165, 189; Abbas al-Saffah, 162; Haroun el-Rashid, 165; Ayyubid dynasty, 184; Saladin, 161–2, 184–6, 189

Mukaddasi, Moslem geographer, 168, 173

Nabateans, 92

Nasser, Gamal Abdul, 259

Nebuchadnezzar, king of Babylon, 70, 73, 76

Negev, 43, 55–7, 91

Nehemiah, 74–7

Nicaea, ecumenical council of, 145

Nicodemus, 117

Omar, Caliph, 152, 155, 165

Omri, king of Israel, 56

Ottoman empire: origins, 199; conquest of Palestine, 196; Suleiman's empire,

199, 201; decline of, 204, 206; fall of, 226, 233

see also Jerusalem – Ottoman; Turkey

Osmanli sultans, 199; Osman I, 199; Selim I, 196, 199; Suleiman the Magnificent, 161, 180, 199–204; Murad III, 204; Abdul Hamid, 233; Pashas: Mohammed Pasha, 206, 217; Mohammed ibn-Farouk, 217, 219

Palestine: Byzantine rule, 145; Persian occupation, 152; Byzantine return, 152; massacre and expulsion of Jews, 152; Moslem occupation, 152, 162; Jews return, 152; Seljuks, 166; First Crusade, 175, 176; Saladin conquers Jerusalem, 184–5; Third Crusade, capture of Acre, 185; treaty with Saladin, 185; Mameluke rule, 189, 191, 196; plague and famine, 196; Ottoman conquest, 196, 199; part of Syria, 199; Jews flee from Europe, 203–4; under Ottomans, 204, 209, 220, 223; Western political interest, 223; Napoleon invades, 223; Egyptian conquest, Ottoman rule restored, 223; Zionist immigration, 229–30; fall of Ottoman empire, 226–7, 233; British Mandate, 233, 235; Jews try to settle, 237; Arab massacre, civil war, 240; Mandate ends, 249; Arabs attack Jerusalem, 240, 245–6; British Royal Commission recommends partition, 240

see also Israel, State of

Parthians, 95–6

Passover, festival of, 68, 111, 113, 246

Paul the Apostle, 118–20

Pekah, king of Israel, 59

Pella, Christian community, 138

Persian empire, 11, 73–4, 77, 79, 148, 152

Peter the Hermit (Peter of Picardy), 179

Petachia, Rabbi, 184

Pharisees, 91, 125

Phasael, governor of Jerusalem, 95–6

Philip, king of France, 185

Philistines, 22, 27, 34

Phoenicia and Phoenicians, 37, 43, 55, 57

Pilate, Pontius, 111, 117, 211

Poland, Jewish community, 226

Pompey, 92–3, 95

Portugal, Jewish community, 204

Procurators, 106–7, 111, 117, 125

Prophets, 15, 41, 67, 113

Prussia, 201, 223

Ptolemys, 79–80

Rabbis, 77, 111, 118, 125, 137, 186

see also names of individual rabbis

Rabin, General Yitzhak, 269

Rachel, tomb of, 229

Red Sea, 11, 34, 43, 56–7

Rehoboam, king of Judah, 55–6

Rezin, king of Syria, 59

Richard I of England, 185

Rivlin, Yosef, 228–9

Roman Catholic Church *see* Latin Church

Romans and Roman empire, 11, 92–3, 95–7, 99, 105–7, 111, 113, 117–8, 120, 125–30, 132, 135, 137–8, 140, 145, 151, 212

Russia, 206, 223, 225, 233; Jewish community, 226

Sadducees, 91, 125

Safad, Jewish community, 204, 220, 240

St John, Knights of, Crusader order, 179

Saladin, 161–2, 184–6, 189

Salome Alexandra, Hasmonean queen, 91

Samaria, 56, 59, 87, 89

Sanhedrin, 97, 137

Saracens *see* Moslem empire

Sargon II, king of Assyria, 59

Saudi Arabia, 249

Saul, king of Israel, 22, 27

Saul of Tarsus *see* Paul the Apostle

Scaurus, Marcus, 92–3

Scrolls of the Law *see* Torah

Seleucids, 11, 79–80, 85–9, 91, 114

Seleucus, king of Seleucids, 79

Seljuks, 11, 166, 189

Sennacherib, king of Assyria, 62, 65

Sephardi Jews, 217, 220, 223, 238

Severus, Julius, Roman general, 138, 140

Shalmaneser V, king of Assyria, 59

Shapiro, Moshe Haim, 274

Shavuot, festival of, 68, 270

Sheshbazzar, governor of Judah, 73

Siloam, 37, 62, 76, 132, 135; valley, 38; inscription, 62

Simon of Cyrene, 212

Sinai peninsula, 259, 261–2

Smith, George Adam, 40, 74

Solomon, 34, 37, 40, 43, 46–7, 50, 52, 55–7, 89, 135

see also Temple

Sophronius, Patriarch of Jerusalem, 152, 155

Sosius, Roman general, 96

Spain, Jewish community, 203–4

Succot, festival of, 68, 76–7, 165

Suleiman the Magnificent, 161, 180, 199–204

Syria and Syrians, 20, 91, 106, 118, 126,

233; Israel defeats, 57; league with Israel, 59; conquered by Seleucus, 79; Herod's auxiliaries, 96; Cestius Gallus governor of, 126; under Fatimid rule, 165–6; under Saladin, 184; under Ottoman empire, 199; attacks Israel, 179; and Christians, 179

Tabernacles, festival of, *see* Succot

Talmud, 88, 106, 137, 142, 193, 238

Tarsus, town in Turkey, 118

Tel-Aviv, 245

Tel el-Amarna letters, 20

Teutonic Knights, Crusader order, 179

Templars, Crusader order of, 156, 161, 179

Tiberias, Jewish community, 204, 220

Tiglath-Pileser, king of Assyria, 59

Titus, Roman commander, 105, 128–30, 132, 135, 179

Toulouse, Raymond of, 175–6

Torah, 77, 85, 91, 111, 135, 193, 217

Transjordan *see* Jordan

Turkey, 11, 28, 30, 118, 145, 165, 223, 233

see also Ottoman empire

Turks, Khwarizmian, 186; Seljuks, 11, 166, 189

Tyre, 37, 43, 92

Tyropoeon valley, 38, 114, 135

United Nations, 240, 250, 252, 260

Uzziah, king of Judah, 57–9

Varus, governor of Syria, 106

Vespasian, Roman emperor, 128, 135

Via Dolorosa *see* Jerusalem – sites

Waleed, 161

Weeks, feast of, *see* Shavuot

Weizmann, Dr Chaim, first president of Israel, 235–6

Wilhelm II, German Kaiser, 201, 233

Willibald the pilgrim, 167

World Zionist Movement, 230

Yadin, Yigael, Professor, 28, 30–1, 140

Yavne, *see* Jamnia

Yellin, David, 228

Zacharias, patriarch of Jerusalem, 152

Zealots, 125–30, 132, 135

Zedekiah, king of Judah, 68, 70

Zerubbabel, governor of Judah, 74

Zionism, 224, 228–30, 233, 235–6

Zionist Commission, 235